D1105463

J
80
A283
1974-77
Index

The Cumulated Indexes to the Public Papers of the Presidents of the United States

U.S. President.
Public papers.

Gerald R. Ford
1974–1977

Kraus International Publications
A U.S. Division of Kraus-Thomson Organization Ltd.
Millwood, New York
1980

Copyright © Kraus International Publications 1980

All rights reserved. No part of this work covered by the copyright hereon may be reproduced or used in any form or by any means—graphic, electronic, or mechanical, including photocopying, recording, or taping, or information storage and retrieval systems—without written permission of the publisher.

ISBN 0-527-20756-X

Composition by Vance Weaver Composition, Inc., New York

First Printing
Printed in the United States of America

PREFACE

Although the words spoken by a president during the course of his administration are directed to the citizens of his own time, they become invaluable to future generations of Americans who look to the past for help in understanding their present world. The Ford administration can perhaps best be characterized by referring to those events that Gerald Ford himself mentions in his "Forewords" to the three volumes of *Public Papers of the Presidents* for which this volume serves as a cumulated index. "No past Administration," he writes, "has begun its tenure in office under more unusual circumstances than this one." Entering into the presidency by a route traveled by no other president before him in United States history, Gerald Ford could write of the 1975 published records of his administration that they "demonstrate how the American people, in the first full year of my Presidency, found a new realism." And of 1976, the year of our national Bicentennial, he wrote, "No American who witnessed, who felt and was caught up in that spontaneous outpouring of unashamed pride in our country, that jubilant reaffirmation of faith in the future of freedom, can ever forget our 200th birthday. . . . These pages record the official words and acts of the Presidency in the 200th year of our independence, a year of peace at home and abroad, a year of economic recovery and receding inflation, a year that closed with an orderly transition of political responsibility befitting a mature and secure Republic." The Ford volumes of the *Public Papers of the Presidents*, like the other volumes in this series, offer a unique view of the American presidents and of American history. The character of a president, the individuals with whom a president interacts, the historical events that are shaped by a president and that, in turn, shape his presidency, are all to be found within the pages of the *Public Papers*. And *The Cumulated Indexes to the Public Papers of the Presidents of the United States* provide, for the first time in one volume, full access to the papers of each presidential administration published in the *Public Papers* series.

A resolution passed by the United States Congress on July 17, 1894, provided that a compilation of "all the annual, special, and veto mes-

sages, proclamations, and inaugural addresses'' of all the presidents from 1789 to 1894 be printed. The publication was to be prepared by James D. Richardson, a representative from Tennessee, under the direction of the Joint Committee on Printing, of which Richardson was a member. The official set was issued in two series of ten volumes each. A joint resolution of May 2, 1896, provided for the distribution of the set to members of Congress, with the remainder to be delivered to the compiler, James Richardson. An act passed about a year later provided that the plates for *A Compilation of the Messages and Papers of the Presidents* be delivered to Richardson ''without cost to him.'' Representative Richardson then made arrangements for the commercial publication of the set. Several other compilations of presidential papers were commercially published in the first half of the nineteenth century; these usually contained only selected documents.

The Richardson edition of the *Messages and Papers*, however, was the only set authorized by Congress and published by the government until 1957, when the official publication of the public messages and statements of the presidents, the *Public Papers of the Presidents of the United States*, was initiated based on a recommendation made by the National Historical Publications Commission (now the National Historical Publications and Records Commission). The Commission suggested that public presidential papers be compiled on a yearly basis and issued in a uniform, systematic publication similar to the *United States Supreme Court Reports* and the *Congressional Record*. An official series thus began in which presidential writings and statements of a public nature could be made promptly available. These presidential volumes are compiled by the Office of the Federal Register of the General Services Administration's National Archives and Record Service.

As might be expected, the ''public papers'' vary greatly in importance and content; some contain important policy statements while others are routine messages. They include, in chronological order, texts of such documents as the president's messages to Congress, public addresses, transcripts of news conferences and speeches, public letters, messages to heads of state, remarks to informal groups, etc. Executive orders, proclamations, and similar documents that are required by law to be published in the *Federal Register* and *Code of Federal Regulations* are not reprinted, but are listed by number and subject in an appendix in each volume.

The *Public Papers of the Presidents* are kept in print, and are available from the Superintendent of Documents, United States Government Printing Office. The *Papers* of each year are published in single volumes, with each volume containing an index for that calendar year. *The Cumulated Indexes to the Public Papers of the Presidents* combines and integrates the separate indexes for a president's administration into one alphabetical listing.

References to all of the volumes of a president's public papers can thus

be found by consulting this one-volume cumulated index. *See* and *see also* references have been added and minor editorial changes have been made in the process of cumulating the separate indexes.

References in *The Cumulated Indexes to the Public Papers of the Presidents* are to item numbers. Individual volumes are identified in the *Index* by year, as are the actual volumes of the *Papers*. The year identifying the volume in which a paper is located appears in boldface type. When page references are used, they are clearly noted in the entry.

Other volumes in the set of *The Cumulated Indexes to the Public Papers of the Presidents* include Herbert Hoover, 1929–1933; Harry S. Truman, 1945–1953; Dwight D. Eisenhower, 1953–1961; John F. Kennedy, 1961–1963; Lyndon B. Johnson, 1963–1969; and Richard M. Nixon, 1969–1974. Forthcoming volumes will index the papers of Jimmy Carter, as well as those of future presidents when their administrations are completed.

Kraus International Publications

GERALD R. FORD
1974–1977

Abdnor, Repr. James, **1974:** 152
Abel, I. W., **1974:** 109; **1976–77:** 1052
Abilene, Tex., **1976–77:** 405–408
ABM's.
  See Antiballistic missile systems.
Abortion, **1976–77:** 67 [7], 68 [21], 189 [15], 210 [6], 287 [2], 333 [16], 674 [34], 763 [5, 19], 769, 770, 947
Abrams, Gen. Creighton W., Jr., **1974:** 51
Accidents.
  See Safety.
ACTION
  Budget deferral, **1976–77:** 1022
  Director, **1975:** 20, 92
Addresses and remarks
  Abilene, Tex.
    Jaycees
      Bicentennial celebration, question-and-answer session, **1976–77:** 406
      Reception, **1976–77:** 408
    President Ford Committee volunteers, **1976–77:** 407
    President's arrival, **1976–77:** 405
  Advertising Council, Inc., conference, **1975:** 212
  Advisory Committee for Trade Negotiations, **1976–77:** 11
  AFL-CIO Building and Construction Trades Department, annual convention, **1975:** 580
  Agriculture Department, resignation of Secretary, **1976–77:** 849
  Aiken, Sen. George D., dinner honoring, **1974:** 118; **1975:** 266
  Air Force Association, convention, **1975:** 567
  Akron, Ohio, President's departure, **1976–77:** 1004
  Alexandria Police Association, picnic, **1974:** 59
  Alfred E. Smith, memorial dinner, **1976–77:** 935
  Alpha Kappa Alpha Sorority, conference, **1975:** 218
  Alton, Ill., whistlestop tour, **1976–77:** 907
Addresses and remarks—*continued*
  Amarillo, Tex.
    Northern Texas Panhandle Lion's Club, dinner, **1976–77:** 332
    President's arrival, **1976–77:** 330, 331
  American Agricultural Editors Association, question-and-answer session, **1976–77:** 272
  American Chamber of Commerce Executives, **1975:** 585
  American Conference on Trade, **1974:** 274
  American Enterprise Institute for Public Policy Research, reception, **1976–77:** 498
  American Football Coaches Association, awards dinner, **1975:** 25
  American Freedom Train, ceremonies, **1974:** 311
  American Hardware Manufacturers Association, convention, **1975:** 500
  American Hellenic Educational Progressive Association, biennial congressional dinner, **1976–77:** 302
  American Indian leaders, meeting, **1976–77:** 670
  American Jewish Committee, annual meeting, **1976–77:** 473
  American leaders of East European ancestry, **1976–77:** 881
  American Legion, national convention, **1975:** 492
  American Lutheran Church, convention, **1974:** 134
  American Mother's Committee, Inc., awards dinner, **1976–77:** 431
  American Retail Federation, annual meeting, **1976–77:** 469
  American Revolution Bicentennial, remarks, **1975:** 752
  American Society of Newspaper Editors, question-and-answer session, **1976–77:** 339
  American Society of Oral Surgeons, reception, **1975:** 617
  American Textile Manufacturers Institute, national convention, **1976–77:** 260

Addresses and remarks—*continued*
Americans of Eastern European background, remarks on meeting, **1975:** 430
Ames, Iowa, Iowa State University, **1976–77:** 904
AMVETS, presentation of the Golden Helmet Award, **1976–77:** 920
Anaheim, Calif., California Peace Officers Association, annual convention, **1976–77:** 513
Anderson Independent and Anderson Daily Mail Building, dedication, **1974:** 171
Angola, Senate action to prohibit U.S. assistance, **1975:** 738
Ann Arbor, Mich., University of Michigan
Address, **1976–77:** 784
Football team, dinner, **1976–77:** 783
Regents luncheon, **1976–77:** 1032
Apollo-Soyuz Test Project crewmembers
Meeting, **1975:** 624
Telephone conversations, **1975:** 412, 428
Arends, Repr. Leslie C., ceremonies honoring, **1974:** 190
Arlington, Va., Northeast Republican Conference, **1976–77:** 62
Armed Forces Week exhibit, Washington Monument, **1976–77:** 448
Asheville, N.C., **1976–77:** 237, 238
Associated General Contractors of America, annual convention, **1976–77:** 195
Association of American Editorial Cartoonists, reception, **1976–77:** 434
Atlanta, Ga.
Dobbins Air Force Base, President's arrival, **1976–77:** 358
Freedom Foundation, dinner, **1976–77:** 361
Military Order of World Wars, Atlanta Chapter, annual service, **1976–77:** 359
President Ford Committee, reception, **1976–77:** 360
Public forum, question-and-answer session, **1976–77:** 362
Atlantic City, N.J.
Boardwalk, **1976–77:** 973
National Aviation Facilities Experimental Center, **1976–77:** 972
New Jersey School Boards Association, **1976–77:** 974
Austria
President's visit, **1975:** 296–300
Visit of Chancellor Kreisky, **1974:** 227, 229
Bakersfield, Calif., President's arrival, **1975:** 165
Battle Creek, Mich., whistlestop tour, **1976–77:** 485
Bay Pines, Fla., Veterans Administration Center Hospital, **1976–77:** 94
Bay St. Louis, Miss., Hancock County Public Library, **1976–77:** 813
Belgium, President's visit, **1975:** 287, 289, 290

Addresses and remarks—*continued*
Bethesda Naval Hospital, annual physical examination, **1976–77:** 29
Beverly Hills, Calif., Republican fundraising dinners, closed-circuit television remarks, **1976–77:** 861
Bicentennial ceremony, National Archives and Records Service, **1976–77:** 639
Bicentennial Exposition on Science and Technology
Meeting, **1976–77:** 71
Telephone call, **1976–77:** 591
Bicentennial Land Heritage program, message signing ceremony, **1976–77:** 745
Big Brothers of America, award ceremony, **1976–77:** 350
Biloxi, Miss., Mavar's Cannery, **1976–77:** 815
Biological and chemical weapons treaties, remarks upon ratification, **1975:** 37
Birmingham, Ala.
President Ford Committee, receptions, **1976–77:** 422, 423
President's arrival, **1976–77:** 419
Public forum and question-and-answer session sponsored by Chamber of Commerce, **1976–77:** 420
Wilson Park, **1976–77:** 421
Birmingham, Mich., public rally, **1976–77:** 462
Bloomington, Ill., whistlestop tour, **1976–77:** 907
B'nai B'rith, **1976–77:** 196, 766
Boca Raton, Fla.
Royal Park Shopping Center, **1976–77:** 160
Spanish River Park, **1976–77:** 159
Bossier City, La.
Ambassador's Club, **1976–77:** 374
Exchange with reporters, **1976–77:** 372
Local officials, question-and-answer session, **1976–77:** 373
President's arrival, **1976–77:** 371
Boston school desegregation violence, remarks, **1974:** 142
Bowling Green, Ohio, Bowling Green State University, question-and-answer session, **1976–77:** 580
Boy Scouts of America
Annual report, **1976–77:** 132
Awards dinner, **1974:** 272
Boy of the Year, award presentation ceremony, **1976–77:** 309
Boynton, Fla., Sunshine Square Shopping Center, **1976–77:** 155
Boys/Girls Nation, joint session, **1976–77:** 714
Boys Nation, convention, remarks on greeting delegates, **1975:** 421
Briney Breezes, Fla., town offices, **1976–77:** 156
Bristol, Tenn., President's arrival, **1976–77:** 475
Brooklyn, N.Y.
Limousine tour, **1976–77:** 886

Addresses and remarks—*continued*
Brooklyn, N.Y.—*continued*
Yeshiva of Flatbush, High School, **1976–77:** 885
Broward County, Fla., Bicentennial delegation, **1976–77:** 175
Budget, Federal
Message, remarks on signing, **1975:** 63; **1976–77:** 21, 244
News briefing, **1976–77:** 23 (p. 50)
Buffalo, N.Y., Republican Party, reception, **1976–77:** 998
Buffalo Grove, Ill., Buffalo Grove High School, question-and-answer session, **1976–77:** 210
Business Council, meeting, **1974:** 290
Busing, message signing ceremony, **1976–77:** 614
Cabinet meeting following Presidential election, **1976–77:** 1016
California State Legislature, joint session, **1975:** 532
Campaign appearances
Alexandria, Va., **1974:** 88
Chicago, Ill., **1974:** 191
Cleveland, Ohio, **1974:** 184
Des Moines, Iowa, **1974:** 188
Detroit, Mich., **1974:** 135
Fresno, Calif., **1974:** 213
Grand Junction, Colo., **1974:** 219
Grand Rapids, Mich., **1974:** 208, 209
Greensboro, N.C., **1974:** 174
Greenville, S.C., **1974:** 173
Indianapolis, Ind., **1974:** 154
Kansas City, Mo., **1974:** 151
Lincoln, Nebr., **1974:** 153
Los Angeles, Calif., **1974:** 211
Louisville, Ky., **1974:** 175
Oklahoma City, Okla.,**1974:** 182, 183
Portland, Oreg., **1974:** 215
Rock Hill, S.C., **1974:** 172
Salt Lake City, Utah, **1974:** 218
Sioux City, Iowa, **1974:** 210
Sioux Falls, S. Dak., **1974:** 152
Spartanburg, S.C., **1974:** 170
Wichita, Kans., **1974:** 220
Canada, visits of Prime Minister Trudeau, **1974:** 278
Canyon, Tex., West Texas State University, public forum, question-and-answer session, **1976–77:** 333
Capitol Club, Overland Park, Kans., **1975:** 556
Capital Page School class, **1975:** 314
Carlinville, Ill., whistlestop tour, **1976–77:** 907
Carter, Jimmy, transition meeting, **1976–77:** 1020
Cederberg, Repr. Elford A., reception honoring, **1976–77:** 178
Centennial safe opening, the Capitol, **1976–77:** 632

Addresses and remarks—*continued*
Central Intelligence Agency, swearing in of Director, **1976–77:** 44
Chamber of Commerce of the United States, meeting, **1975:** 220; **1976–77:** 365
Champaign, Ill., **1976–77:** 188, 189
Charlotte, N.C.
Future Homemakers of America, **1976–77:** 235
President Ford Committee headquarters, President's visit, **1976–77:** 236
President's arrival, **1976–77:** 233
Reception honoring Repr. James G. Martin, **1976–77:** 234
Chicago, Ill.
Chicago Council of Foreign Relations, question-and-answer session, **1976–77:** 208
Ford City Shopping Mall, **1976–77:** 968
Northern Illinois Newspaper Association, question-and-answer session, **1976–77:** 209
President Ford Committee, reception, **1976–77:** 211
President's arrival, **1974:** 15
Chicago State University, commencement ceremonies, **1975:** 397
China, People's Republic of
National women's basketball team, **1975:** 696
President's visit, **1975:** 706, 708
U.S. Liaison Office, Chief
Designation, **1976–77:** 229
Swearing in, **1976–77:** 340
Christmas
Congressional ball, **1976–77:** 1026
National Community Tree lighting, **1974:** 306; **1975:** 736; **1976–77:** 1030
Church of Jesus Christ of Latter-day Saints, gift presentation, **1976–77:** 637
Cincinnati, Ohio
Fountain Square, **1976–77:** 981
Hamilton County Republican Club, breakfast, **1976–77:** 571
Local labor leaders, reception, **1976–77:** 572
President's arrival, **1976–77:** 570
Republican Party and President Ford Committee, reception, **1976–77:** 573
Citizen's Advisory Council on the Status of Women, annual report, **1976–77:** 363
Citizens Conference on State Legislatures, awards ceremony, **1975:** 34
Clemency program
Announcement, **1974:** 77
Executive warrants, signing, **1974:** 266
Cleveland, Ohio
Fleet Avenue parade site, **1976–77:** 982
Golden Agers banquet, **1976–77:** 568
National Conference of Christians and Jews, national awards dinner, **1976–77:** 569

Addresses and remarks—*continued*
Cleveland, Ohio—*continued*
President's arrival, **1976–77:** 566
Republican Party, reception, **1976–77:** 567
Sun Newspaper Good Neighbor Awards banquet, **1976–77:** 984
Taft, Robert Jr., fundraising reception, **1976–77:** 983
CLOSE-UP program, remarks to participants, **1975:** 172
Coal industry, White House meeting, **1975:** 152
Collective bargaining stamp, dinner marking issuance, **1975:** 134
Colombia, visit of President Lopez, **1975:** 586, 587
Columbia, S.C.
Governor's mansion, **1976–77:** 951
South Carolina State Fair, **1976–77:** 950
Columbus, Ohio
Fort Hayes Career Center, **1976–77:** 1006
Governor's Conference on Aging, annual meeting, **1976–77:** 533
Ohio State Capitol, **1976–77:** 534, 1005
Columbus Day ceremony, **1976–77:** 880
Combined Federal Campaign, **1975:** 593
Commerce Department, swearing in of Secretary, **1976–77:** 53
Community Services Administration, swearing in of Director, **1976–77:** 343
Concord, Mass., remarks, **1975:** 198
Concord, N.H.
Budget briefing, **1976–77:** 64
President Ford Committee, reception, **1976–77:** 66
State Capitol
General Court, address, **1975:** 195
President's arrival, **1975:** 194
Conference Board, dinner meeting, **1975:** 39
Conference on Ethnicity and Neighborhood Revitalization, **1976–77:** 426
Conference on Inflation, **1974:** 54, 56, 67, 106, 109
Conference on Security and Cooperation in Europe, **1975:** 459
Congress
Addresses to Joint Sessions, **1974:** 6, 121; **1975:** 28, 179
Democratic leadership, remarks following meeting, **1975:** 115
Former Members, reception, **1975:** 275
House of Representatives, President's visit, **1974:** 27
Senate, President's visit, **1974:** 26
Congressional Medal of Honor, presentation ceremonies, **1974:** 293; **1976–77:** 176
Congressional summer interns, **1975:** 423
Connally, John B., endorsement of the President, **1976–77:** 694

Addresses and remarks—*continued*
Connecticut Association of Realtors, convention, **1975:** 629
Conroe, Tex.
Montgomery County War Memorial, **1976–77:** 389
President Ford Committee, reception, **1976–77:** 390
Coral Springs, Fla., building, **1976–77:** 162
Cotton, Sen. Norris, dinner honoring, **1975:** 266
Council on Environmental Quality, annual report, **1976–77:** 143
Covington, Ky., **1976–77:** 980
Crime
Message, remarks at briefing, **1975:** 340
Radio address, **1976–77:** 988
Cub Scout induction ceremonies, Charleston, W.Va., **1975:** 671
Dallas, Tex.
Chamber of Commerce, public forum and question-and-answer session, **1976–77:** 398
Exchange with reporters, **1976–77:** 872
News conference, **1976–77:** 325
President Ford Committee, breakfast and receptions, **1976–77:** 322, 324, 871
President's arrivals, **1975:** 558; **1976–77:** 320, 396, 868
President's departure, **1976–77:** 399
Rally, **1976–77:** 397
Southern Methodist University School of Business, briefing and question-and-answer session, **1976–77:** 321
Texas State Fair
Board luncheon, **1976–77:** 870
Opening, **1976–77:** 869
Daughters of the American Revolution
84th Continental Congress, **1975:** 186
85th Continental Congress, **1976–77:** 349
Davies, Rodger P., ceremony honoring, **1974:** 22
Day-of-prayer proclamations, remarks on receiving collection, **1975:** 416
Dayton, Ohio, Montgomery County Historical Museum, **1976–77:** 575
Dearborn, Mich., Midwest Republican Conference, **1976–77:** 49
Deerfield, Fla., Deerfield Beach Fishing Pier, **1976–77:** 161
Defense budget meetings, **1976–77:** 172, 194
Defense and foreign policy briefing, **1976–77:** 77
Del Ray Beach, Fla., **1976–77:** 157
Department of Defense Medal for Distinguished Public Service, presentation ceremony, **1976–77:** 267
Destrehan, La., SS *Natchez* tour, **1976–77:** 812
Detroit, Mich.
Economics Club of Detroit, question-and-answer session, **1976–77:** 461
President's arrivals, **1976–77:** 460, 1007

Addresses and remarks—*continued*
Devon, Pa., Valley Forge Music Fair, **1976–77:** 978
Diplomatic Corps, **1976–77:** 682
Disabled American Veterans National Service and Legislative Headquarters, dedication ceremonies, **1976–77:** 174
District of Columbia Masons, Grand Lodge, Masonic Medallion presentation ceremony, **1976–77:** 243
District of Columbia undercover operations, meeting with law enforcement officials, **1976–77:** 664
Dover, N.H.
Chamber of Commerce, question-and-answer session, **1976–77:** 118
Dover High School, **1976–77:** 119
President Ford Committee headquarters, President's visit, **1976–77:** 120
Drug abuse, **1976–77:** 129, 367
Drug Abuse Prevention Week proclamation, signing ceremony, **1974:** 167
Durand, Mich., whistlestop tour, **1976–77:** 485
Durham, N.H.
News conference, **1976–77:** 67
University of New Hampshire, question-and-answer session, **1976–77:** 68
Economic Report of the President, remarks upon signing, **1975:** 68; **1976–77:** 30
Economic statistics, question-and-answer session, **1976–77:** 555
Education Division and Related Agencies Appropriation Act, 1976, remarks on veto, **1975:** 432
Egypt, visit of President Sadat, **1975:** 642–644, 654
Egyptian-Israeli troop disengagement agreement, telephone conversations with Secretary of State Kissinger, Prime Minister Rabin, and President Sadat, **1975:** 516
El Paso, Tex.
Bicentennial commemoration ceremony, **1976–77:** 329
President Ford Committee, reception, **1976–77:** 328
President's arrival, **1976–77:** 326
Texas Grain and Feed Association, annual convention, question-and-answer session, **1976–77:** 327
El Toro Marine Corps Air Station, Calif., President's arrival, **1976–77:** 510
Elder, Lee, reception honoring, **1974:** 268
Election eve remarks, **1974:** 221; **1976–77:** 1011
Elementary and secondary education reform, message signing ceremony, **1976–77:** 168
Elkins, W.Va., **1975:** 611
Emergency housing bill, remarks announcing veto, **1975:** 350

Addresses and remarks—*continued*
Energy, message signing ceremony, **1976–77:** 139
Energy and economic programs
Addresses to the Nation, **1975:** 26, 283
Briefings, **1975:** 32, 54
European trips
President's departures, **1975:** 286, 439
President's return, **1975:** 472
See also specific country; Travel, President's.
Evansville, Ind.
President Ford Committee, reception, **1976–77:** 357
President's arrival, **1976–77:** 355
Public forum, question-and-answer session, **1976–77:** 356
Everett McKinley Dirksen Congressional Leadership Research Center, dedication, **1975:** 495
F. Edward Hébert Library, groundbreaking ceremonies, **1975:** 206
F-15 aircraft, remarks on accepting for the U.S. Air Force, **1974:** 235
"Face the Nation," CBS interview, **1976–77:** 560
Fairbanks, Alaska, **1975:** 703
Far East trip
Anchorage, Alaska, stopover, **1974:** 239
President's departures, **1974:** 238; **1975:** 702
President's return, **1974:** 259
See also specific country; Travel, President's.
Federal-aid highway legislation, remarks upon signing message, **1975:** 382
Federal budget, remarks at briefing, **1975:** 62
Federal Council on Aging, swearing in of members, **1976–77:** 932
Federal Election Commission
Reconstitution, **1976–77:** 102, 145
Swearing in of members, **1976–77:** 500
Federal Energy Administration, National Energy Outlook Report, meeting, **1976–77:** 177
Federal Summer Employment Program for Youth, message and memorandum signing ceremony, **1976–77:** 310
Federal taxes and spending
Addresses to the Nation, **1975:** 164, 614
Bill veto, remarks announcing, **1975:** 731
Financial assistance for health care, message signing ceremony, **1976–77:** 135
Findley, Ohio, Elks Lodge, **1976–77:** 579
Finland, President's visit, **1975:** 455–457, 459
First Continental Congress, remarks concluding reconvening, **1974:** 58
Flint, Mich., whistlestop tour, **1976–77:** 485
Fond du Lac, Wis.
Farm forum, question-and-answer session, **1976–77:** 288
Key to city, presentation, **1976–77:** 289
Foreign assistance legislation, veto, **1976–77:** 436

Addresses and remarks—*continued*
Foreign exchange students, 1975–76, **1976–77:** 665
Foreign policy, address before Joint Session of Congress, **1975:** 179
Fort Chaffee refugee facility, remarks to reporters, **1975:** 484
Fort Lauderdale, Fla.
Budget briefing, **1976–77:** 89
President Ford Committee volunteers, **1976–77:** 90
President's arrival, **1976–77:** 88
Fort McHenry National Monument and Historic Shrine, **1975:** 379
Fort Myers, Fla.
President Ford Committee, reception, **1976–77:** 96
Rally, question-and-answer session, **1976–77:** 95
Fort Wayne, Ind.
President Ford Committee and Friends of Ford, reception, **1976–77:** 416
President's arrival, **1976–77:** 414
Public forum, question-and-answer session, **1976–77:** 415
Fort Worth, Tex.
Fort Worth-Tarrant County Bar Association, luncheon, **1976–77:** 380
President Ford Committee, reception, **1976–77:** 381
President's arrival, **1976–77:** 379
Foster Grandparent program, service award recipients, **1975:** 550
Fountain Valley, Calif., recreation center, **1976–77:** 954
Fourth of July, message, **1976–77:** 641
France
Meetings with President Giscard d'Estaing, **1974:** 297, 300, 301
President's visit, **1975:** 680
Freedom Day celebration, **1975:** 271
Freeland, Mich., President's arrival, **1976–77:** 487
Fresno, Calif., **1976–77:** 263, 264
Future Farmers of America
Annual convention, **1974:** 150
Members' visit to White House, **1975:** 419
General Aviation Manufacturers Association, meeting, **1976–77:** 538
General revenue sharing, briefings, **1975:** 393; **1976–77:** 57, 417, 551, 552
George C. Marshall Memorial Corridor at the Department of Defense, dedication ceremonies, **1976–77:** 348
George Washington Masonic National Memorial, unveiling ceremony, **1975:** 95
Georgine, Robert A., remarks at dinner honoring, **1975:** 35

Addresses and remarks—*continued*
Germany, Federal Republic of
President's visit, **1975:** 440–444
Visit of Chancellor Schmidt, **1974:** 279, 282
Visit of President Scheel, **1975:** 330, 331, 334
Girls Nation, convention, remarks on greeting delegates, **1975:** 414
Glendale, Calif.
"Days of the Verdugos" Festival, **1976–77:** 864
Exchange with reporters, **1976–77:** 865
Goodpaster, Gen. Andrew J., retirement ceremonies, **1974:** 312
Governors dinner, **1975:** 102
Grand Rapids, Mich.
Gerald R. Ford Health and Physical Education Building, dedication, **1976–77:** 1010
Mural unveiling ceremony, **1976–77:** 1013
President's arrivals, **1974:** 207; **1976–77:** 486
Rally, **1976–77:** 1009
Green Bay, Wis.
Green Bay Packers Hall of Fame Building, dedication ceremonies, **1976–77:** 291
President Ford Committee volunteers, **1976–77:** 292
President's arrival, **1976–77:** 290
Public forum, question-and-answer session, **1976–77:** 293
Greensboro, N.C., news conference, **1976–77:** 212
Greenspan, Alan, swearing in ceremony as Chairman of the Council of Economic Advisers, **1974:** 52
Greenville, U.S.S., remarks on greeting crewmembers, **1975:** 426
Guatemala, U.S. disaster assistance, **1976–77:** 103
Guilford, N.C., Courthouse National Military Park, **1976–77:** 213
Gulfport, Miss., Main Post Office, **1976–77:** 814
Handicapped American of the Year, award ceremonies, **1975:** 229; **1976–77:** 369
Harmon International Aviation Trophies, award ceremonies, **1975:** 235
Hartford, Conn., State Republican convention, **1976–77:** 672
Hatch Act amendments, veto, **1976–77:** 334
Hauppauge, N.Y., Colonie Hill, **1976–77:** 1000
Hawthorne, Calif., Rockwell International Cooperation Employees, **1976–77:** 858
Health, Education, and Welfare Department, Commissioner of Education
Nomination, **1976–77:** 792
Swearing in, **1976–77:** 915
Health care, message signing ceremony, **1976–77:** 135
Hempstead, N.Y.
Long Island labor and business leaders, **1976–77:** 1001

Addresses and remarks—*continued*
Hempstead, N.Y.—*continued*
Nassau County Veterans Memorial Coliseum, **1976–77:** 1002
Hickory, N.C., Lenoir Rhyne College, question-and-answer session, **1976–77:** 240
Highland, Fla., Seagate Highland Condominiums, **1976–77:** 158
Holm, Jeanne, appointment as Special Assistant to the President for Women, **1976–77:** 193
Holton-Arms School, graduation ceremonies, **1975:** 307
Honor America program, **1976–77:** 642
Hopkinton, R.I., officials, remarks on greeting, **1975:** 591
House Budget Committee, meeting with Members, **1976–77:** 194
House Judiciary Committee, testimony on decision to pardon Richard Nixon, **1974:** 155
Housing actions, remarks announcing, **1975:** 350
Houston, Tex.
Campaign rally, question-and-answer session, **1976–77:** 385
Greater Houston Builders and Contractors Associations, forum and question-and-answer session, **1976–77:** 383
Houston Chamber of Commerce Conference on Energy and the Economy, **1975:** 82
Houston Music Theatre, **1976–77:** 995
News conference, **1976–77:** 387
President Ford Committee, receptions, **1976–77:** 384, 386
President's arrivals, **1976–77:** 382, 994
Texas Nursing Home Association, annual meeting, **1976–77:** 388
Independence, Mo., Harry S Truman Statue, dedication ceremonies, **1976–77:** 447
Indianapolis, Ind.
Butler University, public forum, question-and-answer session, **1976–77:** 352
Indiana Broadcasters Association, statewide convention, question-and-answer session, **1976–77:** 354
Local officials, briefing on general revenue sharing, **1976–77:** 417
News conference, **1976–77:** 418
President Ford Committee headquarters, President's visit, **1976–77:** 353
President's arrivals, **1976–77:** 351, 609
Scottish Rite Cathedral, **1976–77:** 979
United States Jaycees, annual convention, **1976–77:** 610
Indonesia
President's visit, **1975:** 709
Visit of President Suharto, **1975:** 381
Inland Daily Press Association, question-and-answer session, **1976–77:** 138

Addresses and remarks—*continued*
Intelligence Oversight Board, meeting, **1976–77:** 124
Interlochen Arts Academy, **1975:** 399
International Association of Chiefs of Police, annual convention, **1974:** 96
International Conference on Urban Transportation, **1974:** 65
International Monetary Fund and World Bank Group, Boards of Governors, annual meetings, **1974:** 110; **1975:** 518
International Star Class Yacht Racing Association, dinner, **1975:** 499
Iowa State Fair, **1975:** 490
Iowa State House, **1974:** 187
Iran, visit of Shah, **1975:** 258, 261, 263
Irving, Tex., Bar Association Law Day, dinner, **1976–77:** 323
Israel, visits of Prime Minister Rabin, **1974:** 66, 75; **1975:** 322
Italian-American Foundation, dinner, **1976–77:** 787
Italy
President's visit, **1975:** 301, 302, 304, 305
U.S. disaster assistance, **1976–77:** 493
Visit of President Leone, **1974:** 100, 104
J. Edgar Hoover F.B.I. Building, dedication, **1975:** 596
Jackie Gleason Inverrary Classic, Lauderhill, Fla., **1975:** 110
Jackson, Miss.
Exchange with reporters, **1976–77:** 704
Republican Party, reception, **1976–77:** 703
Jacksonville Naval Air Station, Fla., President's arrival, **1975:** 653
Japan
President's visit, **1974:** 244–248, 250, 251
Visit of Emperor Hirohito, **1975:** 603, 606, 610
Visit of Prime Minister Miki, **1975:** 474
Japanese-American Internment in World War II, proclamation signing ceremony, **1976–77:** 111
Johnson City, Tenn., rally, **1976–77:** 476
Joliet, Ill., whistlestop tour, **1976–77:** 907
Jordan, visits of King Hussein, **1974:** 12; **1975:** 222
Judiciary, Federal and State, dinner honoring, **1975:** 692
Kalamazoo, Mich., whistlestop tour, **1976–77:** 485
Kansas City, Mo.
Acceptance speech, **1976–77:** 733
Campaign workers, **1976–77:** 731
New York delegation, **1976–77:** 729
President Ford Committee, staff, **1976–77:** 728
President Ford Youth Group, **1976–77:** 727
President's arrival, **1975:** 555
Reagan, Ronald, question-and-answer session with, **1976–77:** 730

Addresses and remarks—*continued*
Kansas City, Mo.—*continued*
Republican National Committee, breakfast and visit, **1976–77:** 726, 734
Vice-Presidential running mate, announcement, **1976–77:** 732
Kansas State Capitol, Topeka
Address, **1975:** 84
President's arrival, **1975:** 83
Keene, N.H.
Harper's Acres Retirement Home, **1976–77:** 117
Keene High School, question-and-answer session, **1976–77:** 116
President's arrival, **1976–77:** 115
Remarks, **1975:** 547
Kincheloe Air Force Base, President's departure, **1975:** 401
King, Martin Luther, Jr., remarks commemorating birth, **1975:** 27
Kissinger, Secretary of State Henry A., trips to Soviet Union and Middle East
President's remarks on departure, **1974:** 124
President's remarks following report, **1974:** 226
President's remarks on return, **1975:** 153, 523
Korea, Republic of, President's visit, **1974:** 252–254
Korean and American legislators, meeting, **1975:** 353
Labor Day, **1975:** 514; **1976–77:** 755
Labor Department, Secretary
Nomination, **1976–77:** 25
Swearing in, **1976–77:** 75
Labor Department building, dedication, **1974:** 163
La Crosse, Wis.
Mary E. Sawyer Municipal Auditorium, question-and-answer session, **1976–77:** 266
President's arrival, **1976–77:** 265
Laguna Hills, Calif., Rossmoor Leisure World, **1976–77:** 512
Lake Worth, Fla., City Hall, **1976–77:** 152
La Mesa, Calif., Grossmont Shopping Center, **1976–77:** 955
Langhorne, Pa., Oxford Valley Mall, **1976–77:** 996
Langley Air Force Base, Va., President's arrival, **1976–77:** 50
Lansing, Mich., whistlestop tour, **1976–77:** 485
Lantana, Fla., Bicentennial Park, **1976–77:** 153
Las Vegas, Nev.
International Council of Shopping Centers, convention, **1976–77:** 516
President Ford Committee, reception, **1976–77:** 517
President's arrival, **1976–77:** 515

Addresses and remarks—*continued*
Law Enforcement Assistance Administration, Career Criminal Conference, **1975:** 590
Lawton, Okla., President's arrival, **1976–77:** 866
Lebanon
Assassination of U.S. embassy officials, **1976–77:** 599, 606
Evacuation of American citizens, **1976–77:** 607, 608
Lexington, Mass., remarks, **1975:** 199
Libby Dam, dedication, **1975:** 498
Lilly Endowment Continuing Conference for the Liberal Arts, **1974:** 281
Lima, Ohio, Lima Mall, **1976–77:** 578
Lincoln, Abraham, ceremonies commemorating birth, **1975:** 86; **1976–77:** 80
Lincoln, Ill., whistlestop tour, **1976–77:** 907
Lincoln, Nebr.
Nebraska Educational Secretaries Association, **1976–77:** 445
President Ford Committee, reception, **1976–77:** 446
University of Nebraska, **1976–77:** 444
Lincoln Day Dinner in Grand Rapids, Mich., telephone remarks from White House, **1976–77:** 221
Little League World Series teams, remarks to members, **1974:** 36
Livonia, Mich., Wonderland Center, **1976–77:** 1008
Longview, Tex., President's arrival, **1976–77:** 376
Los Angeles, Calif.
Los Angeles Press Club, question-and-answer session, **1976–77:** 523
President Ford Committee, dinner and reception, **1976–77:** 262, 863
San Fernando Valley Business and Professional Association, **1976–77:** 862
University of Southern California, **1976–77:** 860
Louisville, Ky.
Armed Forces Day, dinner, **1976–77:** 484
Armed Forces Reserve Bill, signing ceremony, **1976–77:** 493
President Ford Committee, reception, **1976–77:** 482
President's arrival, **1976–77:** 481
Loy Norris High School students, **1975:** 337
Lubbock, Tex.
President Ford Committee, receptions, **1976–77:** 403, 404
President's arrival, **1976–77:** 400
Texas Technological University
Public forum, **1976–77:** 401
Students, question-and-answer session, **1976–77:** 402
Lutcher, La., SS *Natchez* tour, **1976–77:** 812

Addresses and remarks—*continued*
Luxembourg, visit of Prime Minister Thorn, **1975:** 674
Lyndon Baines Johnson Memorial Grove
Dedication ceremony, **1976–77:** 304
Groundbreaking ceremonies, **1974:** 107
Magna Carta delegation, **1976–77:** 554
Mahon, Repr. George H., portrait unveiling, **1974:** 287
Maine AFL-CIO Field Day program, **1975:** 508
Manchester, N.H., President's arrivals, **1975:** 193; **1976–77:** 63
Mansfield, Sen. Mike, reception honoring, **1974:** 21
Mao Tse-tung, death, **1976–77:** 767
Marion, Ill.
John A. Logan Community College, question-and-answer session, **1976–77:** 192
President's arrival, **1976–77:** 191
Martin, Repr. James G., reception honoring, **1976–77:** 234
Mayaguez, SS
Remarks following recovery, **1975:** 256
Remarks on greeting captain, **1975:** 426
Medford, Oreg.
Library Park, **1976–77:** 502
President's arrival, **1976–77:** 501
Memorial Day ceremonies, Arlington National Cemetery, **1975:** 278; **1976–77:** 544
Memphis, Tenn.
Commerce Square Fountain, dedication ceremonies, **1976–77:** 478
President Ford Committee, reception, **1976–77:** 479
President's arrival, **1976–77:** 477
Republican Party, reception, **1976–77:** 480
Mexico-United States Interparliamentary Conference, reception, **1976–77:** 137
Miami, Fla.
Naturalization ceremony, **1976–77:** 148
President Ford Committee, receptions, **1976–77:** 99, 149
South Florida Chapter Federal Bar Association, dinner, **1976–77:** 97
Villa Maria Nursing and Retirement Center, **1976–77:** 819
Miami Beach, Fla.
International Association of Chiefs of Police, annual conference, **1976–77:** 818
National Parkinson Institute, fundraising dinner, **1976–77:** 98
Michigan, western, question-and-answer session with businessmen, **1976–77:** 308
Michigan Association of Broadcasters, reception, **1976–77:** 435
Michigan Republican State Convention, **1974:** 35

Addresses and remarks—*continued*
Mid-America Committee for International Business and Government Cooperation, **1975:** 395
Middletown, Ohio, **1976–77:** 574
Midland, Tex., President's arrival, **1975:** 561
Milwaukee, Wis.
Ethnic organizations, question-and-answer session, **1976–77:** 283
Ford-Dole Committee, reception, **1976–77:** 990
News conference, **1976–77:** 282
President Ford Committee volunteers, **1976–77:** 285
Remarks on departure, **1975:** 503
Wisconsin Association of Manufacturers and Commerce, question-and-answer session, **1976–77:** 284
Wisconsin Education Association, annual meeting, **1976–77:** 989
Missing in action in Vietnam, efforts to account for, **1976–77:** 762
Mission Viejo, Calif., 10th anniversary, **1976–77:** 511
Mobile, Ala., Bates Field, Municipal Airport, **1976–77:** 817
Monterey, U.S.S., crewmembers reunion, **1975:** 277
Monticello, Va., naturalization ceremonies, **1976–77:** 649
Multiple Sclerosis Mother and Father of the Year award, **1976–77:** 454
NASA Distinguished Service Medal, award ceremony, **1975:** 482
Nashua, N.H., Chamber of Commerce, dinner, **1976–77:** 65
National Air and Space Museum, dedication ceremonies, **1976–77:** 631
National Alliance of Businessmen, receptions, **1975:**, 174; **1976–77:** 306
National Association for the Advancement of Colored People, **1975:** 369
National Association of Broadcasters
Las Vegas, Nev., **1975:** 171
Portland, Oreg., **1976–77:** 964
National Association of Food Chains, convention, **1975:** 631
National Association for Foreign Students Affairs, **1975:** 250
National Association of Life Underwriters, convention, **1975:** 579
National Association of Realtors, convention, **1974:** 234
National Association of Secondary School Principals, annual convention, **1976–77:** 105
National Baptist Convention, meeting, **1975:** 553
National Bicentennial Conference, **1975:** 105

Addresses and remarks—*continued*
National Bicentennial Salute to Small Business, award luncheon, **1976–77:** 470
National Collegiate Athletic Association, honors luncheon, **1975:** 22
National Commission on the Observance of International Women's Year
Establishment, **1975:** 24
Reception for members, **1975:** 185
Report, **1976–77:** 634
National Community Christmas Tree lighting, **1974:** 306; **1975:** 736; **1976–77:** 1030
National Conference of State Legislatures, **1975:** 216
National Council on the Arts, reception, **1974:** 53
National Council on Crime and Delinquency, meeting, **1974:** 181
National Defense University, dedication ceremonies, **1976–77:** 1075
National Education Association
Bicentennial Commemorative Plaque, presentation ceremony, **1976–77:** 14
Remarks to Members of the Board, **1975:** 234
National Entertainment Conference, luncheon, **1975:** 87
National Environmental Research Center, dedication, **1975:** 373
National Exchange Club, annual convention, **1976–77:** 663
National Explorer Presidents' Congress, **1975:** 177
National Farm Credit Bureau, Directors, **1976–77:** 793
National Farm Family of the Year, remarks on greeting, **1975:** 409
National Federation of Business and Professional Women's Clubs, reception, **1976–77:** 179
National Federation of Independent Business, conference, **1975:** 335
National Federation of Republican Women
Convention, **1975:** 559
Reception, **1976–77:** 791
National Football Foundation and Hall of Fame, awards dinner, **1974:** 289
National Governors' Conference
Dinner, **1976–77:** 131
Winter meeting, **1976–77:** 126
National Guard Association, general conference, **1976–77:** 749
National Hispanic Heritage Week
Proclamation, signing ceremonies, **1974:** 48; **1976–77:** 768
Reception, **1976–77:** 788
National Industrial Council, remarks following briefing, **1975:** 318
National League of Cities, **1976–77:** 216

Addresses and remarks—*continued*
National League of Families of American Prisoners and Missing in Southeast Asia, meeting, **1975:** 411; **1976–77:** 689
National Medal of Science, awards ceremonies, **1975:** 568; **1976–77:** 914
National Multiple Sclerosis Society, awards ceremony, **1975:** 238
National Newspaper Association, question-and-answer session, **1976–77:** 231
National Newspaper Association's Government Affairs Conference, **1975:** 135
National Newspaper Publishers Association, **1975:** 43
National Prayer Breakfast, **1975:** 56; **1976–77:** 37
National Religious Broadcasters Congressional Breakfast, **1975:** 50
National Religious Broadcasters and National Association of Evangelicals, combined convention, **1976–77:** 125
National Republican Club of Capitol Hill
Fundraising reception, **1975:** 543
Portrait unveiling, **1975:** 213
National Republican Heritage Groups Council, **1975:** 262
National Retired Teachers Association and American Association of Retired Persons, **1976–77:** 24
National Rural Electric Cooperative Association, Youth Tour, **1975:** 321
National Teacher of the Year Award, **1976–77:** 219
National Teen-age Republican Leadership Conference, **1975:** 339; **1976–77:** 603
National YMCA Youth Governors Conference, **1975:** 356
Native American Awareness Week, proclamation signing ceremony, **1976–77:** 867
NATO Council, swearing in of U.S. Representative, **1976–77:** 927
Navy League of the United States, convention, **1975:** 207
NBC News interview, **1976–77:** 6
Nessen, Ron, remarks announcing appointment as Press Secretary, **1974:** 92
Netherlands, visit of Prime Minister den Uyl, **1975:** 255
New City, N.Y., Rockland County Courthouse, **1976–77:** 892
New England Council, **1975:** 663
New Orleans, La., SS *Natchez* tour, **1976–77:** 812
New York, N.Y.
Alfred E. Smith Memorial dinner, **1976–77:** 935
Operation Sail, New York Harbor, **1976–77:** 647
Republican National Committee, dinner, **1976–77:** 887

Addresses and remarks—*continued*
New York Society of Security Analysts, remarks and question-and-answer session, **1975:** 90
Newark, N.J., President's arrival, **1976–77:** 561
Newsweek magazine interview, **1974:** Appendix D
Niles, Mich., whistlestop tour, **1976–77:** 485
Nimitz, U.S.S., commissioning ceremony, **1975:** 236
Nixon, Richard M.
Pardon, remarks announcing, **1974:** 60
President's visit with, remarks following, **1974:** 212
Noise standards for commercial aircraft, exchange with reporters, **1976–77:** 934
Norfolk, Va., Southern Baptist Convention, **1976–77:** 595
North Atlantic Treaty Organization Council, address, **1975:** 289
North Carolina Central University, **1975:** 676
Northbrook, Ill., Allstate Insurance Company, **1976–77:** 969
Notre Dame University, convocation, **1975:** 137
Oath of Office, remarks following ceremony, **1974:** 1
Ocean Ridge, Fla., **1976–77:** 154
Office of Science and Technology Policy
Establishment, message signing ceremony, **1976–77:** 244
Swearing in of Director, **1976–77:** 724
Offutt Air Force Base, Nebr., President's arrival, **1975:** 599
Ohio Farm Bureau Federation, remarks and question-and-answer session, **1976–77:** 217
Ohio State University, commencement, **1974:** 42
Oil
Import fees
Proclamations, remarks upon signing, **1975:** 41, 120
U.S. Court of Appeals, remarks following decision, **1975:** 485
Price controls
Bill veto, **1975:** 537
Congress, announcement of compromise plans, **1975:** 402, 429
Oil and gas development, meeting with coastal State Governors, **1974:** 233
Oklahoma State Fair, **1975:** 571
Older Americans, message signing ceremony, **1976–77:** 69
Older Americans Month, proclamation signing cermony, **1976–77:** 300
Old North Church Bicentennial Lantern Service, **1975:** 197

Addresses and remarks—*continued*
Olympics
Funding for 1980 winter games, message signing ceremony, **1976–77:** 438
U.S. team, **1976–77:** 658, 659, 716
Omaha, Nebr.
Bergan-Mercy Hospital, groundbreaking ceremonies, **1976–77:** 440
Farm forum, question-and-answer session, **1976–77:** 442
President Ford Committee, receptions, **1976–77:** 441, 443
President's arrival, **1976–77:** 439
Opportunities Industrialization Centers of America, annual convention, **1975:** 71
Oregon Museum of Science and Industry, auction, **1974:** 216
Organization of American States General Assembly, reception for chiefs of delegation, **1975:** 251
Orlando, Fla., **1976–77:** 86, 87
Pakistan, visit of Prime Minister Bhutto, **1975:** 74
Paramus, N.J., Garden State Plaza, **1976–77:** 893
Pasadena, Calif., **1976–77:** 952, 953
Pascagoula, Miss., Beach Park, **1976–77:** 816
Paterson, N.J.
Bergen County business and civic leaders, reception, **1976–77:** 563
Great Falls National Historic Site, dedication, **1976–77:** 562
Pearl Harbor, Hawaii, memorial ceremonies, **1975:** 715
Pendelton, Oreg.
Agricultural organizations, reception, **1976–77:** 509
Pendleton Memorial Armory, **1976–77:** 508
President's arrival, **1976–77:** 507
Peoria, Ill.
Bradley University, Everett McKinley Dirksen forum, question-and-answer session, **1976–77:** 185
Mohammed Shrine Temple, **1976–77:** 186
President Ford Committee, reception, **1976–77:** 187
President's arrival, **1976–77:** 184
Pepperdine University, dedication ceremonies, **1975:** 574
Permian Basin Petroleum Museum, dedication ceremonies, **1975:** 562
Philadelphia, Pa.
Independence Hall, **1976–77:** 645
International Eucharistic Congress, **1976–77:** 720
Italian Market, **1976–77:** 806
Luncheon honoring the President, **1976–77:** 646

Addresses and remarks—*continued*
Philadelphia, Pa.—*continued*
Pennsylvania, New Jersey, and Delaware President Ford Committees, reception, **1976–77:** 804
Plymouth Meeting Hall, **1976–77:** 977
Polish-American Congress, **1976–77:** 805
Presidential campaign debate, **1976–77:** 803
Republican Party, fundraising dinner, **1976–77:** 976
Philippines, President's visit, **1975:** 711, 712, 714
Pittsburgh, Pa., Pittsburgh Economic Club, question-and-answer session, **1976–77:** 967
Plattsburgh, N.Y., U.S. Olympic Team, **1976–77:** 658, 659
Poland
President's visit, **1975:** 448, 449, 451–453
Visit of First Secretary Gierek, **1974:** 119, 123, 128
Pontiac, Ill., whistlestop tour, **1976–77:** 907
Pope Air Force Base, N.C., President's arrival, **1974:** 69
Portland, Oreg.
National Association of Broadcasters, question-and-answer session, **1976–77:** 964
President's arrivals, **1975:** 528; **1976–77:** 503, 962
President's departure, **1976–77:** 965
Republican Party—President Ford Committee, reception, **1976–77:** 504
Sheraton-Portland Hotel, remarks, **1976–77:** 963
Warner Pacific College, commencement address, **1976–77:** 506
World Affairs Council of Oregon, question-and-answer session, **1976–77:** 505
Portsmouth, N.H.
Newington Plaza Shopping Center, **1976–77:** 121
Remarks, **1975:** 549
President Ford Committee, National
Ethnic Affairs Committee, **1976–77:** 846
Headquarters, President's visits, **1976–77:** 10, 722
Resignation of Chairman, **1976–77:** 273
Presidential debates, question-and-answer session with reporters, **1976–77:** 750
Presidential election
Remarks awaiting results, **1976–77:** 1012
Remarks on eve of the elections, **1976–77:** 1011
Remarks on results, **1976–77:** 1014
Presidential Medal of Freedom, presentation ceremony, **1976–77:** 76, 281, 716, 900, 1052, 1061
Presidential Scholars, **1975:** 371
President's Advisory Committee on Refugees, remarks upon establishing, **1975:** 267

Addresses and remarks—*continued*
President's Committee on Urban Development and Neighborhood Revitalization, interim report, **1976–77:** 931
President's Foreign Intelligence Advisory Board, swearing in of Chairman and members, **1976–77:** 279
Primary election results
Alabama, **1976–77:** 427
California, **1976–77:** 585
Florida, **1976–77:** 198
Georgia, **1976–77:** 427
Indiana, **1976–77:** 427
Maryland, **1976–77:** 497
Michigan, **1976–77:** 497
New Jersey, **1976–77:** 585
Ohio, **1976–77:** 585
Wisconsin, **1976–77:** 307
Professional athletes prayer brunch, **1976–77:** 100
Public Works Employment Act, veto, **1976–77:** 652
Puerto Rico, summit conference, **1976–77:** 550, 618–621
Question-and-answer sessions. *See under* News conferences.
Radio addresses
Crime, **1976–77:** 988
Future Goals for America, **1976–77:** 1003
Inflation, **1976–77:** 957
Peace, **1976–77:** 985
Senior citizens, **1976–77:** 971
Taxes, **1976–77:** 966
Radio and Television Directors' Association, conference, **1974:** 76
Radio-Television News Directors Association
Briefing for members, **1975:** 46
Question-and-answer session, **1976–77:** 48
Raleigh, N.C., North Carolina State Fair, **1976–77:** 949
Rantoul, Ill., Chanute Community Foundation, reception, **1976–77:** 190
Regulatory reform
Meeting with commissioners, **1976–77:** 314
Remarks at a meeting, **1975:** 392
Republican Congressional staff members, reception, **1974:** 98
Republican National Associates, reception, **1975:** 352
Republican National Committee
Executive Committee, **1976–77:** 617
Receptions, **1975:** 536; **1976–77:** 142
Republican National Committee and Republican National Finance Committee, luncheon, **1974:** 79
Republican National Hispanic Assembly, first annual banquet, **1976–77:** 702

Addresses and remarks—*continued*
Republican National Leadership Conference, dinner meeting, **1975:** 129
Republican Party functions. *See under* Republican Party.
Republican Party leaders, meeting, **1976–77:** 1025
Republican Party Senate-House fundraising dinners, **1975:** 187; **1976–77:** 278
Republican Presidential nomination, remarks announcing candidacy, **1975:** 386
Reserve, La., SS *Natchez* tour, **1976–77:** 812
Reserve Officers Association of the United States, **1975:** 103
Richmond, Va., State Capitol grounds, **1976–77:** 948
Rochester, N.Y., President's departure, **1976–77:** 999
Rockefeller, Nelson A.
Dinner honoring, **1975:** 91
Remarks announcing nomination to be Vice President, **1974:** 17, 18
Rockefeller Public Service Awards, luncheon, **1974:** 275
Rockford, Ill.
Cherryvale Mall, **1976–77:** 205
Farm forum, question-and-answer session, **1976–77:** 203
Greater Rockford Tool, Die and Machining Association, **1976–77:** 204
President Ford Committee, reception, **1976–77:** 206
President's arrival, **1976–77:** 202
Romania, President's visit, **1975:** 461–464
Roseville, Mich., **1976–77:** 463
Roudebush, Richard L., swearing in ceremony as Administrator of Veterans Affairs, **1974:** 139
Russell, Kans., picnic honoring Senator Robert Dole, **1976–77:** 735
Sacramento, Calif., remarks following assassination attempt, **1975:** 533
Sacramento Host Breakfast, **1975:** 531
Saginaw, Mich., Saginaw Township Bicentennial Park, **1976–77:** 488
St. Edward Mercy Medical Center, dedication ceremonies, **1975:** 483
St. Louis, Mo.
American Farm Bureau Federation, annual convention, **1976–77:** 8
Exchange with reporters, **1975:** 551
Luther Ely Smith Memorial Park, **1976–77:** 993
Northwest Plaza, **1976–77:** 909
President's arrivals, **1976–77:** 7, 991
St. Petersburg, Fla.
President Ford Committee, reception, **1976–77:** 93

Addresses and remarks—*continued*
St. Petersburg, Fla.—*continued*
President's arrival, **1976–77:** 91
Senior citizens group, **1976–77:** 92
San Antonio, Tex.
Alamo, **1976–77:** 317
President Ford Committee, reception, **1976–77:** 319
President's arrival, **1976–77:** 316
Republican Party, reception, question-and-answer session, **1976–77:** 318
San Diego, Calif.
Chamber of Commerce and San Diego Council of the Navy League, **1976–77:** 519
Exchange with reporters, **1976–77:** 956
President Ford Committee, reception, **1976–77:** 520
President's arrival, **1976–77:** 518
Southwest Border Economic Region, establishment, **1976–77:** 958
Theresa Janene, remarks on board, **1976–77:** 521
San Francisco, Calif.
American Textile Manufacturers Institute, annual convention, **1976–77:** 260
Citizens for Ford Committee, establishment, **1976–77:** 853
Exchange with reporters, **1976–77:** 259, 852, 855, 856
President Ford Committee, luncheon and party, **1976–77:** 261, 857
Presidential campaign debate, **1976–77:** 854
San Francisco Bay Area Council, **1975:** 169
San Jose, Calif.
Center for the Performing Arts, **1976–77:** 525
President Ford Committee, reception, **1976–77:** 526
President's arrival, **1976–77:** 524
President's departure, **1976–77:** 532
San Jose Foreign Trade Zone, luncheon, **1976–77:** 527
Sarasota, Fla.
President's arrival, **1976–77:** 163
Sarasota Shrine Hall, **1976–77:** 164
Savings bonds, Bicentennial-design, first purchase, **1975:** 228
Schaumberg, Ill., Woodfield Shopping Mall, **1976–77:** 970
Scott, Sen. Hugh, reception honoring, **1975:** 265
Scranton, William W., dinner honoring, **1974:** 131
Seattle, Wash.
Pier 57, **1976–77:** 960
President's arrivals, **1975:** 524; **1976–77:** 959
Veterans Administration Hospital, **1976–77:** 961
Senate Armed Services and Appropriations Committees, meeting, **1976–77:** 172

Addresses and remarks—*continued*
SER–Jobs for Progress, meeting, **1975:** 410
Shouse, Catherine Filene, **1976–77:** 559, 1052
Shreveport, La., Louisiana National Guard Military Ball, **1976–77:** 375
Shultz, George P., remarks at ceremony honoring, **1975:** 240
Singapore, visit of Prime Minister Lee, **1975:** 249
Sixth Circuit Judicial Conference, **1975:** 400
Skylab astronauts, remarks on presenting the Robert H. Goddard Memorial Trophy, **1975:** 180
Small Business Administration, swearing in of Administrator, **1976–77:** 82
Small Business Awards, ceremony, **1975:** 272
Social security benefit indexing act, proposed, **1976–77:** 601
Social Security Trust Fund, meeting with administration officials, **1976–77:** 432
Southern Baptist Convention, **1976–77:** 595
Southern Methodist University, special convocation, **1975:** 560
Southern Republican leaders, meeting, **1976–77:** 786
Soviet transpolar aviators, **1975:** 348
Soyuz spacecraft, remarks on launch, **1975:** 406
Spain, President's visit, **1975:** 291–294
Sparkman, Sen. John J., birthday party, **1974:** 315
Springfield, Ill.
Farm forum, question-and-answer session, **1976–77:** 181
Lincoln Home National Visitor's Center, cornerstone unveiling, **1976–77:** 180
President Ford Committee, reception, **1976–77:** 183
Teachers of children with impaired hearing, **1976–77:** 182
Whistlestop tour, **1976–77:** 907
Springfield, Mo.
Missouri Republican Convention, **1976–77:** 589
President's arrival, **1976–77:** 588
Springfield, Ohio
Snyder Park, **1976–77:** 576
Springfield Art Center, **1976–77:** 577
Spruce Pine, N.C., President's arrival, **1976–77:** 239
Stanford University School of Law
Dedication ceremonies, **1975:** 577
Question-and-answer session, **1975:** 578
State Department, swearing in of Chief of Protocol, **1976–77:** 680
State of the Union Address
1975, **1975:** 28
1976, **1976–77:** 19
1977, **1976–77:** 1057

Addresses and remarks—*continued*
Stein, Herbert, farewell party, **1974:** 38
Stevens, Sen. Ted, remarks at birthday party, **1975:** 704
Sullivan, Repr. Leonor K., portrait unveiling, **1974:** 99
Supreme Court of the United States, nomination of Associate Justice, **1975:** 697
Swine flu immunization program, **1976–77:** 257, 718
Syracuse, N.Y., Onondaga County War Memorial Auditorium, **1976–77:** 997
Tampa, Fla.
Austin Building Complex, **1976–77:** 166
President Ford Committee, reception, **1976–77:** 167
President's arrival, **1976–77:** 165
Task Force on Questionable Corporate Payments Abroad, **1976–77:** 277, 592
Teague, Repr. Olin E., portrait unveiling, **1975:** 112
terHorst, J. F., remarks announcing appointment as Press Secretary, **1974:** 2
Teton Dam, Idaho, collapse, **1976–77:** 583, 587
Texas Republican delegation, **1976–77:** 253
Thanksgiving Day, **1975:** 694
"Today" program, NBC interview, **1976–77:** 778
Toledo, Ohio, President's departure, **1976–77:** 581
Travel Program for Foreign Diplomats, luncheon, **1975:** 148
Truman, Harry S, statue dedication, **1976–77:** 447
Tulane University, convocation, **1975:** 208
Tunisia, visit of Prime Minister Nouira, **1975:** 233
Turkey, U.S. military assistance, remarks following meeting with Congressmen, **1975:** 387
Tyler, Tex.
President Ford Committee, reception, **1976–77:** 377
Tyler Junior College, question-and-answer session, **1976–77:** 378
Uniformed Services University of Health Sciences, groundbreaking ceremonies, **1975:** 394
Union, N.J., President Ford Committee, reception, **1976–77:** 894, 895
United Kingdom
U.S. Ambassador
Nomination, **1976–77:** 16
Swearing in, **1976–77:** 112
Visit of Prime Minister Wilson, **1975:** 57, 61
United Nations, U.S. Representative
Nomination, **1976–77:** 133
Swearing in, **1976–77:** 218

Addresses and remarks—*continued*
United Nations General Assembly, **1974:** 81
United States Conference of Mayors, **1976–77:** 38, 216
United States Industrial Payroll Savings Committee, **1976–77:** 28
United States Jaycees
Indianapolis, annual convention, **1976–77:** 610
Officials, **1975:** 540; **1976–77:** 790
United States Military Academy, commencement address, **1975:** 306
United States-Soviet Treaty on Underground Nuclear Explosions for Peaceful Purposes, signing ceremony, **1976–77:** 540
United Way campaign, **1974:** 57
University of Hawaii, **1975:** 716
University of Michigan Club, Congressional dinner, **1975:** 122
University of Pennsylvania, commencement ceremonies, **1975:** 264
Uranium production, remarks about proposed legislation, **1975:** 357
Urban League, dance, **1974:** 217
U.S. Army Bicentennial, ceremonies, **1975:** 329
U.S. Industrial Payroll Savings Committee, remarks to members, **1975:** 33
U.S. Marine Corps Bicentennial, ceremony, **1975:** 667
U.S. Navy Bicentennial, ceremony, **1975:** 619
Vail, Colo.
Exchange with reporters, **1976–77:** 737, 740, 742, 1039, 1040, 1042
President's arrival for Christmas holidays, **1976–77:** 1033
Vail Symposium, **1975:** 488
Valley Forge, Pa., Valley Forge State Park, **1976–77:** 643, 644
Van Nuys, Calif., President's arrival, **1976–77:** 522
Veterans Day, **1974:** 192; **1975:** 641
Veterans of Foreign Wars
Annual Convention, **1974:** 16
Annual congressional dinner, **1976–77:** 197
Vice-Presidential campaign debate, telephone conversation with Senator Robert Dole, **1976–77:** 906
Viking I, landing on Mars, **1976–77:** 679
Villanova, Pa., Villanova University, **1976–77:** 975
Waco, Tex.
Baylor University, question-and-answer session, **1976–77:** 392
President Ford Committee, reception, **1976–77:** 394
President's arrival, **1976–77:** 391
President's departure, **1976–77:** 395
Waco Suspension Bridge, restoration project, **1976–77:** 393

Addresses and remarks—*continued*
Walnut Creek, Calif.
President Ford Committee, reception, **1976–77:** 531
Rossmoor Golden Rain Foundation, **1976–77:** 529
Rossmoor President Ford Committee, reception, **1976–77:** 530
Town square, **1976–77:** 528
Walter Hagen Invitational Golf Tournament, **1975:** 398
Washington Press Club, **1974:** 84
West Bend, Wis., public forum, question-and-answer session, **1976–77:** 287
West Orange, N.J.
Republican Committee members, meeting, **1976–77:** 565
Republican Party, reception, **1976–77:** 564
West Palm Beach, Fla.
President's arrival, **1976–77:** 150
West Palm Beach Mall, **1976–77:** 151
Wheatgrowers organizations, remarks and question-and-answer session, **1975:** 497
Wheaton, Ill., Wheaton College, question-and-answer session, **1976–77:** 207
White House Conference on Domestic and Economic Affairs, **1974:** 214; **1975:** 69, 108, 167, 196, 374, 496, 502, 527, 554, 602, 616
White House Conference on Handicapped Individuals, **1975:** 691
White House Correspondents Association, dinner, **1975:** 237
White House Fellows, reception, **1976–77:** 471
White House Fellowship program, remarks to participants, **1975:** 269
White House News Photographers Association, **1975:** 190
White House staff, Christmas party, **1975:** 728
White Plains, N.Y., City Hall, **1976–77:** 891
Wilkesboro, N.C., West Wilkes High School, question-and-answer session, **1976–77:** 215
Williamsburg, Va.
Dinner toasts with Governor Godwin, **1976–77:** 52
Langley Air Force Base, President's arrival, **1976–77:** 50
Presidential campaign debate, **1976–77:** 947
President's departure from White House, **1976–77:** 942
Virginia General Assembly, **1976–77:** 51
Wimbledon tennis champions, remarks on greeting, **1975:** 417
WIN consumer pledge, remarks on signing, **1974:** 232
Winston-Salem, N.C., Hanes Mall, **1976–77:** 214
Wolf Trap Farm Park, Va., **1976–77:** 559
Women in top-level Government positions, briefing, **1976–77:** 366

Addresses and remarks—*continued*
Women's Forum on National Security, **1975:** 106
World Affairs Council, question-and-answer session, **1975:** 581
World Conference on Law, **1975:** 632
World Energy Conference, **1974:** 94
World Golf Hall of Fame
Dinner, **1974:** 71
Opening ceremony, **1974:** 70
Yale University Law School, convocation, **1975:** 217
Yellowstone National Park, Wyo., **1976–77:** 743
Young Republican Conference, **1976–77:** 39
Young Republican Leadership Conference, **1975:** 116
Youth Bicentennial rally, **1975:** 530
Yugoslavia
President's visit, **1975:** 466–470
Visit of Prime Minister Bijedic, **1975:** 145
Zambia, visit of President Kaunda, **1975:** 200
See also Bill signings; Legislation, remarks and statements on approval; Meetings with foreign leaders; News conferences; News media; Swearing-in ceremonies.
Administration on Aging, **1975:** 280; **1976–77:** 248
Administration's goals and achievements, **1976–77:** 67 [11], 68, 116, 231 [4], 339 [15], 672, 684, 733, 925 [10], 947
Administrative Law Judges, **1974:** 205
Advertising Council, Inc., **1975:** 212
Advisory Committee on Federal Pay, **1974:** 115, 117; **1975:** 328, 506; **1976–77:** 844
Advisory Committee on Refugees, President's, **1975:** 267, 415
Advisory Committee for Trade Negotiations, **1976–77:** 11
Advisory Council on Economic Opportunity, National, **1975:** 544
Advisory Council on Extension and Continuing Education, National, **1975:** 336
Advisory Council on Intergovernmental Personnel Policy, **1974:** 101
Advisory Council on Social Security, **1975:** 126
Aeronautics program, **1975:** 313
AFL-CIO.
See American Federation of Labor-Congress of Industrial Organizations.
AFL-CIO Building and Construction Trades Department, **1975:** 35, 580
Africa
Administration policy, **1975:** 179, 200, 581 [7], 750 [6]
Campaign debate remarks, **1976–77:** 854
Interview remarks, **1976–77:** 778
Kissinger, Henry A., trip, **1976–77:** 396, 406, 770
News conference remarks, **1976–77:** 763 [1, 16]
Security assistance programs, **1975:** 649
University of Michigan, remarks, **1976–77:** 784
Africa—*continued*
U.S. policy, **1976–77:** 372, 378 [7], 420 [5], 552, 566, 576, 807
U.S. trade, **1976–77:** 420 [8]
See also specific country.
African Development Bank, **1974:** 72
African Unity, Organization of, **1975:** 739 [9], 750 [6]
Aged.
See Older persons.
Agency for International Development, Administrator, **1975:** 163
See also other part of title.
Aging, Federal Council on the, **1976–77:** 708, 932
Aging, Ohio Governor's Conference on, **1976–77:** 533
Agreements, international.
See Treaties and other international agreements; *specific subject.*
Agricultural Development, International Fund for, **1976–77:** 1037
Agricultural Marketing Agreement Act, **1975:** 16
Agricultural Policy Committee, **1976–77:** 181, 200
Agricultural resources conservation act, veto, **1976–77:** 922
Agriculture, Department of
Appropriations, **1974:** 72, 240
Budget deferrals and rescissions, **1975:** 59, 437, 541, 607; **1976–77:** 227, 697, 1069
Emergency livestock feed assistance, **1976–77:** 1029
Farm forums.
See Farm forums.
Financial assistance programs, **1976–77:** 558
Forest and Rangeland Renewable Resources Planning Act of 1974, **1976–77:** 170
Grain inspection system, **1976–77:** 939
National Forest System, **1975:** 726
National School Lunch program, **1974:** 210
Predator control reorganization, **1976–77:** 1082
Rabbit meat inspection, **1976–77:** 911
Secretary, **1974:** 41, 109, 132, 195 [18], 210, 241, 276, 277, 291; **1975:** 20, 92, 159, 311, 600 [3, 6]; **1976–77:** 181, 200, 272, 288, 327, 415, 626, 793, 849, 852
Texas Grain and Feed Association, **1976–77:** 327
Under Secretary, **1975:** 311
See also specific constituent agencies.
Agriculture and agricultural programs
Administration policy, **1976–77:** 333 [6], 507, 735
Agricultural Policy Committee, **1976–77:** 181, 200
American Agricultural Editors Association, **1976–77:** 272
American Farm Bureu Federation, remarks, **1976–77:** 8
Commodities prices limitations, **1976–77:** 327 [4]
Commodity exports, **1975:** 85 [9], 502 [3], 554 [2]

Agriculture—*continued*
Commodity futures trading, **1974:** 189
Conservation, **1975:** 15
Dairy products, **1974:** 152, 153
Emergency agricultural bill, **1975:** 232, 252, 332
Employment opportunities, **1976–77:** 287 [7]
Energy requirements, **1975:** 84, 502 [17]
Energy tax rebate, **1975:** 121
Environmental protection, **1975:** 15
Farm forums.
See Farm forums.
Federal assistance, **1975:** 85 [9], 138 [3]
Federal restrictions, **1975:** 64, 70
Food, foreign assistance, **1974:** 102; **1975:** 600 [5]
Food stamp program, **1975:** 28, 36 [22], 64, 89, 620 [14], 622 [5, 19], 626, 634, 647
Future Farmers of America, presentation of plaque to President, **1976–77:** 287 [8]
Grain sales, **1974:** 210; **1975:** 460, 511 [3, 12], 528, 539, 548, 552 [8], 571, 581 [6], 582 [8], 598, 600 [1, 6], 602 [1, 5, 7, 13], 616 [5], 620 [7], 622 [1], 636, 650, 750 [7]
Investment tax credit, **1975:** 84
Iowa State University, remarks, **1976–77:** 904
Legislation, **1976–77:** 685
Loans, exemption from State usury laws, **1974:** 199
National Farm Credit Directors, remarks, **1976–77:** 793
Ohio Farm Bureau Federation, **1976–77:** 217
President's assessment, **1975:** 490, 497 [1]
President's views, **1976–77:** 321 [1]
Prices, **1975:** 232, 602 [16], 616 [17], 636
Production, **1975:** 571, 602 [1], 616 [5, 17, 18]
Rural development legislation, **1976–77:** 301
State of the Union Address, **1976–77:** 19
Sugar production, **1974:** 241
Texas Grain and Feed Association, **1976–77:** 327
Tobacco price support levels, **1975:** 601
Trade agreements, **1976–77:** 189 [1]
Vocational education programs, **1975:** 602 [11]
Agronsky, Martin, **1975:** 479
Aguirre, Edward, **1976–77:** 792, 915
AID.
See Agency for International Development.
Aid to families with dependent children, legislation, **1976–77:** 685
Aiken, Sen. George D., **1974:** 118; **1975:** 266
Aikens, Joan D., **1975:** 184
Ailes, Stephen, **1976–77:** 107 [1, 10], 124, 199
Ainsworth, W. Eugene, Jr., **1974:** 310
Air Force, U.S.
F-15 aircraft, **1974:** 235
R.O.T.C. programs, Bradley University, **1976–77:** 185 [2]
Secretary, **1976–77:** 1076
Air Force Association, **1975:** 567
Air Law, International Conference on, **1974:** 86
Air and Space Museum, National, **1976–77:** 631
Air Transportation Policy, Economic Policy Board Task Force on International, **1976–77:** 765
Aircraft and aviation
Airline safety, **1975:** 725
Airport and airway development, **1975:** 64, 136
B-1 bomber, **1974:** 271 [16]; **1975:** 600 [11]; **1976–77:** 356 [12], 385 [4], 401 [7], 405
B-52 bomber, **1976–77:** 385 [4]
Backfire bomber, **1975:** 666 [25]
Bombers, arms limitations, **1974:** 271 [1]
Concorde, **1976–77:** 356 [10]
F-15, **1974:** 235
F-26, **1975:** 565 [2], 578 [5]
Hijacking, mandatory prison terms, **1975:** 341
Industry regulation, **1976–77:** 1072
International carriage, **1976–77:** 1063
International transportation policy, **1976–77:** 765
Legislation, **1976–77:** 685
Manufacturers, **1976–77:** 538
News conference remarks, **1976–77:** 67 [3]
Noise standards, **1976–77:** 862, 934, 941, 959
Regulatory reform, **1975:** 618; **1976–77:** 1060
Report to Congress, transmittal, **1975:** 313
Soviet transpolar aviators, **1975:** 348
Airport and Airway Development Act Amendments, **1976–77:** 661, 662
Airport and Airway Trust Fund, **1975:** 64, 136
Akron, Ohio, **1976–77:** 1004
Alabama
Birmingham Chamber of Commerce, public forum, **1976–77:** 420
Birmingham President Ford Committee, **1976–77:** 422, 423
President's visit, **1976–77:** 419–423, 817
Primary results, **1976–77:** 427
Alaska
Disaster assistance, **1974:** 239
Naval petroleum reserves, **1974:** 72; **1975:** 28
Pipelines
Natural gas, **1975:** 527 [16]
Oil, **1975:** 703, 704; **1976–77:** 657 [12], 685
President's visits, **1974:** 239; **1975:** 703, 704
Wilderness areas, **1974:** 276, 277
Alaska Conservation Act, proposed, **1976–77:** 746
Alaska Natural Gas Transportation Act, **1976–77:** 945
Albert, Repr. Carl, **1976–77:** 33, 551
Alcohol Abuse and Alcoholism Prevention Treatment, and Rehabilitation Act Amendments, Comprehensive, **1976–77:** 693
Alcohol and Drug Abuse Education Act Amendments of 1974, **1974:** 93
Alexander Hamilton Award, **1975:** 240
Alexandria, Va., **1974:** 88, 311; **1975:** 95, 218, 219
Alexandria Police Association, **1974:** 59
Aliens, Domestic Council Committee on Illegal, **1975:** 20
Aliens, illegal, **1976–77:** 373 [8]

Allende Gossens, Salvador, **1974:** 80 [5]
Alliance of Businessmen, National, **1974:** 192
Allied wartime veterans medical benefits bill, remarks upon signing, **1976–77:** 897
Allison, Lt. Col. Edgar L., **1975:** 235
Allstate Insurance Company, **1976–77:** 969
Alpha Kappa Alpha Sorority, **1975:** 218
Alton, Ill., **1976–77:** 907
Amarillo, Tex., **1976–77:** 330–332
Ambassador, U.S.
See country to which assigned.
America, President's assessment, **1976–77:** 389
American Agricultural Editors Association, **1976–77:** 272
American Association of Retired Persons, **1976–77:** 24
American Bar Association, **1975:** 695 [17]
American Chamber of Commerce Executives, **1975:** 585
American Conference on Trade, **1974:** 274
American Enterprise Institute for Public Policy Research, **1976–77:** 498
American families, President's views, **1976–77:** 266 [15]
American Farm Bureau Federation, **1976–77:** 8
American Federation of Labor-Congress of Industrial Organizations, **1975:** 85 [5], 497 [1], 508, 539, 580; **1976–77:** 23 (p. 65)
American Field Service, **1976–77:** 665
American Folklife Center, **1976–77:** 5
American Football Coaches Association, **1975:** 25
American Freedom Train Foundation, **1974:** 311
American Friends of Lubavitch, **1975:** 265
American G.I. Forum, **1975:** 410
American Hardware Manufacturers Association, **1975:** 500
American Hellenic Educational Progressive Association, **1976–77:** 302
American Jewish Committee, **1976–77:** 473
American Legion, **1975:** 421, 492
American Legion Auxiliary, **1975:** 414
American Lutheran Church, **1974:** 134
American Mother's Committee, Inc., **1976–77:** 431
American National Red Cross, **1974:** 11
American-Polish Trade Commission, Joint, **1974:** 129, 130, 143
American Retail Federation, **1976–77:** 469
American Revolution, **1975:** 264, 329
American Revolution Bicentennial
  Bicentennial activities
    Abilene (Tex.) Jaycees Bicentennial celebration, **1976–77:** 406
    American Freedom Train, **1974:** 311
    Army ceremony, Fort Benning, Ga., **1975:** 329
    First Continental Congress, reconvening, **1974:** 58
    Fort McHenry National Monument and Historic Shrine, Baltimore, Md., **1975:** 379

American Revolution Bicentennial—*continued*
  Bicentennial activities—*continued*
    Freedom Day, Charlotte, N.C., **1975:** 271
    John J. McCloy Fund for German-American Exchanges, **1975:** 331
    Lexington Green, Lexington, Mass., **1975:** 199
    Marine Corps ceremony, Arlington, Va., **1975:** 667
    Navy ceremony, **1975:** 619
    Old North Bridge, Concord, Mass., **1975:** 198
    Old North Church Bicentennial Lantern Service, Boston, Mass., **1975:** 197
    Savings bonds, Bicentennial-design, purchase, **1975:** 228
    Song presented by officials from Hopkinton, R.I., **1975:** 591
    Youth rally, Portland, Oreg., **1975:** 530
  Bicentennial Charter for Older Americans, **1976–77:** 300
  Bicentennial delegation, Broward County, Fla., **1976–77:** 175
  Bicentennial Exposition on Science and Technology, **1976–77:** 71
  Bicentennial gifts to U.S.
    Canada, **1976–77:** 600
    Church of Jesus Christ of Latter-day Saints, **1976–77:** 637
    France, **1976–77:** 499
    Japan, **1976–77:** 624
    Norway, **1976–77:** 636
  Bicentennial Independence Day, Proclamation 4446, **1976–77:** 623
  Bicentennial Land Heritage program, **1976–77:** 743, 745, 746, 1084
  Bicentennial Year, **1975:** 752
  B'nai B'rith International Bicentennial Convention, **1976–77:** 196
  Centennial safe opening at the Capitol, **1976–77:** 632
  Columbus Day, **1976–77:** 880
  Commemoration ceremony, El Paso, Tex., **1976–77:** 329
  Commercialization, **1975:** 530
  Diplomatic Corps, remarks, **1976–77:** 682
  Fourth of July message, **1976–77:** 641
  Guilford Courthouse National Military Park, remarks, **1976–77:** 213
  Honor America program, **1976–77:** 642
  Independence Day statement, **1975:** 377
  Italian-American Foundation, **1976–77:** 787
  Nashua, N.H., Chamber of Commerce dinner, **1976–77:** 65
  National Archives and Records Service, ceremony, **1976–77:** 639
  National Bicentennial Conference, **1975:** 105
  National Education Association Bicentennial Commemorative Plaque, **1976–77:** 14

American Revolution Bicentennial—*continued*
National Teacher of the Year, presentation of Bicentennial Medal, **1976–77:** 219
Naturalization ceremonies at Monticello, Va., **1976–77:** 649
Operation Sail, U.S.S. *Forrestal*, New York Harbor, **1976–77:** 647
Philadelphia, Pa., **1976–77:** 645, 646
Saginaw, Mich., **1976–77:** 488
Science and Technology Exposition, **1976–77:** 591
Small business, salute to, **1976–77:** 470
Third century goals, **1975:** 377, 379, 400, 512, 525, 530, 554 [17], 559, 560, 577
Valley Forge State Park, Pa., **1976–77:** 643
Virginia General Assembly, Williamsburg, **1976–77:** 51
Waco Suspension Bridge, **1976–77:** 393
American Revolution Bicentennial Administration, **1974:** 58; **1976–77:** 1046
American Society of Newspaper Editors, **1975:** 189; **1976–77:** 339
American Society of Oral Surgeons, **1975:** 617
American States, Organization of, **1974:** 39 [23], 179 [5]; **1976–77:** 682
American Telephone and Telegraph, **1974:** 271 [19]
American Textile Manufacturers Institute, national convention, **1976–77:** 260
Ames, Iowa, **1976–77:** 904
Amnesty.
See Executive clemency.
Amtrak, **1976–77:** 95
Amtrak Improvement Act of 1974, **1974:** 72, 201
Amtrak Improvement Act of 1975, **1975:** 279
AMVETS, **1976–77:** 920
Anaheim, Calif., **1975:** 579; **1976–77:** 513
Anchorage, Alaska, **1974:** 239; **1975:** 704
Anders, William A., **1974:** 195 [1]; **1976–77:** 315
Anderson, George W., **1976–77:** 199
Anderson, Gwen, **1974:** 79
Anderson, Jack, **1975:** 582 [7]
Anderson, Repr. John B., **1974:** 191
Anderson, S.C., **1974:** 171
Andreotti, Giulio, **1976–77:** 1023, 1024
Andrews Air Force Base, Md., **1975:** 523, 702
Andrus, Ethel Percy, **1976–77:** 24
Anemia programs, Cooley's, **1975:** 545
Angola
Administration policy, **1975:** 739 [7]
Cuban involvement, **1975:** 738, 750 [5, 21]; **1976–77:** 160, 266 [7, 12], 385 [2]
Farm forum remarks, Rockford, Ill., **1976–77:** 203
Letter to the Speaker of the House, **1976–77:** 33
National Front for the Liberation of Angola [FNLA], **1976–77:** 266 [7], 505, 523 [5]
NBC News interview, **1976–77:** 6
News conference remarks, **1976–77:** 282 [8], 387 [32], 535 [5]

Angola—*continued*
Popular Movement for the Liberation of Angola [MPLA], **1976–77:** 266 [7], 505, 523 [5]
Radio-Television News Directors Association, **1976–77:** 48 [5, 16]
Soviet Union, involvement, **1975:** 695 [22], 738, 739 [7, 8], 750 [5, 21]; **1976–77:** 266 [7, 12]
Union for the Total Independence of Angola [UNITA], **1976–77:** 266 [7], 505, 523 [5]
U.S. military assistance, **1975:** 738, 750 [6]
U.S. policy, **1976–77:** 7, 8, 68 [6], 116, 118, 138 [4], 266 [7, 12]
Anguilla.
See St. Christopher-Nevis-Anguilla.
Animal health
Disease control agreement, **1974:** 270
Research legislation, veto, **1974:** 9
Ann Arbor, Mich., **1976–77:** 783, 784, 1032
Anthony, Susan B., **1976–77:** 85
Antiballistic missile systems, **1974:** 85; **1975:** 119
Antitrust Improvements Act, Hart-Scott-Rodino, **1976–77:** 836
Antitrust laws
Enforcement, **1974:** 121, 271 [19], 317
Legislation, **1976–77:** 224, 240 [7], 398 [8], 417, 836
Reform, **1974:** 218, 240, 317
Violations, **1975:** 70, 496 [8], 689; **1976–77:** 68 [7], 95, 185 [1]
Antitrust Procedures and Penalties Act, **1974:** 317
Apollo-Soyuz Test Project, **1974:** 59; **1975:** 405, 406, 412, 428, 482, 624
Appointments and nominations
Cabinet, personnel changes, **1975:** 666 [12]
Central Intelligence Agency, Director, **1975:** 657 [1]
Combined Federal Campaign, Chairman, **1975:** 564
Commerce Department, Secretary, **1975:** 657 [1]; **1976–77:** 53
Commission on CIA Activities Within the United States, Chairman and members, **1975:** 19
Commission on Federal Paperwork, membership, **1975:** 335
Council on Wage and Price Stability
Chairman and members, **1974:** 41
Director, **1974:** 109
Defense Department, Secretary, **1975:** 657 [1]
Domestic Council
Deputy Director, **1975:** 91, 92
Executive Director, **1975:** 91, 92
Vice Chairman, **1975:** 91, 92
Domestic Council Committee on Illegal Aliens, Chairman and members, **1975:** 20
Energy Research and Development Administration, Administrator, **1974:** 195 [1]
Energy Resources Council, Chairman, **1974:** 138

Appointments and nominations—*continued*
Federal Energy Administration, Administrator, **1974:** 195 [1]
Federal Home Loan Bank Board, Chairman, **1975:** 678 [11]
Federal Power Commission, member, withdrawal of nomination, **1974:** 243
Health, Education, and Welfare Department, Commissioner of Education, **1976–77:** 792
Interdepartmental Committee for the Voluntary Payroll Savings Plan for the Purchase of United States Savings Bonds, Chairman, **1975:** 159, 627
Labor Department, Secretary, **1976–77:** 25
National Center for Productivity and Quality of Working Life, Chairman, **1975:** 721
National Commission on the Observance of International Women's Year, 1975, presiding officer, **1976–77:** 634
Nuclear Regulatory Commission, Chairman, **1974:** 195 [1]
President's Commission on Olympic Sports, Chairman and members, **1975:** 338
President's Economic Policy Board, Chairman and members, **1974:** 109
President's Labor-Management Committee, members, **1974:** 109
President's Panel on Federal Compensation, Chairman and members, **1975:** 328
Procedures for selection, **1974:** 236 [24]
State Department
Assistant Secretary, **1974:** 195 [1]
U.S. Ambassadors
India, **1974:** 295
Spain, withdrawal of nomination, **1974:** 237
United Kingdom, **1975:** 23; **1976–77:** 16
Supreme Court of the United States, Associate Justice, **1975:** 697
Tennessee Valley Authority, member, **1975:** 678 [17]
Textile Trade Policy Group, Chairman and members, **1975:** 311
Veterans Administration, Administrator, **1974:** 16
Vice President of the United States, **1974:** 17, 18
White House Conference on Handicapped Individuals, National Planning and Advisory Council, **1975:** 691
White House Staff
Assistant to the President for Domestic Affairs, **1975:** 91, 92
Assistant to the President for Economic Affairs, **1974:** 109
Assistant to the President for National Security Affairs, **1975:** 657 [1]
News conference response, **1974:** 80 [12]
Press Secretary to the President, **1974:** 2, 92

Appointments and nominations—*continued*
White House Staff—*continued*
Special Assistant to the President for Women, **1976–77:** 193
Special Assistants, **1976–77:** 741
Special Coordinator for Disaster Relief, **1975:** 163
Appropriations
Agriculture, **1974:** 72, 240
Agriculture-environmental and consumer protection, **1974:** 240; **1975:** 59
Defense Department, **1974:** 72, 126, 240, 271 [2, 4, 7, 16, 21, 22]; **1975:** 64
Education, **1975:** 432, 433, 511 [7]
Executive Office of the President, **1975:** 160
First supplemental, **1974:** 240; **1975:** 59
Fiscal year transition period, **1975:** 100
Foreign assistance, **1974:** 72; **1975:** 161
Health, Education, and Welfare Department, **1974:** 72, 240, 285; **1975:** 201, 681, 737
Health revenue sharing and health services, **1974:** 319
Labor Department, **1974:** 72, 240, 285; **1975:** 737
Labor-Health, Education, and Welfare, **1975:** 59
Military construction and foreign assistance, **1974:** 72, 240
Second continuing appropriations resolution, **1974:** 156, 164
State Department, **1975:** 681
State-Justice-Commerce, **1974:** 72
Treasury Department, **1975:** 681
United States Arms Control and Disarmament Agency, **1975:** 96
Urgent supplemental, **1975:** 59
See also specific programs.
Arabian-American Oil Company, **1974:** 39 [14]
Arabs
Boycott of American businesses, **1976–77:** 766, 854, 859, 925 [5, 8]
Oil embargo, **1976–77:** 925 [9]
Aranda, Thomas, Jr., **1976–77:** 702
Areeda, Phillip E., **1975:** 93
Arends, Repr. Leslie C., **1974:** 190; **1976–77:** 199
Arias Navarro, Carlos, **1975:** 292n., 293, 459n.
Arizona
Page, transfer to non-Federal status, **1974:** 202
President's visits, **1974:** 178–180, 235, 236
Wilderness areas, **1974:** 276, 277
Arizona, U.S.S., Memorial, **1975:** 715
Arkansas
President's visit, **1975:** 483, 484
Wilderness area, **1974:** 277
Arlington, Va., **1975:** 410, 411, 667; **1976–77:** 62
Arlington National Cemetery, **1974:** 192; **1975:** 278; **1976–77:** 544
Armed Forces, U.S.
All-volunteer services, **1976–77:** 352 [4], 362 [16]

Armed Forces, U.S.—*continued*
Bicentennial ceremonies
El Paso, Tex., **1976–77:** 329
U.S. Army, **1975:** 329
U.S. Marine Corps, **1975:** 667
U.S. Navy, **1975:** 619
Budget news briefing, **1976–77:** 23 (p. 54, 59, 67, 71, 73, 74)
Cambodia, evacuation of U.S. Mission, **1975:** 182, 183
Campaign issue, **1976–77:** 378
Combined Federal Campaign, **1974:** 103; **1975:** 413, 564
Congressional Medal of Honor, presentation ceremonies, **1974:** 293; **1976–77:** 176
Deployment in Europe, **1974:** 20, 242; **1975:** 101, 186, 281
F-15 aircrft, U.S. Air Force acceptance, **1974:** 235
Federal cost reduction campaign, **1975:** 244, 245, 722
Incentive awards programs
1974, **1975:** 139
1975, **1976–77:** 1058
1976, **1976–77:** 1059
Korea, Republic of
President's visit, **1974:** 253
U.S. presence, **1974:** 255; **1975:** 316 [7], 354 [9]
Legislation, **1976–77:** 685
Mayaguez, SS, recovery, **1975:** 256, 257
Memorial Day ceremonies, **1975:** 278
Middle East intervention, **1975:** 36 [10], 45 [2], 109 [2], 204 [7], 276 [5], 502 [16], 581 [7]
Military capabilities, **1976–77:** 266 [5], 283, 308
Military construction bill, veto, **1976–77:** 638
Military deserters, clemency, **1975:** 36 [14], 58, 113, 243 [5], 566, 573 [12]; **1976–77:** 68 [20]
Military installations, closing, **1976–77:** 116, 293 [8]
Military Order of World Wars, Atlanta Chapter, **1976–77:** 359
National Guard Association, remarks, **1976–77:** 749
NATO participation, **1975:** 186, 276 [2], 442
News conference remarks, **1976–77:** 212 [13], 282 [14]
One percent add-on in retirement systems, **1976–77:** 254
Pay and allowances, **1976–77:** 736, 837
Pay increase, **1974:** 39 [26], 43, 72, 82, 87, 115, 117, 262; **1975:** 26, 28, 32, 46, 64, 143, 506, 554 [15], 573 [12]
President's assessment, **1975:** 488 [14]; **1976–77:** 118, 197, 371, 1075
Prisoners of war and missing in action, **1975:** 411, 522 [9], 600 [13], 716
Reduction of personnel, **1976–77:** 417

Armed Forces, U.S.—*continued*
Reserve forces, **1976–77:** 378, 483
Reserve Officers Association of the United States, **1975:** 103
Retirement benefits, pay increase, **1975:** 26, 28, 32, 64; **1976–77:** 215 [14]
South Pacific action, **1975:** 204 [1]
Training, **1975:** 678 [10]
Turkey
Suspension of operations in, **1975:** 434, 447, 457, 460 [2]
U.S. bases in, **1975:** 387, 390
Uniformed Services University of Health Sciences, **1975:** 394
U.S. and Soviet manpower, comparison, **1976–77:** 398 [11]
Veterans.
See Veterans.
Vietnam conflict, **1975:** 36 [21]
Draft evaders and military deserters, clemency, **1974:** 16, 77, 78, 80 [10], 236 [13], 266, 329; **1975:** 36 [14], 58, 113, 243 [5], 566, 573 [12]; **1976–77:** 585
Missing in action, **1974:** 192; **1975:** 411, 552 [9], 600 [13], 716; **1976–77:** 762
Selective service discharge, **1976–77:** 1076
Veterans, **1974:** 192, 263
See also Veterans; *specific branch of service.*
Armed Forces Week, **1976–77:** 448
Arms control and disarmament.
See Strategic arms limitation.
Arms Control and Disarmament Agency, United States, **1975:** 96, 119; **1976–77:** 701
Arms Export Control Act, International Security Assistance and, **1976–77:** 630
Arms and weapons
B-1 aircraft, **1974:** 271 [1, 16]
Biological and chemical weapons, **1975:** 37, 38
Budget news briefing, **1976–77:** 23 (p. 54, 59, 67, 71, 73, 74)
F-15 aircraft, **1974:** 235
Federal spending, **1974:** 271 [2, 4, 7, 16, 21, 22]; **1976–77:** 321 [11]
Foreign assistance, **1975:** 161
Fort Worth/Tarrant County Bar Association, **1976–77:** 380
Military assistance.
See specific country.
Military construction programs, **1976–77:** 736
News conference responses, **1974:** 271 [1, 2, 5, 11, 22]
Nuclear weapons, **1975:** 290 [3], 354 [2, 9], 475
President's assessment, **1976–77:** 283, 322, 349, 398 [11]
Research and development, **1974:** 138
Sales to foreign countries, **1975:** 101, 109 [11], 260, 565 [2, 11], 649, 719; **1976–77:** 20, 212 [2], 766, 854, 925 [13]

Arms and weapons—*continued*
Tactical use, **1975:** 354 [9]
Trident submarine, **1974:** 271 [16]
Union of Soviet Socialist Republics
Joint statements, **1974:** 257, 258
Treaty with United States, protocol, **1974:** 85
See also Missiles; Strategic arms limitations; *specific weapons systems.*
Armstrong, Anne L., **1974:** 41, 265; **1976–77:** 16, 112, 318
Armstrong, Repr. William L., **1974:** 219
Army, U.S.
Bicentennial ceremonies, **1975:** 329
Corps of Engineers, **1976–77:** 181
Enlistment bonuses, **1976–77:** 736
Secretary, **1975:** 376; **1976–77:** 738, 1076
Training stations, **1975:** 678 [10]
United States Military Academy, **1975:** 306
Arthritis, Diabetes, and Digestive Diseases Amendments, **1976–77:** 924
Arts and Artifacts Indemnity Act, **1975:** 740
Arts and humanities
Administration policy, **1975:** 554 [18]
Federal assistance, **1975:** 346, 740
Arts, Humanities, and Cultural Affairs Act of 1976, **1976–77:** 875
Arts, National Council on the, **1974:** 53; **1976–77:** 744
Arts, National Endowment for the, **1976–77:** 744
Ash, Roy L., **1974:** 41, 109, 115, 303; **1975:** 63
Ashbrook, Repr. John M., **1974:** 184
Ashe, Arthur, **1975:** 417
Asheville, N.C., **1976–77:** 237, 238
Ashley, Repr. Thomas L., **1974:** 29
Asia
Administration policy, **1975:** 475
See also specific country.
Asian Americans, **1975:** 477
Asian Development Bank, **1974:** 72
Asian Development Fund, **1976–77:** 685
Askew, Gov. Reubin, **1975:** 654
Assassination attempts on foreign leaders, **1976–77:** 107 [11]
Assassination attempts on the President, **1975:** 533, 534, 551, 583, 615 [6], 616 [10], 655 [2]
Associated General Contractors of America, **1976–77:** 195
Association.
See other part of title.
Athanasakos, Betty, **1976–77:** 634
Athletic Association, National Collegiate, **1975:** 22
Atiyeh, Vic, **1974:** 215
Atlanta, Ga., **1975:**, 69, 71, 72, 678, 679; **1976–77:** 359–362
Atlantic Alliance.
See North Atlantic Treaty Organization.
Atlantic City, N.J., **1976–77:** 972, 973
Atlantic Fisheries, International Commission for the Northwest, **1975:** 584
Atlantic Relations, Declaration on, **1974:** 105
Atmospheric Region Program, Global, **1976–77:** 824
Atomic energy.
See Nuclear energy.
Atomic Energy Act amendments, **1974:** 141, 240
Atomic Energy Agency, International, **1975:** 520; **1976–77:** 987
Atomic Energy Commission, **1974:** 40, 138
Atomic Energy Commission Appropriation Act, 1975, Public Works and Power Development and, **1974:** 40, 72
Augusta, Maine, **1975:** 508
Auschwitz, Poland, **1975:** 454
Australia
Christmas Island, Generalized System of Preferences beneficiary, **1975:** 668
Extradition treaty with United States, **1974:** 28
Joint statement, **1976–77:** 698
Prime Minister J. Malcolm Fraser, **1975:** 727; **1976–77:** 692, 696, 698
Austria
Chancellor Bruno Kreisky, **1974:** 227, 229; **1975:** 296, 298
President's visit, **1975:** 296–300
Auto Workers, United, **1976–77:** 778, 947
Automobiles.
See Motor vehicles.
Aviation Administration, Federal, **1976–77:** 661
Aviation Conference, International Civil, **1976–77:** 959
Aviation Facilities Experimental Center, National, **1976–77:** 972
Aviation Organization, International Civil, **1974:** 86
Aviation Trophies, Harmon International, **1975:** 235
Awards and citations
Congressional Medal of Honor, **1974:** 293; **1976–77:** 176
Defense Distinguished Service Medal, **1974:** 312
National Medal of Science for 1975, **1976–77:** 557, 914
Presidential Medal of Freedom, **1976–77:** 76, 281, 716, 900, 1052, 1061
Sun Newspaper Good Neighbor Awards, **1976–77:** 984

B-1 bomber, **1974:** 271 [1, 16]; **1975:** 600 [11]; **1976–77:** 95, 356 [12], 385 [4], 401 [7], 405, 858, 960, 967
B-52 bomber, **1976–77:** 385 [4], 858, 960, 967
Backfire bomber, **1975:** 666 [25]
Backus, John W., **1976–77:** 557, 914

Bagley, William T., **1974:** 211; **1976–77:** 314
Baidukov, Col. Gen. Georgi, **1975:** 348
Bailey, Douglas, **1976–77:** 740
Bailey, Pearl, **1976–77:** 672
Baker, Sen. Howard H., Jr., **1976–77:** 476, 740
Baker, James A., III, **1976–77:** 740
Baker, William O., **1976–77:** 199
Bakersfield, Calif., **1975:** 165
Bakke, Karl E., **1976–77:** 314
Balance of payments, **1974:** 20, 242; **1975:** 602 [8], 650
Baltimore, Md., **1975:** 379; **1976–77:** 671
Bank, African Development, **1974:** 72
Bank, Asian Development, **1974:** 72
Bank for Reconstruction and Development, International, **1974:** 110
Banking and finance
  Arab investment in the United States, **1975:** 72 [11]
  Consumer protection, **1974:** 200
  Credit.
  See Loans; Mortgages.
  Discriminatory practices, international, **1975:** 109 [1, 15], 689, 690
  Federal deposit insurance increase, **1974:** 200
  Federal regulation, **1975:** 70
  Financial institutions
    Credit availability, **1974:** 121
    Legislation, **1976–77:** 3
  Foreign investment, **1975:** 147
  Interest rates, **1974:** 199, 234; **1975:** 138 [9], 144, 171, 527 [10]
  Minority banks, Federal deposits, **1975:** 639
  Mortgage foreclosures, **1975:** 372
  Mortgage insurance, **1975:** 351
  Municipal bankruptcy legislation, **1975:** 645, 646, 655 [8], 683, 695 [1]
  Municipal bonds, **1975:** 655 [8]
  Regulatory reform, **1974:** 199, 200, 240; **1975:** 144, 192, 196, 220
  Stock market transactions, **1975:** 308, 616 [14]
Baptist Convention, National, **1975:** 553
Baptist Convention, Southern, **1976–77:** 595
Barcelo, Carlos Romero, **1976–77:** 1042
Bardeen, John, **1976–77:** 1052
Barnum, John W., **1976–77:** 657 [12]
Baroody, William J., Jr., **1975:** 20
Bartlett, Sen. Dewey F., **1974:** 182
Battle Creek, Mich., **1976–77:** 485
Baudouin I, King, **1975:** 287, 289n., 290 [1]
Bay Pines, Fla., **1976–77:** 94, 95
Bay St. Louis, Miss., **1976–77:** 813
Baylor University, **1976–77:** 392
Beame, Abraham D., **1975:** 254
Bechtel, Stephen D., **1974:** 109
Becker, Benton, **1974:** 155
Beef industry, **1976–77:** 287 [11], 376
Belgium
  Bilateral meetings, **1975:** 290 [4, 9, 10]
Belgium—*continued*
  King Baudouin I, **1975:** 287, 289n., 290 [1]
  President's visit, **1975:** 287, 289, 290
  Prime Minister Leo Tindemans, **1975:** 287
  Representative to NATO, **1976–77:** 267
Belgrade, Yugoslavia, **1975:** 466, 467, 468, 469, 470
Bell, Jack, **1975:** 563
Bellmon, Sen. Henry L., **1974:** 182, 183
Belyakov, Lt. Gen. Aleksandr, **1975:** 348
Benedict, Manson, **1976–77:** 557, 914
Bennett, Bob, **1974:** 220
Bennett, Sen. Wallace F., **1974:** 218
Benny, Jack, **1974:** 322
Bensinger, Peter B., **1974:** 191; **1976–77:** 128, 129
Bergan-Mercy Hospital, **1976–77:** 440
Berlin, Irving, **1976–77:** 1052
Berlin, Four-Power Agreement on, **1975:** 459
Berlin, West, **1975:** 276 [3]
Bernardin, Archbishop Joseph L., **1976–77:** 769
Bethe, Hans A., **1976–77:** 557, 914
Bethesda, Md., **1975:** 307, 394
Bethesda Naval Hospital, **1976–77:** 29
Beverly Hills, Calif., **1976–77:** 861
Bhutto, Zulfikar Ali, **1975:** 74
Bicentennial.
  See American Revolution Bicentennial.
Bicentennial Administration, American Revolution, **1974:** 58
Big Brothers of America, **1976–77:** 350
Bijedic, Dzemal, **1975:** 145, 146, 468n.
Bill signings.
  See Legislation, remarks and statements on approval.
Bill vetoes.
  See Veto messages and memorandums of disapproval.
Biloxi, Miss., **1976–77:** 815
Biological and chemical weapons, **1975:** 37, 38
Birmingham, Ala., **1976–77:** 419–423
Birmingham, Mich., **1976–77:** 462
Birth Defects Prevention Month, March of Dimes, **1975:** 734
Black, Shirley Temple, **1976–77:** 680
Black History Month, **1976–77:** 74
Black History Week, **1975:** 67
Black lung legislation, **1976–77:** 192 [7]
Black lung program, **1974:** 205
Black Press Week, **1975:** 130
Blackburn, Ben B., **1975:** 678 [11]
Blacks
  Administration policy, **1975:** 369
  Black History Month, message, **1976–77:** 74
  Black vote, **1976–77:** 325 [6, 12]
  Consideration as 1976 Republican Vice-Presidential nominee, **1975:** 678 [5]
  Economic situation, **1975:** 552 [6]
  Education, **1975:** 676
  National Association for the Advancement of Colored People, **1975:** 369

Blacks—*continued*
National contributions, **1975:** 553
National Newspaper Publishers Association, **1975:** 43
Sickle cell anemia, **1975:** 77, 530
Voting rights, **1975:** 422
Youth unemployment, **1975:** 243 [11]
Bliss, Ray C., **1976–77:** 734
Block grant programs, **1976–77:** 22, 38
Bloembergen, Nicolaas, **1975:** 568
Blood disease, **1974:** 97
Bloomington, Ill., **1976–77:** 907
Blue collar workers, **1976–77:** 354 [3]
B'nai B'rith, **1976–77:** 196, 766
Boca Raton, Fla., **1976–77:** 159, 160
Bolles, Don, **1976–77:** 609
Bolton, Charlie, **1974:** 184
Bolton, Frances P., **1976–77:** 569
Bond, Gov. Christopher S., **1974:** 151
Bonn, Federal Republic of Germany, **1975:** 440, 441
Bonneville Power Administration, **1974:** 176
Boorstin, Daniel J., **1975:** 672
Bork, Robert H., **1975:** 485n.
Borlaug, Norman, **1976–77:** 1052
Bossier City, La., **1976–77:** 371–374
Boston, Mass., **1975:** 197, 663, 664, 665
School desegregation, **1974:** 127 [20], 142; **1975:** 552 [10], 554 [3]
Bowling Green State University, **1976–77:** 580
Boy Scouts of America, **1974:** 272; **1975:** 177, 530, 671; **1976–77:** 132, 240 [6]
Boy of the Year, **1976–77:** 309
Boycott practices, foreign, **1975:** 109 [1, 15], 689, 690
Boynton Beach, Fla., **1976–77:** 155
Boys Clubs of America, **1976–77:** 309
Boys Nation, **1975:** 421
Boys/Girls Nation, joint session, **1976–77:** 714
Bradley, Gen. Omar N., **1976–77:** 1052
Bradley University, Ill., **1976–77:** 185
Brand, Vance D., **1975:** 412, 428, 482
Brandon, Henry, **1975:** 276
Bratteli, Trygve, **1975:** 290n.
Bray, Repr. William G., **1974:** 154
Brazil, shrimp agreement with United States, **1975:** 320
Brennan, Peter J., **1974:** 41, 109; **1975:** 80
Bretton Woods Agreement Act amendment, **1976–77:** 926
Brezhnev, L. I., **1974:** 127 [7], 256, 257, 258, 259, 271 [1], Appendix D; **1975:** 36 [23], 72 [4], 316 [5], 456, 460 [1, 8, 13], 622 [4], 657 [14], 666 [25], 695 [16]; **1976–77:** 766
Brinegar, Claude S., **1974:** 109, 308
Briney Breezes, Fla., **1976–77:** 156
Bristol, Tenn., **1976–77:** 475
Broadcasters, Michigan Association of, **1976–77:** 435
Broadcasters, National Association of, **1976–77:** 964
Broadcasting, public, **1976–77:** 2
Broder, David S., **1975:** 666
Brokaw, Tom, **1975:** 45; **1976–77:** 6, 778
Brooke, Sen. Edward W., **1974:** 161; **1975:** 678 [5]; **1976–77:** 270
Brooklyn, N.Y., **1976–77:** 886
Brooks, Repr. Jack, **1975:** 192; **1976–77:** 552
Brotzman, Repr. Donald G., **1974:** 219
Broward County, Fla., **1976–77:** 175
Brown, Repr. Clarence J., **1974:** 184
Brown, Repr. Garry E., **1974:** 29
Brown, Gen. George S., **1974:** 236 [7]; **1976–77:** 925 [3], 947
Brown, L. Dean, **1976–77:** 560 [8], 599
Brown v. *Board of Education of Topeka, Kansas*, **1975:** 565 [8]
Broyhill, Repr. James T., **1974:** 174
Bruce, David K. E., **1976–77:** 76, 267
Brussels, Belgium, **1975:** 288, 289, 290
Bryant, Paul (Bear), **1976–77:** 817
Bucharest, Romania, **1975:** 461, 462, 463
Buchen, Philip W., **1974:** 80 [2ftn.], 155
Buckley amendment, **1976–77:** 333 [12]
Budget, Federal
Briefings for State and local officials
Florida, **1976–77:** 89
New Hampshire, **1976–77:** 64
Campaign debate remarks, **1976–77:** 947
Chamber of Commerce of the United States, **1976–77:** 365
Congressional oversight, **1975:** 166 [5], 171, 223, 731, 732
Defense spending.
See under Defense and national security.
Deferrals and rescissions, **1974:** 40, 89, 90, 121, 240, 262, 285, 318, Appendix B; **1975:** 11, 59, 72 [9], 133, 173, 201, 202, 248, 367, 437, 541, 607, 635, 681, 705; **1976–77:** 9, 27, 61, 227, 269, 336, 364, 467, 633, 651, 697, 699, 739, 757, 779, 802, 822, 843, 1017, 1022, 1046, 1069
Deficits, **1975:** 3, 26, 28, 32, 36 [12, 24], 39, 46, 54, 62, 63, 64, 70, 72 [8, 16], 85 [17], 89, 90 [1, 7], 125 [14], 164, 166 [5], 167, 169, 171, 187, 195, 252, 288, 318, 354 [17], 436, 478, 511 [3], 527 [2], 565 [17], 573 [5], 602 [14, 18], 626, 647, 707; **1976–77:** 210 [4], 284 [7]
Economic Report of the President, **1976–77:** 1070
Education, **1976–77:** 378 [12]
Efforts to balance, **1976–77:** 116, 401 [3], 803
Energy message, **1976–77:** 1045
Executive, legislative, and judicial salary increases, **1976–77:** 1068
Fiscal policy, **1975:** 602 [4]

Budget, Federal—*continued*
Fiscal Year 1975, reductions, **1974:** 39 [19], 72, 121, 127 [11], 132, 195 [7], 262, 271 [13, 21], Appendix D
Fiscal Year 1976, **1974:** 195 [23]
Fiscal Year 1977, requests, **1976–77:** 244, 245
Growth of expenditures, **1976–77:** 333 [14]
Medical research funding, **1976–77:** 333 [13]
Messages to Congress, **1975:** 63, 64; **1976–77:** 21, 22, 1066
News conference remarks, **1976–77:** 325 [11]
Oceans program, annual report to Congress, transmittal, **1976–77:** 1081
Presidential news briefing, **1976–77:** 23 (p. 50)
President's assessment, **1976–77:** 95, 195, 308, 862
Reporting procedures, **1974:** 189
Science and technology, **1976–77:** 245
Spending ceiling, **1975:** 379 [1, 2, 10], 622 [13, 18], 630, 652, 666 [26], 731, 732, 737, 750 [10]; **1976–77:** 327 [3], 339 [10], 472
State and local assistance, **1976–77:** 373
See also Appropriations; Federal spending; Appendix B, **1974**.
Budget and Impoundment Control Act of 1974, Congressional, **1974:** 40, 72, 89, 262, 318; **1975:** 59, 62, 64, 166 [5], 167, 171, 367, 437
Buffalo, N.Y., **1976–77:** 998
Buffalo Grove, Ill., **1976–77:** 210
Building and Construction Trades Department, AFL-CIO, **1975:** 35, 580
Bulgaria
Consular convention with United States, **1974:** 73
Fishery agreement with U.S., **1976–77:** 1067
Burch, Dean, **1974:** 79, 269; **1975:** 343; **1976–77:** 740
Burditt, George, **1974:** 191
Bureau of Alcohol, Tobacco and Firearms, **1975:** 341
Bureau of Economic Analysis, **1974:** 195 [13]
Bureau of Indian Affairs, **1975:** 10, 488 [4]
Bureau of Reclamation, **1976–77:** 201
Burger, Warren E., **1974:** 1; **1975:** 692
Burke, Arleigh, **1976–77:** 1052
Burlington, Vt., **1974:** 118
Burns, Arthur F., **1974:** 109; **1975:** 204 [9], 602 [15]; **1976–77:** 23 (p. 65), 118
Burt, Alvin V., Jr., **1974:** 203
Bush, George H., **1974:** 79; **1975:** 657 [1, 3, 5, 6, 11], 663, 666 [5], 678 [18], 733; **1976–77:** 44, 107 [1, 2]
Bush, Gwen, **1974:** 170, 173
Business, National Federation of Independent, **1975:** 335
Business Amendments of 1974, Small, **1974:** 34, 72
Business Council, **1974:** 290

Business and industry
Administration policy, **1975:** 335
Advertising, **1975:** 212, 554 [13]
American Revolution Bicentennial, commercialization, **1975:** 530
Antitrust laws, **1974:** 121, 218, 240, 271 [19], 317; **1975:** 70, 496 [8], 689; **1976–77:** 224, 240 [7], 398 [8]
Arab boycotts of American businesses, **1976–77:** 854, 859, 925 [5, 8]
Arab investments, **1975:** 72 [11]
Business Council meeting, **1974:** 290
Chamber of Commerce of the United States, **1976–77:** 365
Collective bargaining, **1975:** 134
Corporate investment, **1975:** 39
Corporate payments abroad, questionable, **1976–77:** 275–277, 580 [3], 592, 593
Corporate tax reduction, **1975:** 614, 666 [1]
Defense production, **1974:** 114
Domestic International Sales Corporation, **1975:** 554 [7]
Energy research and development, **1975:** 580, 582 [10], 600 [7], 616 [1], 621, 622 [13], 742
Fair trade laws, **1975:** 192, 196, 220, 723, 724
Federal paperwork reduction, **1975:** 595, 602 [2], 631
Federal role in private industry, **1976–77:** 231 [6], 321 [13], 398 [9]
Foreign activities, **1976–77:** 266 [17]
Foreign boycott practices, **1975:** 689
Foreign investment, **1975:** 147
Government-sanctioned monopolies, **1975:** 500
Housing, **1974:** 161, 162, 234
Interest rates, **1975:** 171
Investment tax credit, **1975:** 69, 70, 71, 84, 602 [8], 614, 616 [1], 623
Job creation, **1975:** 502 [6], 508, 531, 579, 614, 616 [14], 631
Job market responsibility, **1976–77:** 116
Loans, exemption from State usury laws, **1974:** 199
Metric system conversion, **1975:** 744
Minority enterprise, **1974:** 291; **1975:** 369, 502 [9]; **1976–77:** 321 [3]
Monopolies, **1976–77:** 321 [12]
Municipal bonds, **1975:** 655 [8]
National Alliance of Businessmen, **1976–77:** 306
National Center for Productivity and Quality of Working Life, **1975:** 721
Overseas bribes, **1975:** 396 [10]
Payroll savings plans, **1975:** 33
Pension funding, **1974:** 45, 46
Pollution, **1975:** 527 [15]
President's assessment, **1975:** 395, 500
Price fixing legislation, **1974:** 218
Price increases, **1975:** 64, 68
Productivity, **1975:** 602 [8], 616 [18], 742

Business and industry—*continued*
Regulatory reform, **1974:** 127 [9]; **1975:** 70, 220, 335, 392, 496 [8], 500, 502 [2], 527 [13], 531, 585, 602 [2], 618, 675, 723, 724
Small business, **1976–77:** 333 [9], 398 [2]
Small Business Awards, **1975:** 272
Stock market transactions, **1975:** 616 [14]
Task Force on Questionable Corporate Payments Abroad, **1976–77:** 275–277, 580 [3], 592, 593
Tax reduction, **1975:** 26, 28, 32, 34, 64, 90 [3, 4], 623, 629, 630, 631
Taxes on industry, **1976–77:** 362 [4]
Trademark Registration Treaty, **1975:** 519
Trucking, compensatory legislation, **1974:** 240
Windfall profits tax, **1975:** 32, 60, 64, 70, 85 [6], 109 [7], 283, 488 [7], 538
See also specific business or industry.
Businessmen, National Alliance of, **1975:** 174
Busing, school, **1974:** 24, 25, 127 [20], 142; **1975:** 496 [6], 511 [6], 552 [10], 554 [3], 565 [7, 8], 573 [10], 578 [9], 620 [5], 622 [17], 648 [2]; **1976–77:** 48 [15], 209 [9], 210 [13], 240 [10], 282 [1], 378 [12], 402 [7], 415 [4], 497, 507, 523 [6], 535 [2, 13, 17], 543, 560 [6], 610, 614, 615, 685
Butler University, **1976–77:** 352
Butterfield, Alexander P., **1975:** 396 [20]
Butz, Earl L., **1974:** 41, 109, 195 [18]; **1975:** 159, 600 [3, 6]; **1976–77:** 181, 200, 272, 288, 327, 415, 626, 793, 849, 852
Byrnes, John W., **1976–77:** 831

Cabinet
Changes, personnel, **1974:** 195 [18]; **1975:** 666 [12]
Members, **1976–77:** 23 (p. 50), 1016
Newsweek magazine interview, **1974:** Appendix D
Relations with Congress, **1975:** 750 [18]
See also specific department.
Cabinet Committee on Crime Prevention and Rehabilitation, **1975:** 341
Cabinet Committee on Drug Abuse Prevention, **1976–77:** 633
Cabinet Committee for Drug Law Enforcement, **1976–77:** 633
Caglayangil, Sabri, **1976–77:** 60
Calder, Alexander, **1976–77:** 1018, 1052
California
Cannery strike, **1976–77:** 695
"Days of the Verdugos" Festival, **1976–77:** 864
"Expo 81," **1976–77:** 1034
Los Angeles Press Club, **1976–77:** 523
Naval petroleum reserves, **1974:** 72; **1975:** 28, 189 [11]

California—*continued*
Peace Officers Association, convention, **1976–77:** 513
President Ford Committees
Los Angeles, **1976–77:** 863
Rossmoor, **1976–77:** 530
San Diego, **1976–77:** 520
San Jose, **1976–77:** 526
Walnut Creek, **1976–77:** 531
President's travel, **1975:** 657 [17]
President's visits, **1974:** 211–213; **1975:** 165–167, 169, 531–533, 573, 574, 577–581, 647, 648, 650; **1976–77:** 259–264, 510–513, 518–532, 852–858, 860–865, 952–956, 958
Primary results, **1976–77:** 497, 585
Remarks on departure, **1976–77:** 532
Republican fundraising dinners, closed-circuit television remarks, **1976–77:** 861
Rossmoor Golden Rain Foundation, **1976–77:** 529
San Diego Harbor, **1976–77:** 523
San Jose Foreign Trade Zone, **1976–77:** 527
State legislature, address, **1975:** 532
10th anniversary of Mission Viejo, **1976–77:** 511
Wilderness areas, **1974:** 277
Callaghan, James, **1976–77:** 621, 807
Callahan, Nicholas P., **1976–77:** 674 [35]
Callaway, Howard H. (Bo), **1975:** 376, 396 [19], 620 [6], 657 [12], 678 [1], 739 [6], 750 [13]; **1976–77:** 10, 48 [3], 212 [1, 4, 8], 273, 325 [18], 360
Cambodia
Administration policy, **1975:** 125 [11], 138 [2]
Assistance appropriations, **1974:** 325
Cease-fire, **1975:** 189 [2]
Executions, **1975:** 243 [12]
Fall of government, **1975:** 191
Mayaguez, SS, seizure, **1975:** 256, 257, 276 [2]; **1976–77:** 287 [10]
President Lon Nol, **1975:** 125 [11]
Prince Norodom Sihanouk, **1975:** 189 [2]
Refugees, **1975:** 182, 183, 347, 530; **1976–77:** 611
U.S. humanitarian assistance, **1975:** 36 [13], 125 [1, 2, 4, 11], 161, 179, 347
U.S. military assistance, **1975:** 36 [13], 53, 107, 109 [3, 21], 125 [1, 2, 4, 11], 138 [13], 179
U.S. personnel, evacuation, **1975:** 182, 183, 243 [10]
Camp, Repr. John N. Happy, **1974:** 182, 183
Camp Casey, Korea, **1974:** 253
Camp David, Md., **1975:** 516, 517
Campaign.
See Elections, 1976.
Campbell, Carroll A., Jr., **1974:** 170, 173
Canada
Bicentennial gift to U.S., **1976–77:** 600
Extradition treaty with United States, **1974:** 74
Natural gas pipeline, **1975:** 527 [16]

Canada—*continued*
Oil and natural gas exports, **1975:** 498, 648 [3]
Prime Minister Pierre Elliott Trudeau, **1974:** 278; **1975:** 290n.
Relations with U.S., **1976–77:** 308
Summit conference in Puerto Rico, **1976–77:** 621
Trans-Canada gas pipeline, possibility, **1976–77:** 657 [21]
Cancer Act Amendments of 1974, National, **1974:** 222
Cancer Advisory Board, National, **1974:** 169, 186
Cancer Institute, National, **1974:** 186, 222
Cancer Program, National, **1974:** 222
Candidacy, President's, 1976 elections, **1974:** 39 [4], 127 [19]; **1975:** 45 [7], 72 [3], 129, 166 [12], 204 [10], 243 [4], 316 [10], 343, 386, 501 [7], 600 [15], 622 [24], 666 [21], 739 [6, 11]
Cannery strike, **1976–77:** 695
Cannon, James M., **1975:** 91, 92
Cape Canaveral-Kennedy Space Center, **1976–77:** 71
Cape Verde, Republic of
Generalized System of Preferences beneficiary, **1975:** 668
U.S. recognition, **1975:** 404
Capital Housing Authority, National, **1974:** 231
Capital punishment, **1976–77:** 215 [12]
Capitol Club, Kans., **1975:** 556
Capitol Page School, **1975:** 314
Caplin, Mortimer M., **1975:** 111
Caramanlis, Constantine, **1975:** 289n., 456n.
Cardwell, James B., **1974:** 275
Career Criminal Conference, **1975:** 590
Career Criminal Impact program, **1974:** 96; **1975:** 341, 590
Carey, William A., **1975:** 142
Carlinville, Ill., **1976–77:** 907
Carr, Col. Gerald P., **1975:** 180
Carter, Jimmy, **1975:** 678 [9, 19]; **1976–77:** 339 [12], 387 [2], 392 [8], 406, 418 [1, 6], 585, 657 [14], 674 [3, 6, 36], 737, 763 [18], 766, 778, 803, 846, 854, 861, 863, 864, 871, 887, 891, 895, 908, 925 [4, 7], 947, 972, 1014, 1020, 1068
Carter, John, **1974:** 111
Carter, Martha B., **1974:** 111
Carter, Tim Lee, **1974:** 175
Cartoonists, Association of American Editorial, **1976–77:** 434
Case, Sen. Clifford P., **1976–77:** 893
Casey, William J., **1975:** 569; **1976–77:** 199
Casselman, William E., II, **1975:** 481
Castro, Fidel, **1975:** 243 [8]; **1976–77:** 702
Catholic Bishops, National Conference of, **1976–77:** 769
Catton, Bruce, **1976–77:** 1052
Cavaiani, S. Sgt. Jon R., **1974:** 293
CBS News interview, **1975:** 204
Ceausescu, Nicolae, **1975:** 460 [14], 461, 462, 463, 464, 465
Cedar Point National Wildlife Reserve, **1976–77:** 535 [9]
Cederberg, Repr. Elford A., **1976–77:** 178
Census
Ethnic inclusion, **1976–77:** 283
Florida budget briefing, **1976–77:** 89
Mid-decade, **1976–77:** 913
Centennial safe opening, **1976–77:** 632
Center for Disease Control, **1976–77:** 823
Central Intelligence Agency
Budget news briefing, **1976–77:** 23 (p. 65)
Chile, activities in, **1974:** 80 [5]; **1975:** 204 [6], 565 [3]
Congressional investigations, **1975:** 125 [3], 138 [15], 179, 316 [1, 4], 551, 565 [5], 573 [8, 9], 600 [4], 615 [5], 657 [1, 8], 659, 750 [9]; **1976–77:** 68 [18]
Congressional oversight, **1975:** 204 [6], 479 [6]
Director, **1975:** 324, 657 [1, 4], 733; **1976–77:** 44
Domestic intelligence activities, **1975:** 582 [7], 695 [3]
Florida budget briefing, **1976–77:** 89
Foreign covert activities, **1975:** 204 [6], 565 [3], 582 [7]
Foreign leaders, alleged assassination attempts, **1975:** 695 [3]
Intelligence activities and international law, **1974:** 80 [16]
Investigatory commission, **1975:** 19, 45 [4], 125 [3], 138 [4, 16], 166 [13], 204 [6], 243 [8], 316 [1, 4, 8], 323, 324, 479 [6], 565 [3]
Legislative proposals, **1975:** 573 [9], 750 [9]
News conference remarks, **1976–77:** 107 [1, 2, 4, 7, 13, 16]
President's views, **1976–77:** 118
Station Chief, **1975:** 745
White House, clandestine employees, **1975:** 396 [18, 20]
Century Club, **1975:** 664
CETA.
See Comprehensive Employment and Training Act.
Chafee, Susan, **1976–77:** 1039
Chamber of Commerce, International, **1976–77:** 86 [1]
Chamber of Commerce Executives, American, **1975:** 585
Chamber of Commerce of the United States, **1975:** 220; **1976–77:** 365
Champaign, Ill., **1976–77:** 188, 189
Chance, Britton, **1975:** 568
Chancellor, John, **1975:** 45; **1976–77:** 6
Chargaff, Erwin, **1975:** 568
Charleston, W.Va, **1975:** 669, 670, 671
Charlotte, N.C., **1975:** 271; **1976–77:** 233–236

Charter of Economic Rights and Duties of States, **1974:** 179 [1, 7]
Chase, Chevy, **1976–77:** 262
Chemical and biological weapons, **1975:** 37, 38
Cheney, Richard B., **1975:** 657 [1]; **1976–77:** 740
Chern, Shiing-Shen, **1976–77:** 914
Cherne, Leo, **1976–77:** 107 [1, 10], 124, 199
Cheverton, Dick, **1974:** 76
Chiang Kai-shek, **1975:** 170, 189 [7]
Chicago, Ill., **1974:** 15, 191; **1975:** 395, 396, 397, 499, 500, 598; **1976–77:** 208, 209, 211, 968
Chicago Council of Foreign Relations, **1976–77:** 208
Chicago State University, **1975:** 397
Chien-Shiung Wu, **1976–77:** 557
Child Nutrition Act of 1966 Amendments of 1975, National School Lunch Act and, **1975:** 609, 615 [8], 616 [15], 620 [11]
Child Nutrition Reform Act of 1976, proposed, **1976–77:** 251, 685
Children
  Aid to families with dependent, **1976–77:** 685
  Birth defects, **1975:** 734
  Child support programs, **1975:** 14, 487; **1976–77:** 116
  Day care, **1975:** 502 [13]; **1976–77:** 305, 333 [8], 424, 430, 759, 760
  See also Youth.
Chile
  Central Intelligence Agency, involvement, **1974:** 80 [5]
  Military assistance, suspension, **1974:** 325
China, People's Republic of
  Administration policy, **1974:** 6; **1975:** 179, 189 [3, 7], 581 [3], 650, 716; **1976–77:** 569
  Campaign debate remarks, **1976–77:** 854
  Chairman Mao Tse-tung, **1975**: 706n.; **1976–77:** 767
  Computer sale, **1976–77:** 991
  Democratic Republic of Vietnam, assistance, **1975:** 189 [5]
  National women's basketball team, **1975:** 696
  News conference remarks, **1976–77:** 86 [16], 107 [3, 15], 325 [21]
  Nixon, Richard M., trip, **1976–77:** 63, 116, 138 [3], 185 [7], 192 [6]
  Premier Chou En-lai, death, **1976–77:** 12
  President's intention to visit, **1974:** 259 [1ftn.]
  President's visit, **1975:** 581 [3], 657 [18], 695 [6], 696, 706, 708
  Secretary of State's visit, **1974:** 259, 271 [1]
  Shanghai communique, **1975:** 706, 716
  Trade agreement with U.S., **1975:** 622 [14]; **1976–77:** 674 [17]
  U.S. Ambassador, **1976–77:** 340
  U.S. Liaison Office, Chief, **1975:** 657 [12]; **1976–77:** 229
  U.S. relations, **1976–77:** 185 [5], 207 [8], 210 [5], 339 [5], 505
  Vice Premier Teng Hsiao-ping, **1975:** 706, 708
China, Republic of
  Administration policy, **1975:** 189 [7]; **1976–77:** 116
  Campaign debate remarks, **1976–77:** 854
  Fishery agreement with United States, **1976–77:** 1047
  Little League World Series team, **1974:** 36
  Military sales credits, **1975:** 649
  News conference remarks, **1976–77:** 212 [12]
  President Chiang Kai-shek, **1975:** 170, 189 [7]
Chinese New Year, **1975:** 66; **1976–77:** 42
Chkalov, Col. Igor, **1975:** 348
Choi Young Hi, **1975:** 353
Chou En-lai, **1976–77:** 12
Christmas
  Message, **1974:** 304; **1975:** 747
  National Community Christmas Tree, lighting, **1974:** 306; **1975:** 736; **1976–77:** 1030
  White House staff party, **1975:** 728
Christmas Island.
  See under Australia.
Chrome imports, **1976–77:** 420 [5]
Church of Jesus Christ of Latter-day Saints, **1976–77:** 637
Church property, taxation, **1976–77:** 846
CIA.
  See Central Intelligence Agency.
CIA Activities Within the United States, Commission on, **1975:** 19, 45 [4], 125 [3], 138 [4, 16], 166 [13], 204 [6], 243 [8], 316 [1, 4, 8], 323, 324, 479 [6]
Cigarettes, Federal regulation, **1974:** 169, 186
Cincinnati, Ohio, **1975:** 373, 374; **1976–77:** 570–573, 981
Cioara, Gheorghe, **1975:** 462
Citizens' Action Committee to Fight Inflation, **1974:** 109, 121, 146, 150, 232
Citizen's Advisory Council on the Status of Women, **1976–77:** 363
Citizens Conference on State Legislatures, **1975:** 34
Citizens for Ford Committee, **1976–77:** 852
Civil Aeronautics Board, **1975:** 203, 392; **1976–77:** 314, 400, 765, 862
Civil Aviation Organization, International, **1974:** 86
Civil Service, memorandum, **1974:** 91; **1976–77:** 539
Civil Service Commission, United States, **1974:** 91, 115, 117; **1975:** 111, 124, 328, 690
Civitan International, **1976–77:** 43
Claims, United States Court of, **1974:** 203
Clancy, Repr. Donald D., **1974:** 184
Clean Air Act, **1974:** 121, 131; **1975:** 28, 64, 70, 72 [15], 364, 527 [15], 616 [11]
Clemency.
  See Executive clemency.
Clements, William P., **1976–77:** 23 (p. 59, 67, 73)
Cleveland, Ohio, **1974:** 184; **1975:** 375; **1976–77:** 556–569, 982–984

CLOSE-UP program, **1975:** 172
Coaches Association, American Football, **1975:** 25
Coal, **1976–77:** 140, 640, 1045
Environmental impact, **1975:** 28, 152
Gasification, **1974:** 121, 138
Mining, **1974:** 72, 131, 240, 326; **1975:** 28, 64, 75, 152, 270, 488 [9, 11], 615 [10], 616 [16], 682
Powerplants, conversion, **1975:** 741, 742
Replacement for oil, **1975:** 72 [15], 418, 527 [6], 616 [11]
Research and development, **1974:** 138; **1975:** 152, 670
White House meeting, **1975:** 152
Coal leasing amendments bill, Federal, veto, **1976–77:** 640
Coast Guard, United States, **1976–77:** 64, 1076
Coastal zone management, **1975:** 274; **1976–77:** 537
Coastal Zone Management Act Amendments, **1976–77:** 537, 690, 691
Cobb, Gail A., **1974:** 96
Cocos (Keeling) Island, Generalized System of Preferences, **1975:** 668
Coffee Agreement of 1968, International, **1975:** 188
Colby, William E., **1975:** 125 [3], 657 [1, 4]; **1976–77:** 44
Cole, Kenneth R., Jr., **1974:** 294
Coleman, William T., Jr., **1975:** 678 [18], 725; **1976–77:** 38, 58, 661, 934, 941, 959, 972, 1073
Collective bargaining commemorative stamp, **1975:** 134
Colleges and universities
Administration relations, **1975:** 138 [14]
Commencement and convocation addresses
Chicago State University, **1975:** 397
North Carolina Central University, **1975:** 676
Notre Dame University, **1975:** 137
Southern Methodist University, **1975:** 560
Tulane University, **1975:** 208
United States Military Academy, **1975:** 306
University of Pennsylvania, **1975:** 264
Yale University Law School, **1975:** 217
Concord, N.H., budget briefing, **1976–77:** 64
Federal aid, **1974:** 127 [13]
Graduates, employment outlook, **1976–77:** 580 [1]
Junior colleges, President's assessment, **1976–77:** 378 [2]
Lilly Endowment Continuing Conference for the Liberal Arts, remarks to, **1974:** 281
Ohio State University, remarks at, **1974:** 42
Pepperdine University, **1975:** 574
Private institutions, support, **1975:** 574, 616 [3]
Stanford University
Hoover Institution, **1975:** 6
School of Law, **1975:** 577, 578
Colleges and universities—*continued*
Student loans, **1975:** 502 [19], 554 [4], 602 [12], 616 [4, 9]; **1976–77:** 685
University of Hawaii, **1975:** 716
See also Education.
Collier, Calvin J., **1976–77:** 314
Colombia
Illicit drug trafficking, **1975:** 748
Joint communique, **1975:** 589
President Alfonso Lopez Michelsen, **1975:** 586, 587, 589
U.S. Ambassador, **1976–77:** 702
Colonial Williamsburg Foundation, **1976–77:** 51
Colorado
Flat Tops Wilderness, **1975:** 726
Hydroelectric project, **1974:** 202
President's visits, **1974:** 219; **1975:** 485, 488, 497; **1976–77:** 737, 740, 742, 1033, 1039, 1040, 1042
Wilderness areas, **1974:** 277
Columbia, S.C., **1976–77:** 950, 951
Columbia River Transmission System Act, Federal, **1974:** 176
Columbus, Ohio, **1974:** 42; **1976–77:** 533, 534, 1005, 1006
Columbus Day, **1976–77:** 880
Combined Federal Campaign, **1974:** 103; **1975:** 413, 564, 593; **1976–77:** 449, 450, 590
Commerce, Department of
Appropriations, **1974:** 72
Budget deferrals and rescissions, **1976–77:** 227, 1046, 1069
"E" award, **1975:** 490
Foreign investment activity in the United States, study, **1974:** 193
Maritime Administration, **1974:** 327
National Fire Prevention and Control Administration, **1974:** 197
Secretary, **1974:** 41, 42, 109, 132, 233, 291; **1975:** 18, 20, 92, 227, 311, 627, 657 [1], 689; **1976–77:** 53, 67 [18], 116, 277, 580 [3], 592, 626, 691, 709, 829, 859, 958, 1034
Under Secretary, **1975:** 311
See also specific constituent agencies.
Commission.
See also other part of title.
Commission on CIA Activities Within the United States, **1975:** 19, 45 [4], 125 [3], 138 [4, 16], 166 [13], 204 [6], 243 [8], 316 [1, 4, 8], 323, 324, 479 [6]
Commission of the European Communities, **1975:** 290n.
Commission on Federal Paperwork, **1974:** 323; **1975:** 220, 335
Commission on Marijuana and Drug Abuse, **1975:** 565 [19]
Commission on the Observance of International Women's Year, 1975, National, **1975:** 24, 185

Commission on Olympic Sports, President's, **1975:** 338
Commission on Productivity and Work Quality, National, **1974:** 121
Commission on Regulatory Reform, National, **1974:** 121, 240
Commission to Report Upon the Assassination of President John F. Kennedy, **1975:** 166 [13], 243 [8], 558, 695 [19]
Commission on Revision of the Federal Court Appellate System, **1975:** 342
Commission on Supplies and Shortages, National, **1974:** 114
Commission on White House Fellowships, President's, **1975:** 269
Committee.
See also other part of title.
Committee on Crime Prevention and Rehabilitation, Cabinet, **1975:** 341
Committee on Federal Pay, Advisory, **1975:** 328, 506
Committee for the Implementation of Textile Agreements, **1975:** 311
Committee on Refugees, President's Advisory, **1975:** 267, 415
Commodity Futures Trading Commission, **1975:** 392; **1976–77:** 315
Commodity Futures Trading Commission Act of 1974, **1974:** 189, 240
Common situs picketing legislation, **1975:** 501 [3], 554 [16], 739 [4, 12], 743; **1976–77:** 4
Communications
  Radio regulations agreement, **1975:** 408
  Satellites, **1975:** 313
Communism, Western Europe, **1976–77:** 402 [1]
Community Action program, **1974:** 39 [21]; **1975:** 12
Community Chest, **1974:** 57
Community Development Act, **1974:** 29, 30, 72; **1976–77:** 415 [5]
Community Development Block Grant Assistance program, **1975:** 167
Community development program, **1976–77:** 23 (p. 60), 38, 126, 138 [11], 415 [5]
Community Improvement Corps, **1974:** 121, 135
Community Partnership Act of 1974, Headstart, Economic Opportunity and, **1975:** 12
Community Services Administration, **1975:** 12, 248, 437
Community Services Administration, Director, **1976–77:** 343, 626, 702
Community services legislation, **1976–77:** 127
Competition in America, President's views, **1976–77:** 333 [7]
Comprehensive Alcohol Abuse and Alcoholism Prevention, Treatment, and Rehabilitation Act Amendments, **1976–77:** 693
Comprehensive Employment and Training Act, **1974:** 67; **1975:** 32, 209, 554 [8], 616 [4, 7], 662, 666 [13], 678 [8]; **1976–77:** 23 (p. 74), 95, 310, 356 [4]
Comprehensive health insurance plan, **1974:** 240
Comprehensive Oil Pollution Liability and Compensation Act of 1975, **1975:** 388
Concord, Mass., **1975:** 198
Concord, N.H., **1975:** 194, 195, 196; **1976–77:** 64, 66
Concorde, **1976–77:** 67 [3], 356 [10]
Conference.
See also other part of title.
Conference on Air Law, International, **1974:** 86
Conference Board, **1975:** 39
Conference on Inflation, **1974:** 6, 54, 56, 67, 106, 109, 121, 150, 236 [21]
Conference on the Law of the Sea, **1975:** 450, 511 [8], 527 [5]
Conference on Security and Cooperation in Europe, **1974:** 129, 258, 284, 302; **1975:** 289, 290 [8], 316 [5], 354 [11], 430, 439, 450, 459, 460 [13, 14, 15], 463, 472, 479 [7], 581 [8]
Conference on Trade, American, **1974:** 274
Conference on Urban Transportation, International, **1974:** 65
Congaree Swamp, S.C., **1976–77:** 918
Congo, People's Republic of the, **1976–77:** 1086
Congress
  American Hellenic Educational Progressive Association, Bicentennial dinner, **1976–77:** 302
  Bipartisan leadership, meetings with the President, **1974:** 19, 290
  Budgetary oversight, **1975:** 166 [5], 171, 223, 731, 732
  Christmas ball, **1976–77:** 1026
  Combined Federal Campaign, **1975:** 593
  Defense appropriations, **1976–77:** 339 [2]
  Democratic Caucus, **1975:** 36 [9]
  Democratic leadership, meeting with the President, **1975:** 115
  Democratic Party control, **1974:** 135, 151, 153, 154, 173, 174, 175, 182, 183, 184, 188, 191, 209, 211, 219, 236 [17]
  Disclosure of classified material, **1976–77:** 107 [9]
  Exemption of Members from local income taxes, veto of bill, **1976–77:** 710
  Federal Election Commission, **1976–77:** 145, 383
  Federal regulations, review, **1975:** 487
  Federal spending ceiling, **1976–77:** 472
  Foreign policy role, **1976–77:** 6
  Former Members, reception, **1975:** 275
  House of Representatives
    Appropriations Committee, **1975:** 347
    Government Operations Committee, **1975:** 192

Congress—*continued*
House of Representatives—*continued*
International Relations Committee, **1975:** 347, 387, 597
Interstate and Foreign Commerce Committee, **1975:** 192, 446
Judiciary Committee, **1974:** 112, 155; **1975:** 347
Minority leader, **1974:** 236 [5]; **1975:** 597
President's visits, **1974:** 27, 99, 287; **1975:** 112
President's voting record as former Member, **1976–77:** 68 [23]
Select Committee on Intelligence, **1975:** 551, 565 [5], 573 [8], 581 [9], 582 [7], 600 [4], 615 [5], 678 [2], 685; **1976–77:** 40
Speaker, **1974:** 276; **1975:** 48, 60, 75, 96, 100, 107, 143, 154, 157, 160, 175, 181, 183, 210, 215, 224, 225, 247, 257, 260, 312, 359, 368, 390, 445, 447, 522, 597, 621, 646, 668, 719, 720; **1976–77:** 33
Joint Sessions, **1974:** 6, 121; **1975:** 28, 179
Korean war veterans, meeting with President, **1975:** 353
Legislative priorities of the administration, **1976–77:** 684
Limitation of terms served, President's views, **1976–77:** 378 [9]
Limitations of executive powers, **1976–77:** 118
Messages and letters to.
See Congress, communications to.
News conference remarks, **1976–77:** 387 [26, 28], 535 [1, 10 11]
94th Congress, statement, **1976–77:** 851
Pay increase, **1974:** 195 [17], **1975:** 620 [10]; **1976–77:** 116
President's relations, **1974:** 236 [18]; **1975:** 45 [1], 316 [12], 501 [5], 573 [7]
Republican Senate-House fundraising dinner, **1975:** 187; **1976–77:** 278
Republican staff, **1974:** 98
Senate
Appropriations Committee, **1975:** 347, 719, 720
Armed Services Committee, **1975:** 733
Energy conservation resolution, **1975:** 149
Filibuster ruling, **1975:** 125 [6]
Foreign Relations Committee, **1975:** 347, 597, 719, 720
Government Operations Committee, **1975:** 192
Israel, support, letter to President, **1975:** 299
Judiciary Committee, **1975:** 347
Majority leader, **1974:** 21, 135; **1975:** 597, 686
Minority leader, **1975:** 422, 597, 686
President, **1975:** 48, 60, 75, 96, 100, 143, 154, 160, 175, 181, 183, 210, 215, 224, 225, 247, 260, 312, 359, 368, 445, 522, 621, 646, 668
President pro tempore, **1974:** 276; **1975:** 157, 257

Congress—*continued*
Senate—*continued*
President's visits, **1974:** 21, 26, 315
Public Works Committee, **1975:** 446
Select Committee To Study Government Operations with Respect to Intelligence Activities, **1975:** 657 [8], 659, 686
Senate Subcommittee on Internal Security, **1976–77:** 352 [10]
Statement by the President, **1974:** 316
Summer intern program, **1975:** 423
Veterans of Foreign Wars, dinner, **1976–77:** 197
Congress, communications to
Addresses to Joint Session, **1974:** 6, 121
Administration on Aging, report transmittals, **1975:** 280; **1976–77:** 248
Advisory Council on Intergovernmental Personnel Policy, report transmittal, **1974:** 101
Aeronautics and space activities, report transmittals, **1975:** 313; **1976–77:** 622
Airline industry regulations, messages, **1975:** 618; **1976–77:** 1060, 1072
Angola, letter to the Speaker of the House, **1976–77:** 33
Antarctic Seals, Convention for the Conservation of, transmittal to Senate, **1975:** 730
Antiballistic missile systems, protocol to U.S.-Soviet treaty, transmittal to Senate, **1974:** 85
Antitrust bill, letter to House Minority Leader on certain provisions of proposed legislation, **1976–77:** 224
Assassinations report, letter to chairman and members of Senate Select Committee on Intelligence, **1975:** 659
Atomic energy, amendment to agreement with United Kingdom, transmittal to Senate, **1974:** 10
Automobile emission standards legislation, letters
Congressional committee chairmen, **1975:** 446
Speaker of the House and President of the Senate, **1975:** 445
Bicentennial Land Heritage Act, letter to Speaker of the House and President of the Senate, **1976–77:** 1084
Bicentennial Land Heritage program, message, **1976–77:** 746
Budget, messages, **1975:** 63, 64; **1976–77:** 22, 245, 1066
Budget deferrals and rescissions, messages, **1974:** 89; **1975:** 59, 201, 202, 248, 367, 437, 541, 607, 635, 681, 705; **1976–77:** 9, 27, 61, 227, 269, 336, 364, 467, 633, 651, 697, 699, 739, 757, 779, 802, 822, 843, 1017, 1022, 1046, 1069
Budget restraint, message, **1974:** 262
Busing legislation, message, **1976–77:** 615

Congress, communications to—*continued*
Cambodia
U.S. assistance
Letter to Speaker of the House, **1975:** 107
Message, **1975:** 53
U.S. Mission, evacuation, letter to Speaker of the House and President of the Senate, **1975:** 183
Central Intelligence Agency, nomination of Director, letter to chairman of Senate Armed Services Committee, **1975:** 733
Child Nutrition Reform Act of 1976, message, **1976–77:** 251
Citizenship requirements for Federal employment, letter to Speaker of House and President of Senate, **1976–77:** 752
Coal mine health program, report transmittal, **1975:** 682
Coastal zone management, report transmittals, **1975:** 274; **1976–77:** 537
Community services, message, **1976–77:** 127
Compensation for Federal Reserve Board and Office of Management and Budget officials, letter to committee chairmen, **1976–77:** 1074
Consular convention with Bulgaria, transmittal to Senate, **1974:** 73
Consumer protection, letter to committee chairmen, **1975:** 192
Convention on Registration of Objects Launched Into Outer Space, transmittal, **1976–77:** 228
Cooley's anemia programs, report transmittals, **1975:** 545; **1976–77:** 823
Cost of Living Council, final report transmittal, **1974:** 116
Council of Economic Advisers, annual report, **1975:** 70
Council on Environmental Quality, report transmittals, **1974:** 292; **1976–77:** 144, 838
Council on Wage and Price Stability, report transmittals, **1975:** 31, 176, 438, 687; **1976–77:** 220, 466, 764, 1055
Crime, special message, **1975:** 341
Cyprus conflict, messages, **1975:** 718; **1976–77:** 60, 315, 582, 717, 850, 1051
Day's Sportswear, Inc., relief disapproval, **1976–77:** 896
Defense budget, message, **1976–77:** 736
Developing countries
Development coordination, report transmittal, **1975:** 273
Generalized trade preferences, letters to Speaker of the House and President of the Senate, **1975:** 154, 668
Diplomats, convention on prevention and punishment of crimes against, transmittal to Senate, **1974:** 230

Congress, communications to—*continued*
District of Columbia, budget, **1975:** 660
Drug abuse, message, **1976–77:** 368
Early warning system in Sinai, U.S. participation, letter to Speaker of the House and President of the Senate, **1975:** 522
Economic Report of the President, annual messages, **1975:** 68, 70; **1976–77:** 31, 1070
Electronic surveillance, letter to Speaker of the House and President of the Senate, **1976–77:** 252
Elementary and secondary education, message, **1976–77:** 169
Energy
Emergency contingency plans, letter to congressional leaders, **1976–77:** 1083
Legislation, proposed
Energy independence act, letter to Speaker of the House and President of the Senate, **1975:** 60
Independence authority, letters to Speaker of the House and President of the Senate, **1975:** 621; **1976–77:** 1078
Special message, **1976–77:** 140
Reorganization of Federal energy functions, report transmittal, **1976–77:** 1054
Special message, **1976–77:** 1045
Energy Research and Development Administration, defense-related programs, report transmittal, **1976–77:** 459
Enriched uranium production legislation
Letter to Speaker of the House and President of the Senate, **1975:** 359
Message, **1975:** 358
Executive, legislative, and judicial salary increases, message, **1976–77:** 1068
Executive branch activities under the Privacy Act of 1974, report transmittal, **1976–77:** 681
Executive Office of the President, appropriations, letter to Speaker of the House and President of the Senate, **1975:** 160
Executive reorganization authority, letter to Speaker of the House and President of the Senate, **1975:** 175
Extradition treaties, transmittal to Senate
Australia, **1974:** 28
Canada, **1974:** 74
Federal Advisory Committees status, report transmittal, **1975:** 162
Federal-aid highway legislation, message, **1975:** 382, 383
Federal airport and airway development programs, message, **1975:** 136
Federal civilian and military retirement systems, message, **1976–77:** 254
Federal Council on the Aging, report transmittals, **1975:** 424; **1976–77:** 708

Congress, communications to—*continued*
Federal Election Commission, reconstitution, message, **1976–77:** 103
Federal employment reduction, message, **1974:** 43
Federal Energy Administration, letter to Speaker of the House and President of the Senate, **1976–77:** 101
Federal oceans program, report transmittal, **1976–77:** 1081
Federal pay and benefits ceiling legislation, letter to Speaker of the House and President of the Senate, **1975:** 143
Federal pay increase, messages, **1974:** 43, 117; **1975:** 506; **1976–77:** 844
Federal Prevailing Rate Advisory Committee, report transmittal, **1976–77:** 751
Federal summer youth employment and public service jobs programs
Letter to President of the Senate, **1976–77:** 313
Memorandum, **1976–77:** 312
Message, **1976–77:** 311
Federal travel, letter to Speaker of the House and President of the Senate, **1976–77:** 45
Financial institutions, regulatory reform legislation, message, **1975:** 144
Fiscal year 1976–77 transition period appropriations, letter to Speaker of the House and President of the Senate, **1975:** 100
Food for Peace program, report transmittals, **1974:** 102; **1976–77:** 36
Food stamp program
Letter to Senate and House committee chairmen, **1975:** 435, 634; **1976–77**: 122
Footwear industry, adjustment assistance, message, **1976–77:** 347
Foreign assistance appropriations bill
Letter to Sen. Edward W. Brooke, **1976–77:** 270
Letter to Speaker of the House, **1976–77:** 303
Veto, **1976–77:** 437
Foreign assistance authorization legislation, letter to Speaker of the House and President of the Senate, **1975:** 260
Foreign Payments Disclosure Act, proposed, message, **1976–77:** 709
Forest and Rangeland Renewable Resources Planning Act of 1974, letter to Speaker of the House and President of the Senate, **1976–77:** 170
Freedom of Information Act amendments, letter to conference committee chairmen, **1974:** 31
General revenue sharing legislation
Letter to Speaker of the House and President of the Senate, **1975:** 215
Message, **1975:** 214

Congress, communications to—*continued*
Generalized system of preferences
Congo, People's Republic of, withdrawal, letter to Speaker of the House and President of the Senate, **1976–77:** 1086
Laos, withdrawal, letter to Speaker of the House and President of the Senate, **1976–77:** 141
Government reform, agenda transmittal, message, **1976–77:** 468
Greece, economic and military assistance, letter to Speaker of the House and Senate committee chairmen, **1975:** 719
Guatamala disaster relief, **1976–77:** 114
Health care reform legislation, message, **1976–77:** 136
Highway, traffic, and motor vehicle safety programs, report transmittals, **1974:** 50; **1975:** 613; **1976–77:** 616
House Select Committee on Intelligence, contempt resolutions, letter to chairman, **1975:** 685
Indochina
Refugees, status of, report transmittals to committee chairmen, **1975:** 347; **1976–77:** 247, 611, 797, 1053
Retrieval of assistance funds, report transmittal to committee chairmen, **1975:** 347
Inter-American Treaty of Reciprocal Assistance (Rio Treaty), transmittal of protocol to Senate, **1975:** 700
Intergovernmental Maritime Consultative Organization convention, amendments, transmittal to Senate, **1975:** 391
International Coffee Agreement of 1968, protocol, transmittal to Senate, **1975:** 188
International Convention for the Safety of Life at Sea amendments, transmittal to Senate, **1974:** 157
International Economic Report of the President, transmittals, **1975:** 147; **1976–77:** 223, 1071
International exhibitions, report transmittal, **1976–77:** 492
International Office of Epizootics agreement, transmittal to Senate, **1974:** 270
International Telecommunication Convention, transmittal to Senate, **1974:** 158
International whaling operations and conservation programs, report, **1975:** 30
International Wheat Agreement, 1971, protocols, transmittal to Senate, **1975:** 319
Italy, U.S. disaster assistance, message, **1976–77:** 453
Legislative priorities, messages, **1974:** 72, 240; **1976–77:** 685
Little Beaver Creek, Ohio, report transmittal, **1976–77:** 72

Congress, communications to—*continued*
Manpower Report of the President, transmittal, **1975:** 209
Mayaguez, SS, U.S. actions to recover, letter to Speaker of the House and President pro tempore of the Senate, **1975:** 257
Military assistance program, message, **1976–77:** 20
Military incentive awards program, report transmittals, **1975:** 139; **1976–77:** 1058, 1059
Motor carrier reform legislation, message, **1975:** 675
Municipal bankruptcy legislation, letter to Speaker of the House and President of the Senate, **1975:** 646
Narcotic sentencing and seizure legislation, letter to Speaker of the House and President of the Senate, **1976–77:** 413
National Advisory Council on Economic Opportunity, report transmittal, **1975:** 544
National Advisory Council on Extension and Continuing Education, report transmittals, **1974:** 133; **1975:** 336
National Cancer Advisory Board, report transmittal, **1974:** 186
National Cancer Program, report transmittals, **1974:** 222; **1976–77:** 296
National Capital Housing Authority, report transmittal, **1974:** 231
National Council on Educational Research, report transmittal, **1975:** 253
National Endowment for the Arts and National Council on the Arts, report transmittals, **1975:** 346; **1976–77:** 744
National Endowment for the Humanities, report transmittal, **1975:** 325
National Heart and Lung Advisory Council, report transmittals, **1975:** 259; **1976–77:** 496
National Heart and Lung Institute, report transmittals, **1974:** 97; **1975:** 361; **1976–77:** 491
National Science Board, report transmittals, **1975:** 150; **1976–77:** 130, 839
National Science Foundation, report transmittals, **1975:** 114; **1976–77:** 246
1977 Budget requests and creation of Office of Science and Technology Policy, message, **1976–77:** 245
North Atlantic Treaty, balance of payments, report transmittals, **1974:** 20, 242; **1975:** 101, 281
Northern Marianas Islands, Commonwealth status, letter to Speaker of the House and President of the Senate, **1975:** 368
Nuclear exports and safeguards, U.S. laws and regulations, report transmittal, **1975:** 241
Nuclear materials, international safeguards, report transmittal, **1975:** 520

Congress, communications to—*continued*
Nuclear-powered Navy, letter to Speaker of the House and President of the Senate, **1976–77:** 84
Occupational safety and health activities, report transmittal, **1975:** 363
Office of Science and Technology, letter to Speaker of the House and President of the Senate, **1975:** 315
Oil import fees and price controls, letter to Speaker of the House and President of the Senate, **1975:** 225
Oil pollution control legislation, message, **1975:** 388
Older Americans, message, **1976–77:** 70
Organization for Economic Cooperation and Development Financial Support Fund, U.S. participation, letter to Speaker of the House and President of the Senate, **1975:** 312
Pardon of Richard Nixon
Letter to House Judiciary subcommittee chairman, **1974:** 112
Testimony before House Judiciary subcommittee, **1974:** 155
Polar Bears, Agreement on the Conservation of, transmittal to Senate, **1975:** 699
Predator control reorganization, letter to Speaker of the House and President of the Senate, **1976–77:** 1082
Public trust in Government, letter to Speaker of the House and President of the Senate, **1976–77:** 675
Puerto Rico, proposed statehood, letter to Speaker of the House and President of the Senate, **1976–77:** 1065
Radiation Control for Health and Safety Act of 1968, report transmittals, **1975:** 362; **1976–77:** 584
Radio Regulations (Geneva 1959), partial revision, transmittal to Senate, **1975:** 408
Railroad regulation reform legislation, message, **1975:** 268
Railroad Retirement Board, report transmittal, **1976–77:** 536
River Basins Commissions, report transmittals, **1975:** 425; **1976–77:** 594
Romania-United States Trade Agreement
Letter to Speaker of the House and President of the Senate, **1975:** 210
Report, **1975:** 211
Saint Lawrence Seaway Development Corporation, report transmittal, **1975:** 535
Secret Service protection, letter to Speaker of the House and President of the Senate, **1976–77:** 1064
Security assistance programs, message, **1975:** 649

Congress, communications to—*continued*
Senate Select Committee to Study Governmental Operations With Respect to Intelligence Activities, report, letter to Senate leadership, **1975:** 686
Shrimp agreement with Brazil, transmittal to Senate, **1975:** 320
Sickle cell anemia, report transmittals, **1975:** 77; **1976–77:** 425
Social security benefit indexing act, message, **1976–77:** 602
Southeast Asia, U.S. missing in action, letter to Speaker of the House and President of the Senate, **1976–77:** 546
Special international exhibits, report transmittal, **1974:** 8
Stainless steel flatware industry, adjusted assistance, message, **1976–77:** 412
State of the Union Address, **1975:** 28; **1976–77:** 19, 1057
Surface mining legislation, letter to Speaker of the House and President of the Senate, **1975:** 75
Swine flu immunization program
Letter to Interstate and Foreign Commerce Subcommittee on Health and the Environment Chairman, **1976–77:** 688
Letter to Speaker of House and Majority Leader of Senate, **1976–77:** 715
Message requesting vaccine appropriations, **1976–77:** 258
Tax reductions
Legislation, letter to Speaker of the House and President pro tempore of the Senate, **1975:** 157
Proposals for 1977, **1976–77:** 1044
Taxation conventions, transmittal to Senate
Iceland, **1975:** 385
Poland, **1975:** 40
Trade Agreements Program, report transmittal, **1975:** 226
Trademark Registration Treaty, transmittal to Senate, **1975:** 519
Treaties and other international agreements
Convention Abolishing the Requirement of Legislation for Foreign Public Documents, message to Senate, **1976–77:** 676
Fishery agreements, transmittals
Bulgaria, **1976–77:** 1067
China, Republic of, **1976–77:** 1047
German Democratic Republic, **1976–77:** 1049
Poland, **1976–77:** 785
Romania, **1976–77:** 1048
Union of Soviet Socialist Republics, **1976–77:** 1050
Interim Convention on Conservation of North Pacific Fur Seals, message to the Senate, **1976–77:** 677

Congress, communications to—*continued*
Treaties—*continued*
International carriage by air, transmittal of protocols to the Senate, **1976–77:** 1063
International Coffee Agreement, 1976, message to the Senate, **1976–77:** 295
International Convention for the Safety of Life at Sea, 1974, message to the Senate, **1976–77:** 748
International Tin Agreement, message to the Senate, **1976–77:** 612
International Wheat Agreement, message to the Senate, **1976–77:** 605
Romania, waiver authority extension, message to Congress, **1976–77:** 548
Turkey, defense cooperation agreement with U.S., request for appropriations, message to Congress, **1976–77:** 598
Union of Soviet Socialist Republics, treaties on the limitation of underground nuclear explosions, message to the Senate, **1976–77:** 700
United States-Egypt Convention on Income Tax, message to Senate, **1976–77:** 79
United States-Israel Convention on Income Tax, message to Senate, **1976–77:** 78
United States-Korea Convention on Taxation and Fiscal Evasion, **1976–77:** 754
United States-Philippines Convention on Income Taxation, message to Senate, **1976–77:** 1080
United States-Spain Extradition Treaty, message, **1976–77:** 56
United States-Spain Friendship and Cooperation Treaty, message to the Senate, **1976–77:** 108
United States-Switzerland Treaty on Mutual Assistance in Criminal Matters, message to the Senate, **1976–77:** 109
United States-Turkey Defense Cooperation Agreement, retransmittal, letter to Speaker of the House and President of the Senate, **1976–77:** 1074
United States-United Kingdom Convention on Taxation and Fiscal Evasion, message to the Senate, **1976–77:** 613, 799
United States-United Kingdom Extradition Treaty, message to the Senate, **1976–77:** 55
Turkey
Opium poppies control, letter to Speaker of the House and Senate committee chairmen, **1975:** 720
U.S. military assistance, letter to Speaker of the House, **1975:** 390, 447
Uniform Relocation Assistance and Real Property Acquisition Policies Act of 1970, report transmittal, **1975:** 49

Congress, communications to—*continued*
Uniformed services, basic allowances for quarters, letter to Speaker of House and President of Senate, **1976–77:** 837
United Nations, U.S. participation, report transmittals, **1974:** 86; **1975:** 656; **1976–77:** 842
United States Arms Control and Disarmament Agency
Appropriations legislation, letter to Speaker of the House and President of the Senate, **1975:** 96
Report transmittals, **1975:** 119; **1976–77:** 701, 1085
United States foreign intelligence community, message, **1976–77:** 110
United States-Japan Cooperative Medical Science Program, report transmittal, **1975:** 384
United States Sinai Support Mission, report transmittals, **1976–77:** 411, 1056
Vietnam, Republic of, U.S. assistance
Letters to Speaker of the House and President of the Senate, **1975:** 181, 224
Message, **1975:** 53
Vietnam era veterans educational benefits, legislation terminating eligibility period, letter to Speaker of the House and President of the Senate, **1975:** 247
Voting Rights Act of 1965, extension, letters
Senate minority leader, **1975:** 422
Speaker of the House and President of the Senate, **1975:** 48
War Risk Insurance Program, report transmittal, **1976–77:** 230
Wilderness area proposals
Letter to President pro tempore of the Senate and Speaker of the House, **1974:** 276
Message, **1974:** 277
World Weather Program
Annual report transmittal, **1976–77:** 824
U.S. participation, plan transmittal, **1975:** 317
See also Veto messages and memorandums of disapproval; Appendix B, 1974.
Congress, First Continental, **1974:** 58
Congressional Budget and Impoundment Control Act of 1974, **1974:**, 40, 72, 89, 262, 318; **1975:** 59, 62, 64, 166 [5], 167, 171, 367, 437
Congressional Budget Office, **1975:** 573 [5]
Congressional City Conference of the U.S. Conference of Mayors and National League of Cities, **1976–77:** 216
Congressional Leadership Research Center, Everett McKinley Dirksen, **1975:** 495
Congressional Legal Counsel, Office of, proposed, **1976–77:** 675
Congressional Medal of Honor, **1974:** 293; **1976–77:** 176
Connally, John B., **1975:** 85 [8], 204 [12], 354 [12]; **1976–77:** 199, 282 [6], 318, 325 [7, 14], 339 [4], 387 [27], 694, 740, 742, 1025
Connecticut, President's visit, **1975:** 217, 629, 630; **1976–77:** 672
Connecticut Association of Realtors, **1975:** 629
Connor, John T., **1975:** 19
Conrad, Capt. Charles, Jr., **1975:** 235
ConRail, **1976–77:** 59
Conroe, Tex., **1976–77:** 389, 390
Conservation
Agricultural production, **1975:** 15
Energy, **1975:** 26, 28, 41, 46, 64, 69, 70, 85 [3, 7], 120, 149, 354 [15], 364, 421, 488 [1, 3], 600 [14], 616 [1], 741, 742; **1976–77:** 1045
Fishery stocks, **1975:** 584
Gasoline rationing, **1975:** 32, 36 [1, 16, 24], 45 [1], 71, 82, 109 [8]
Wilderness areas, proposed, **1974:** 276, 277
Wildlife, **1975:** 30, 699, 730
Youth Conservation Corps, **1974:** 47
See also Energy; Environment.
Conservation Act, Emergency Highway Energy, **1974:** 240
Considine, Bob, **1975:** 588
Constitution, U.S.
Equal rights amendment, **1975:** 24, 185, 307, 396 [14], 578 [2], 616 [21]
25th Amendment, **1974:** 195 [12], 236 [2]; **1975:** 109 [19]
Construction industry
Common situs picketing legislation, **1975:** 501 [3], 554 [16], 739 [4, 12], 743
Highways, **1975:** 84, 85 [3], 108, 622 [21]
Housing, **1975:** 351; **1976–77:** 383
National Association of Realtors, convention, **1974:** 234
President's assessment, **1975:** 580
Consular convention, U.S.-Bulgarian, **1974:** 73
Consumer Advisory Council, **1975:** 230
Consumer affairs
Agency for consumer protection, proposed, **1975:** 220, 527 [12]
Energy efficiency labeling, **1975:** 742
Federal departments and agencies, representation plans, **1975:** 527 [12], 658
Regulatory reforms, **1975:** 192, 220, 341, 392, 675, 678 [6]
Consumer Goods Pricing Act of 1975, **1975:** 723, 724
Consumer Leasing Act of 1976, **1976–77:** 249
Consumer price index, **1976–77:** 31, 118, 555
Consumer Product Safety Commission, **1975:** 392
Chairman, **1976–77:** 314
Consumer Product Safety Commission Improvements Act of 1976, **1976–77:** 458
Consumer protection, **1974:** 189, 200, 240; **1976–77:** 240 [7], 249, 250, 820

Continental Congress, First, **1974:** 58
Conventions.
See Treaties and other international agreements; *specific subject.*
Cook, Sen. Marlow W., **1974:** 175
Cooke, Terence Cardinal, **1976–77:** 935
Cooley's anemia programs, report transmittals, **1975:** 545; **1976–77:** 823
Cooper, Theodore, **1975:** 370; **1976–77:** 674 [20], 688
Coral Springs, Fla., **1976–77:** 162
Corporate Payments Abroad, Task Force on Questionable, **1976–77:** 275–277, 592, 593, 709
Corporation for Public Broadcasting, **1975:** 88
Corps of Engineers, **1976–77:** 181, 583, 802
Corts, Tom, **1974:** 184
Cosgrave, Liam M., **1976–77:** 222, 225, 226
Cost of Living Council, economic stabilization program, **1974:** 116
Costa Gomes, Francisco da, **1974:** 168
Cotton, Sen. Norris, **1975:** 266
Cotton, price support, **1975:** 232
Council.
See also other part of title.
Council on the Arts, National, **1974:** 53
Council on Crime and Delinquency, National, **1974:** 181
Council of Economic Advisers
Chairman, **1974:** 38, 39 [13], 52, 109; **1975:** 20, 92, 311, 328, 626
Economic Report of the President, **1975:** 68, 70
Council on Environmental Quality, **1974:** 233, 292; **1975:** 20, 554 [6]
Council on International Economic Policy, Executive Director, **1974:** 109, 321; **1975:** 311
Council on Wage and Price Stability, **1974:** 41, 109, 121, 152, 241; **1975:** 31, 176, 328, 438, 486, 687
Council on Wage and Price Stability Act, **1974:** 6, 19, 32, 33, 72
Council on Wage and Price Stability Act Amendments of 1975, **1975:** 486
County executives, telegram on inflation-fighting efforts, **1974:** 146, 151
Courts, United States
Appellate system, revision, **1975:** 342
District court judgeships, legislation increasing, **1974:** 72, 240; **1975:** 7, 341, 400
Document declassification, **1974:** 160, 236 [1]
Evidentiary rules legislation, **1974:** 240; **1975:** 5
Federal and State judges, dinner honoring, **1975:** 692
Judge William H. Hastie, **1976–77:** 344
Lumber industry, decisions, **1976–77:** 383
Municipal bankruptcy, jurisdiction, **1975:** 645, 646, 648 [1], 655 [8]
Presidential documents and materials, **1974:** 313
Prosecution standards, **1975:** 7, 341
Courts, United States—*continued*
School busing, decisions, **1975:** 511 [6], 552 [10], 554 [3], 565 [7], 573 [10], 622 [17]
Sentencing procedures, **1975:** 341
State courts, Federal assistance, **1975:** 400
Supreme Court of the United States, **1975:** 565 [8], 578 [1], 673, 678 [4, 7, 18], 692, 695 [9, 14, 17], 697, 750 [1]
Covington, Ky., **1976–77:** 980
Crane, Repr. Philip M., **1974:** 191
Cranston, Sen. Alan, **1974:** 161
Crawford, H. R., **1976–77:** 35
Credit.
See Loans; Mortagages.
Crime.
See Law enforcement and crime.
Crime and Delinquency, National Council on, **1974:** 181
Criminal Code, District of Columbia, **1976–77:** 761
Criminal Code, Federal, **1976–77:** 685, 803, 827
Criminal Impact program, Career, **1974:** 96
Criminal Justice Reform Act of 1975, **1975:** 341
Cronkite, Walter, **1975:** 204
CSCE.
See Conference on Security and Cooperation in Europe.
Cub Scouts, induction ceremonies, **1975:** 671
Cuba
Administration policy, **1974:** 39 [23], 179 [5]; **1975:** 109 [10], 655 [9], 739 [8, 9], 750 [8]
Angola, involvement, **1975:** 738, 750 [5, 21]; **1976–77:** 138 [14], 159, 385 [2]
Foreign intervention, **1976–77:** 339 [14]
News conference remarks, **1976–77:** 282 [8], 325 [5], 387 [32], 535 [5]
Premier Fidel Castro, **1975:** 243 [8]
Puerto Rican independence movement, **1975:** 739 [9]
Rhodesia, involvement, **1976–77:** 415 [2]
U.S. policy, **1976–77:** 68 [12], 148, 702
Cullinane, Maurice J., **1976–77:** 664
Cultural Affairs Act of 1976, Arts, Humanities, and, **1976–77:** 875
Cultural Challenge Grant Program, **1976–77:** 899
Curtis, Thomas B., **1975:** 184; **1976–77:** 657 [7]
Cuyahoga Valley National Recreation Area, **1974:** 324
Cyprus
Death of U.S. Ambassador, **1974:** 16, 22
Generalized System of Preferences, beneficiary, **1975:** 668
Greece-Turkey dispute, **1974:** 81, 113, 120, 135, 144, 145, 147, 151, 156, 164, 195 [21], 236 [21], 258, 284, 325; **1975:** 73, 91, 166 [15], 179, 387, 390, 427, 447, 479 [10], 608, 718; **1976–77:** 60, 68 [9], 118, 283, 315, 582, 717, 850, 1051
Security assistance programs, **1975:** 649

Dairy products
Dry milk mixtures, imports, **1976–77:** 268
Farm forum, Rockford, Ill., **1976–77:** 203
Imports, **1974:** 152, 153, 210, 219; **1975:** 232, 502 [3]; **1976–77:** 288
Price supports, **1975:** 4; **1976–77:** 47
Daley, Richard J., **1975:** 396 [11, 12]; **1976–77:** 1035
Dallas, Tex., **1975:** 558, 559, 560; **1976–77:** 320–322, 324, 396–399, 868–872
Damman, James J., **1974:** 135
Danforth, Jack, **1975:** 557
Daniel, David H., **1976–77:** 663
Daniel, Repr. Robert W., Jr., **1974:** 88
Daniel, Repr. W. C. (Dan), **1974:** 88
Dantzig, George B., **1976–77:** 557, 914
Data collection by the Federal Government, **1976–77:** 173
Daughters of the American Revolution, **1975:** 186; **1976–77:** 349
Davies, Rodger P., **1974:** 16, 22
Davis, Hallowell, **1976–77:** 557, 914
Davis, Joe, **1975:** 421
Davis-Bacon Act, **1976–77:** 383
Day, Col. George E., **1976–77:** 176
Day care centers, **1975:** 502 [13]
Days of observance
Black History Week, message, **1975:** 67
Black Press Week, message, **1975:** 130
Chinese New Year, message, **1975:** 66
Christmas, messages, **1974:** 304; **1975:** 747
Day-of-prayer proclamations, **1975:** 416
Drug Abuse Prevention Week, proclamation, **1974:** 167
Independence Day, **1975:** 377
Jewish High Holy Days, messages, **1974:** 55; **1975:** 521
King, Martin Luther, Jr., birthday, **1975:** 27
Labor Day, remarks, **1974:** 44; **1975:** 513, 514
Lincoln, Abraham, birthday, **1975:** 86
March of Dimes Birth Defects Prevention Month, **1975:** 734
Memorial Day, ceremonies, **1975:** 278
National Epilepsy Month, statement, **1975:** 638
National Hispanic Heritage Week, proclamation, **1974:** 48, 49
National Saint Elizabeth Seton Day, proclamation, **1975:** 546
New Year's Day, message, **1975:** 751
Ramadan, message, **1974:** 159; **1975:** 605
Red Cross Month, **1975:** 104
Thanksgiving Day, **1975:** 694, 695 [24]
Veterans Day
Ceremonies, **1974:** 192
Redesignating November 11 as, **1975:** 575
Remarks for, **1975:** 641
Women's Equality Day, 1975, message, **1975:** 504
Days of observance—*continued*
World Environment Day, **1975:** 310
See also Appendix B, 1974.
Day's Sportswear, Inc., relief disapproval, **1976–77:** 896
Dayton, Ohio, **1976–77:** 575
de Medici, Marino, **1975:** 276
de Rosa, François Pierre Tricornot, **1976–77:** 267
de Segonzac, Adalbert, **1975:** 276
de Staercke, André M., **1976–77:** 267
de Valera, Eamon, **1975:** 507
Dean, Mrs. John W., **1974:** 68
Dearborn, Mich., **1976–77:** 49
Deardourff, John, **1976–77:** 740
Death penalty, Supreme Court decision, **1976–77:** 657 [25]
Debates.
See Elections, 1976.
Declaration on Atlantic Relations, **1974:** 105
Deepwater Port Act of 1974, **1975:** 8
Deepwater ports, **1974:** 72, 240
Deerfield, Fla., **1976–77:** 161
Defense, Department of
Appropriations, **1974:** 72, 126, 240, 271 [2, 4, 7, 16, 21, 22]; **1975:** 64, 612; **1976–77:** 73
Assistant Secretary, **1974:** 14
Assistant Secretary of Defense for Manpower and Reserve Affairs, **1975:** 328
Budget deferrals and rescissions, **1976–77:** 822, 1022, 1069
Deputy Secretary, **1976–77:** 23 (p. 59, 67, 73)
Joint Chiefs of Staff, **1976–77:** 23 (p. 59)
Joint Chiefs of Staff
Chairman, **1974:** 236 [7]
Medal for Distinguished Public Service, **1976–77:** 267
Medical and dental education, financial assistance, **1975:** 602 [12]
Secretary, **1974:** 77, 78, 132, 239, 291; **1975:** 324, 600 [17], 657 [1, 4, 14], 666 [1, 7], 688
See also specific service branch.
Defense Appropriations Act, 1975, Department of, **1974:** 126
Defense Appropriations Act, 1977, Department of, **1976–77:** 800
Defense Appropriations Authorization Act, 1977, Department of, **1976–77:** 667
Defense Distinguished Service Medal, **1974:** 312
Defense and national security
Administration policy, **1975:** 186, 187, 306, 567, 663; **1976–77:** 215 [8], 362 [11]
Armed Forces Week, exhibit, **1976–77:** 448
Budget news briefing, **1976–77:** 23 (p. 54, 59, 67, 71, 73, 74)
Congressional action on spending, **1975:** 72 [7]; **1976–77:** 209 [2]
Contingency plans, **1976–77:** 378 [5]
Defense Production Act, extension, **1974:** 72, 114

Defense and national security—*continued*
Document classification, **1974:** 31, 60, 160, 236 [1]
40 Committee, **1974:** 80 [5]
Funding, **1974:** 126, 262, 271 [2, 4, 7, 16, 21, 22]; **1975:** 39, 64, 85 [10], 103, 106, 167, 179, 186, 207, 306, 393, 492, 619, 622, 626, 663, 666 [6]; **1976–77:** 22, 116, 118, 172, 194, 215 [7], 283, 284 [7, 8], 321 [11], 339 [2], 362 [11, 12], 380, 394, 484
Great Lakes, military cargo, **1975:** 502 [20]
Intelligence activities, **1974:** 80 [5]; **1976–77:** 110
Legislation, **1976–77:** 685
Military capability, **1976–77:** 327 [11], 398 [11], 414, 416, 420 [1], 519
Military construction authorization, **1974:** 39 [17], 72
Naval forces, **1975:** 207
NBC News interview, **1976–77:** 6
News conference remarks, **1976–77:** 282 [14], 387 [21, 22]
Nuclear-powered Navy, **1976–77:** 84
President's assessment, **1975:** 492; **1976–77:** 39, 77, 197, 210 [9], 293 [1], 349, 371, 1075
Radio address, **1976–77:** 985
Radio-Television News Directors Association, **1976–77:** 48 [1, 6]
Security assistance programs, **1975:** 649
Spending, **1976–77:** 209 [2], 415 [7], 417, 667, 736, 749, 766, 790, 854, 858, 920, 925 [16]
State of the Union Address, **1976–77:** 19, 1057
See also Intelligence activities.
Defense Production Act Amendments of 1974, **1974:** 72, 114
Defense Production Act of 1950, **1974:** 121
Deferrals, budget.
See under Budget, Federal.
Del Ray Beach, Fla., **1976–77:** 157
Delaware, wilderness area, **1974:** 277
Dellenback, Repr. John, **1974:** 215
Delta Queen, **1976–77:** 912
Demirel, Süleyman, **1975:** 289n., 457, 720
Democratic National Committee, **1974:** 149
Democratic Party
Congressional leadership, **1975:** 115
Control of Congress, **1974:** 135, 151, 153, 154, 173, 174, 175, 182, 183, 184, 188, 191, 209, 211, 219, 236 [17]
News conference remarks, **1976–77:** 387 [2, 13, 26], 535 [14]
1976 Presidential candidates, **1975:** 655 [11], 678 [9, 19], 750 [16]; **1976–77:** 159, 262, 308, 339 [11], 376, 392 [7], 461
President's views, **1976–77:** 278, 308
den Uyl, Johannes, **1975:** 255
Denmark
Prime Minister Anker Jorgenson, **1975:** 289n.
Visit of Queen Margrethe II, **1976–77:** 455
Dennis, Repr. David W., **1974:** 154, 155
Dent, Frederick B., **1974:** 41, 109, 233
Department.
See also other part of title.
Department of Defense Appropriations Act, 1975, **1974:** 126
Departmental Consumer Representation Plans, **1975:** 527 [12], 658
Departments of Labor and Health, Education, and Welfare Appropriation Act, 1975, **1974:** 285
Derwinski, Repr. Edward J., **1974:** 191; **1976–77:** 810
Des Moines, Iowa, **1974:** 187, 188; **1975:** 490, 491
Desegregation, school, **1974:** 24, 25, 127 [20], 142; **1975:** 496 [6], 511 [6], 552 [10], 554 [3], 565 [7, 8], 573 [10], 578 [9], 620 [5], 622 [17], 648 [2]; **1976–77:** 560 [6, 7], 609
Destrehan, La., **1976–77:** 812
Détente, **1975:** 36 [15], 189 [4, 5], 276 [3], 289, 290 [2], 354 [10], 459, 492, 501 [8], 502 [5], 530, 581 [8], 657 [7], 663, 666 [19, 22], 695 [22], 739 [8], 750 [5]; **1976–77:** 138 [14], 283, 287 [4], 362 [2]
Detroit, Mich.
American Lutheran Church, convention, **1974:** 134
Economic Club of Detroit, question-and-answer session, **1976–77:** 461
Federal assistance, **1975:** 622 [3]
News conference, **1975:** 622
President's arrivals, **1976–77:** 460, 1007
Republican Party fundraising dinner, **1974:** 135; **1975:** 623
World Energy Conference, **1974:** 94
Developing countries
Administration policy, **1975:** 137, 179
Development coordination, **1975:** 273
Generalized System of Preferences, **1975:** 154, 226, 668
Natural resources, exports, **1975:** 581 [5], 602 [18]
Trade adjustment assistance, **1974:** 72, 274
Trade policy, **1975:** 147
U.S. assistance, **1975:** 273, 518, 649
U.S.-Japanese cooperation, **1975:** 475
Development Association, International, **1974:** 110
Development Coordination Committee, **1975:** 273
Devereux, Mrs. John William, **1976–77:** 932
Devine, Repr. Samuel L., **1974:** 184
Devon, Pa., **1976–77:** 978
Diabetes, and Digestive Diseases Amendments, Arthritis, **1976–77:** 924
Dick, Charles, **1974:** 188
Diego Garcia, **1974:** 39 [17], 72
Digestive Diseases Amendments, Arthritis, Diabetes, and, **1976–77:** 924
Dillon, C. Douglas, **1975:** 19
DiMaggio, Dominic, **1976–77:** 852

DiMaggio, Joe, **1976–77:** 1052
Diplomatic Agents, Convention on the Prevention and Punishment of Crimes against Internationally Protected Persons, including, **1974:** 86 230
Diplomatic Corps, **1976–77:** 682
Diplomatic missions, foreign, **1975:** 701
Dirksen, Sen. Everett McKinley, **1974:** 191; **1975:** 495; **1976–77:** 185
Dirksen Congressional Leadership Research Center, Everett McKinley, **1975:** 495
Disabled American Veterans National Service and Legislative Headquarters, **1976–77:** 174
Disadvantaged persons, Federal aid, **1976–77:** 95
Disaster Assistance Administration, Federal, **1976–77:** 1029
Disaster loans, **1974:** 34, 265
Disaster Relief, Special Coordinator for, **1975:** 163
DISC.
See Domestic International Sales Corporation.
Discrimination, credit, **1974:** 30, 200; **1976–77:** 3
Disease Control, Center for, **1976–77:** 823
District of Columbia
Budget
Deferral, **1976–77:** 697
Fiscal Year 1976, amendment, **1976–77:** 345
Transmittal message, **1975:** 660
Criminal Code, **1976–77:** 761
Employees, pay increase, **1975:** 143
National Capital Housing Authority, report, **1974:** 231
Shop-Book Rule bill, **1976–77:** 146, 147
Undercover operations, exchange with law enforcement officials, **1976–77:** 664
District of Columbia Medical and Dental Manpower Act of 1970, bill extending, **1974:** 72
Djakarta, Indonesia, **1975:** 709
Djibouti, French involvement, **1976–77:** 207 [7]
DNA experiments, recombinant, **1976–77:** 801
Dobbins Air Force Base, Ga., **1976–77:** 358
Documents Commission, Public, **1974:** 313
Documents and recordings, Presidential, **1974:** 80 [2, 4, 8], 195 [19], 313
Dole, Sen. Robert, **1974:** 220; **1976–77:** 719, 732–735, 740, 742, 763 [2, 10], 906, 925 [6]
Domenici, Sen. Pete V., **1976–77:** 846
Domestic Council
Advisory Council on Social Security, **1975:** 126
Crime message, **1975:** 341
Deputy Director, **1975:** 91, 92
Executive Director, **1974:** 294; **1975:** 91, 92, 311, 328; **1976–77:** 627
Public meetings, **1975:** 554 [9]
Vice Chairman, **1975:** 91, 92
Domestic Council Committee on Illegal Aliens, **1975:** 20
Domestic Council Committee on the Right of Privacy, **1974:** 39 [11], 125
Domestic Council Drug Abuse Task Force, **1975:** 628, 748
Domestic Council Review Group on Regulatory Reform, **1976–77:** 1062
Domestic International Sales Corporation, **1975:** 554 [7]
Dominican Republic, **1974:** 203
Dominick, Sen. Peter H., **1974:** 219
Domino theory, **1975:** 750 [23]
Douglas, William O., **1975:** 72 [2, 10], 673
Dover, N.H., **1976–77:** 118–120
Draft evaders.
See Military deserters and draft evaders.
Drew, Elizabeth, **1976–77:** 803
Drug Abuse Education Act Amendments of 1974, Alcohol and, **1974:** 93
Drug Abuse Office and Treatment Act Amendments, **1976–77:** 232
Drug Abuse Policy, Office of, **1976–77:** 633
Drug Abuse Prevention, Treatment, and Rehabilitation, Cabinet Committee on, **1976–77:** 465, 633
Drug Abuse Prevention Week, **1974:** 167
Drug Enforcement Administration, **1976–77:** 129, 818
Drug Law Enforcement, Cabinet Committee for, **1976–77:** 464, 633
Drugs and narcotics
Customs inspection, **1974:** 201
Dealers, prison sentences, **1975:** 341, 532
Domestic Council Drug Abuse Task Force, **1975:** 628, 748
Drug abuse message, remarks, **1976–77:** 367, 368
Fort Worth/Tarrant County Bar Association, **1976–77:** 380
Heroin, **1976–77:** 325 [13]
Illicit drug trafficking, **1975:** 341, 655 [10], 720, 748
International Association of Chiefs of Police, Conference of the, **1976–77:** 818
Irving (Tex.) Bar Association Law Day, dinner, **1976–77:** 323
Law enforcement, **1975:** 341; **1976–77:** 128, 129
Legislation, **1976–77:** 413, 685
Marijuana, decriminalization, **1975:** 565 [19]
News conference remarks, **1976–77:** 325 [8, 13, 17]
President's views, **1976–77:** 513
Sentencing and seizure, **1976–77:** 413
State of the Union Address, **1976–77:** 19
Turkish opium poppies, control, **1975:** 720
Duke, Paul, **1975:** 479
Dunham, Richard L., **1975:** 91, 92; **1976–77:** 314
Dunlop, John T., **1974:** 109; **1975:** 140, 600 [2], 739 [12], 743; **1976–77:** 15
Durand, Mich., **1976–77:** 485

Durant, Ariel, **1976–77:** 1052
Durant, Will, **1976–77:** 1052
Durham, N.C., **1975:** 676
Durham, N.H., **1976–77:** 68
Durkin, Sen. John, **1975:** 573 [2]

"E" award, **1975:** 490
Eads, Leaborne, **1976–77:** 663
Eagleton, Sen. Thomas F., **1974:** 113
Eastern Europe
Administration policy, **1976–77:** 339 [6], 881
Campaign debate remarks, **1976–77:** 854
News conference remarks, **1976–77:** 325 [16], 898 [14]
President's views, **1976–77:** 283
Soviet domination, **1976–77:** 862, 865
Eastland, Sen. James O., 611, 797
Eberle, William D., **1974:** 109, 121, 321
Echeverría Alvarez, Luis, **1974:** 127 [1], 177, 178, 179, 180; **1976–77:** 137
Economic Advisers, Council of, **1974:** 38, 39 [13], 52, 109; **1976–77:** 23 (p. 70), 30, 314, 964
Economic Analysis, Bureau of, **1974:** 195 [13]
Economic Cooperation and Development, Organization for, **1974:** 284; **1975:** 312; **1976–77:** 621, 685
Economic democracy, President's views, **1976–77:** 266 [10]
Economic Development Administration, **1974:** 108
Economic Impact Statements program, **1976–77:** 1043
Economic Opportunity, and Community Partnership Act of 1974, Headstart, **1975:** 12
Economic Opportunity, National Advisory Council on, **1975:** 544
Economic Opportunity, Office of, **1974:** 39 [21]; **1975:** 12
Economic Policy, Council on International, **1974:** 109
Economic Policy Board, President's, **1974:** 109, 121, 241; **1975:** 92, 539; **1976–77:** 81, 82
Economic Report, International, **1975:** 147
Economic Report of the President, **1975:** 68, 70; **1976–77:** 30
Economic Rights and Duties of States, Charter of, **1974:** 179 [1, 7]
Economic stabilization program, report transmittal, **1974:** 116
Economic Summit Meeting, **1975:** 680
Economy, international
American Conference on Trade, **1974:** 274
Balance of payments, **1974:** 20, 242; **1975:** 101, 281
Campaign issue, **1975:** 72 [3, 13]
Congress, address to Joint Session, **1974:** 6
Economic Summit Meeting, **1975:** 680

Economy, international—*continued*
Financial Support Fund, **1975:** 312
Joint statements
France, **1974:** 302
Germany, Federal Republic of, **1974:** 284
Japan, **1974:** 249
Natural resources, distribution, **1975:** 602 [18]
New York City default, effect, **1975:** 657 [20]
President's assessment, **1975:** 440, 518
Recovery rates, **1975:** 460 [12]
Report of the President, transmittals, **1975:** 147; **1976–77:** 223, 1071
Task Force on Questionable Corporate Payments Abroad, **1976–77:** 275–277
United Nations General Assembly, address, **1974:** 81
U.S. economy, effect, **1975:** 518
U.S.-Japanese role, **1975:** 475
U.S. trade policy, **1975:** 2
Economy, national
Administration policy, **1975:** 26, 28, 32, 318, 395
American Conference on Trade, **1974:** 274
Business Council, meeting, **1974:** 290
Campaign debate remarks, **1976–77:** 803, 947
CBS News interview, **1976–77:** 560 [9]
Chamber of Commerce of the United States, **1976–77:** 365
Common situs picketing legislation, effect, **1975:** 743
Congress, addresses to Joint Session, **1974:** 6, 121
Congressional action, **1975:** 54, 129
Conference on Inflation, **1974:** 6, 54, 56, 67, 106, 109, 150
Cost of living, **1976–77:** 231
Council on Wage and Price Stability, **1974:** 19, 32, 33, 41, 72, 109, 121, 241
Depression, **1974:** 80 [14]
Economic indicators, **1976–77:** 921
Economic proposals, foreign reaction, **1975:** 54
Economic Report of the President, remarks, **1975:** 68, 70; **1976–77:** 30, 1070
Energy shortage, effect, **1975:** 537, 538
Environmental concerns, **1975:** 527 [9]
Foreign investment activity, study, **1974:** 193
Foreign investments in U.S., **1975:** 72 [11], 615 [3]
Income tax rebate, effect, **1975:** 36 [29]
Inflation.
See Inflation.
Monetary policy, **1975:** 138 [8], 204 [9], 511 [3]
National Center for Productivity and Quality of Working Life, **1975:** 721
New York City default, effect, **1975:** 657 [20], 666 [13]
News conference remarks, **1976–77:** 387 [10], 418 [13], 763 [9], 898 [7]
Newsweek magazine interview, **1974:** Appendix D

Economy, national—*continued*
Northeast Republican Conference, **1976–77:** 62
Oil price increase, effect, **1975:** 354 [14]
Political issue, **1975:** 36 [5]
President's assessment, **1975:** 36 [19], 69, 90 [1], 316 [6], 335, 369, 374, 410, 479 [1, 2], 496 [1], 502 [1], 511 [4], 526, 527 [1], 554 [1], 573 [5, 6], 579, 598, 650, 666 [9, 21], 670, 677; **1976–77:** 49, 138 [6], 209 [15], 352 [1], 362 [10], 392 [1], 512, 527, 967
Public confidence, **1975:** 72 [13]
Recession, **1974:** 127 [2], 195 [13], 236 [3]; **1975:** 36 [12, 27], 62, 64, 70, 72 [8], 85 [4], 147, 166 [8], 167, 189 [10], 204 [8], 410
Regulatory reform, **1975:** 500
State of the Union Address, **1975:** 28; **1976–77:** 19, 1057
Statistics, **1976–77:** 555
Tax reduction, effect, **1975:** 626
Unemployment, effect, **1975:** 496 [3]
Wage and price controls, **1975:** 36 [26]
White House Conference on Domestic and Economic Affairs, **1974:** 214
Editorial Cartoonists, Association of American, **1976–77:** 434
Education
Administration policy, **1975:** 234, 552 [10], 554 [3]
Alcohol and drug abuse programs, **1974:** 93
Basic Education Opportunity Grant program, **1976–77:** 402 [4]
Buckley amendment, **1976–77:** 333 [12]
Budget news briefing, **1976–77:** 23 (p. 54, 60, 62)
Busing, **1976–77:** 402 [7], 415 [4], 507, 523 [6], 543, 560 [6], 610, 614, 615
Cabinet-level department, **1976–77:** 402 [9]
Campaign debate remarks, **1976–77:** 803
CLOSE-UP program, **1975:** 172
Concord, N.H., budget briefing, **1976–77:** 64
Consolidation of Federal programs, **1976–77:** 185 [14]
Department of Education, proposed, **1975:** 602 [3]
Desegregation.
See Desegregation, school.
Education Division and Related Agencies Appropriation Act, 1976, veto, **1975:** 432, 433
Elementary and secondary education, reform legislation, **1976–77:** 168, 169
Ethnic programs, **1976–77:** 283
Federal assistance, **1974:** 24, 25, 127 [13]; **1975:** 234, 502 [11], 511 [7], 554 [4], 578 [9], 602 [3], 616 [4], 648 [3]; **1976–77:** 95, 189 [13], 192 [2], 210 [15], 212 [20, 21], 284 [2], 293 [7], 352 [12], 378 [12], 846
Florida budget briefing, **1976–77:** 89
Foreign students, **1975:** 716
Education—*continued*
Grant programs, **1976–77:** 116
Handicapped youth, **1975:** 707
Harry S Truman Memorial Scholarship Act, **1975:** 6
Impact Aid program, **1975:** 433
Indian communities, **1975:** 10
Legislation, **1976–77:** 685
Lilly Endowment Continuing Conference for the Liberal Arts, **1974:** 281
Medical and dental education, **1975:** 602 [12], 616 [9]
Mentally retarded, **1974:** 136
National Association of Secondary School Principals, **1976–77:** 105
National Teacher of the Year Award, **1976–77:** 219
New Jersey School Boards Association, remarks, **1976–77:** 974
News conference remarks, **1976–77:** 67 [9], 282 [9], 418 [19]
Nurse training, **1975:** 3, 436
Ohio State University commencement, **1974:** 42
Presidential Scholars program, **1975:** 371
Private schools, assistance, **1975:** 496 [7], 502 [11], 560, 574; **1976–77:** 406, 769, 975
Public schools, prayer, **1976–77:** 947
Report to Congress, transmittal message, **1975:** 336
State and local government roles, **1976–77:** 126, 402 [3]
Student loans, **1975:** 55, 502 [19]
Tax credit, **1974:** 127 [13]
Teachers education, financial assistance, **1975:** 616 [9]
University of Michigan, remarks, **1976–77:** 784
Veterans benefits, **1974:** 16, 39 [18], 72, 195 [6], 240, 263; **1975:** 247
Veterinarian programs, **1976–77:** 422
Vocational education, **1975:** 71, 234, 496 [9], 554 [8], 602 [11], 616 [4, 7]
Women's programs, **1976–77:** 402 [8]
Youth Conservation Corps, **1974:** 47
See also Colleges and universities; Schools.
Education, National Advisory Council on Extension and Continuing, **1974:** 133; **1975:** 336
Education, National Institute of, **1975:** 253
Education, Office of, **1974:** 93
Education for All Handicapped Children Act of 1975, **1975:** 707
Education Amendments of 1974, **1974:** 6, 24, 25, 72; **1975:** 565 [7], 578 [9]
Education Association, National, **1975:** 234; **1976–77:** 14
Education Amendments of 1976, **1976–77:** 888
Educational Research, National Council on, **1975:** 253

Edwards, Repr. Don, **1974:** 155
Edwards, James B., **1974:** 170, 173
Edwards, Marvin, **1974:** 183
Egan, John Patrick, **1975:** 117, 118
Egypt
B'nai B'rith Biennial Convention, remarks, **1976–77:** 766
Nuclear reactors, **1975:** 655 [1]
President Anwar el-Sadat, **1975:** 243 [2], 297, 298, 299, 300, 316 [9, 11], 516, 522, 565 [11], 642, 643, 644, 654, 657 [25]
Security assistance programs, **1975:** 649
Troop disengagement agreement with Israel, **1975:** 515, 516, 517, 522, 530, 552 [7], 600 [8], 625
United States-Egypt Convention on Income Tax, **1976–77:** 79
U.S. arms sales, **1976–77:** 210 [2], 420 [4]
U.S. military assistance, **1975:** 657 [25]
See also Middle East.
Eielson Air Force Base, Alaska, **1975:** 703
Eisenhower, John S. D., **1975:** 267
El Paso, Tex., **1976–77:** 326–329
El Salvador, U.S. Ambassador, **1976–77:** 702
El Toro Marine Corps Air Station, Calif., **1976–77:** 510
Elder, Lee, **1974:** 268
Elderly persons.
See Older persons.
Election Campaign Act Amendments of 1974, Federal, **1974:** 148, 149
Election Commission, Federal, **1974:** 149; **1975:** 184, 527 [4], 565 [13]; **1976–77:** 418 [4]
Elections, 1974
Campaign appearances.
See under Addresses and remarks.
Election eve remarks, **1974:** 221
Results
News conference responses, **1974:** 195 [9], 236 [6]
Statement, **1974:** 225
Voter apathy, **1974:** 184, 186, 195 [3], 209, 215, 219
Elections, 1976
Administration goals and achievements, **1976–77:** 523 [1, 4]
Alabama primary, results, **1976–77:** 427
California primary, results, **1976–77:** 497, 555, 585
Campaign
Contributions, **1975:** 620 [6]
Debates, **1975:** 204 [10], 552 [11], 695 [7]
Health and age considerations, **1975:** 666 [17, 24], 750 [24]
Issues, **1975:** 72 [3], 166 [9], 204 [2], 219, 243 [9], 354 [6], 488 [8], 573 [10], 582 [11], 622 [16]
News conference remarks, **1976–77:** 212 [15], 282 [7], 831, 898 [9]
Elections, 1976—*continued*
Campaign—*continued*
Plans, **1975:** 243 [4], 354 [13], 530, 620 [12], 655 [3, 7], 657 [24], 665, 666 [14, 16], 695 [15], 739 [6], 750 [2, 11, 13, 22, 26]; **1976–77:** 116
Primaries, **1975:** 189 [14], 548, 573 [1], 750 [13]
Citizens for Ford Committee, **1976–77:** 852
Connally, John, Presidential endorsement, **1976–77:** 694
Debates
Announcement, **1976–77:** 750
Comments on, **1976–77:** 737, 763 [4, 14, 16], 804, 855, 856, 967
News conference remarks, **1976–77:** 898 [20]
Philadelphia, Pa., **1976–77:** 803
San Francisco, Calif., **1976–77:** 854
Williamsburg, Va., **1976–77:** 947
Defense spending, **1976–77:** 863, 871
Democratic Presidential candidates, **1975:** 655 [11], 678 [9, 19], 750 [16]; **1976–77:** 392 [8]
Election eve address to the Nation, **1976–77:** 1011
Election reform, **1975:** 129, 527 [4]
Federal Election Commission, **1976–77:** 103, 123
First Family, involvement, **1976–77:** 95
Florida primary, results, **1976–77:** 198
Foreign policy, **1976–77:** 209 [14]
General elections results, remarks awaiting, **1976–77:** 1012
Georgia primary, results, **1976–77:** 427
Indiana primary, results, **1976–77:** 427
Interview remarks, **1976–77:** 778
Law enforcement and crime, **1976–77:** 513
Maryland primary, results, **1976–77:** 497
Michigan primary, results, **1976–77:** 497
National Federation of Republican Women, **1976–77:** 791
New Jersey primary, results, **1976–77:** 585
News conference remarks, **1976–77:** 67 [1, 5, 12–15], 282 [10], 418 [1, 10–12], 387 [3, 6, 11, 15, 16, 20, 30], 535 [3], 657 [2, 3, 5, 8, 11, 13, 14, 20, 26, 27], 674 [2, 3, 5–10, 16, 18, 24–27, 30, 31, 33, 36–38], 763 [3, 7, 8, 20, 21], 831, 925 [4, 11]
Nonvoting youths, role, **1976–77:** 266 [16]
Ohio primary, results, **1976–77:** 585
President Ford Committee, **1975:** 343, 620 [6], 657 [12], 678 [1], 739 [6], 750 [13]
Presidential primaries, President's assessment, **1976–77:** 221, 339 [8], 352 [5], 362 [6]
President's candidacy, **1974:** 39 [4], 127 [19]; **1975:** 45 [7], 72 [3], 129, 166 [12], 204 [10], 243 [4], 316 [10], 343, 386, 501 [7], 600 [15], 622 [24], 666 [21], 739 [6, 11]
President's departure for Williamsburg, Va., **1976–77:** 942
President's post-election plans, **1976–77:** 68 [24]

Elections, 1976—*continued*
Public opinion polls, **1975:** 750 [3]
Republican National Convention
Candidates' accommodations, distribution, **1976–77:** 657 [7]
Delegates' selection of Vice-Presidential candidate, **1976–77:** 706
Headquarters, President's arrival, **1976–77:** 726
Nomination acceptance, **1976–77:** 733
Remarks to
Campaign supporters, **1976–77:** 731
New York State delegation, **1976–77:** 729
President Ford Committee staff, **1976–77:** 728
"Presidentials" youth group, **1976–77:** 727
Republican National Committee, **1976–77:** 734
Ronald Reagan, exchange of remarks with reporters, **1976–77:** 730
Vice-Presidential running mate, **1976–77:** 732
Voting rules, **1976–77:** 674 [25]
Republican Party leaders, exchange of remarks with reporters, **1976–77:** 742
Southern influence, **1975:** 678 [20]
Southern Republican leaders, meeting with the President, **1976–77:** 786
Taxation, **1976–77:** 862, 864, 893, 895
Third party, effect, **1975:** 678 [15], 695 [11], 750 [17]; **1976–77:** 159
Vice-Presidential campaign debate, telephone exchange with Sen. Dole following, **1976–77:** 906
Vice-Presidential running mate, **1975:** 138 [11], 204 [11], 396 [9], 501 [15], 511 [11], 551, 552 [5], 565 [12, 14], 655 [4], 657 [2, 5, 26], 662, 666 [18], 678 [5], 733, 750 [14]; **1976–77:** 138 [2], 392 [3], 406, 580 [5], 732
See also Republican Party.
Electric and hybrid vehicle research, development, and demonstration bill, veto, **1976–77:** 777
Electric utilities, **1975:** 321, 326, 615 [2]
Electricity, legislation, **1976–77:** 685
Electronic Fund Transfers, National Commission on, **1976–77:** 3
Electronic surveillance to obtain foreign intelligence information, **1976–77:** 252
Elizabeth II, Queen, **1976–77:** 654, 656
Elk Hills, Calif., **1975:** 28
Elkins, W. Va., **1975:** 611
Ellsworth, Robert, **1974:** 14
Elwyn-Jones, Lord, **1976–77:** 554
Emergencies Act, National, **1976–77:** 781
Emergency Compensation and Special Unemployment Assistance Extension Act of 1975, **1975:** 366
Emergency Food Stamp Vendor Accountability Act, **1976–77:** 650
Emergency Highway Energy Conservation Act, **1974:** 240
Emergency Home Purchase Assistance Act of 1974, **1974:** 161, 162, 234; **1975:** 351, 354 [1]
Emergency Housing Act of 1975, **1975:** 372
Emergency Jobs and Unemployment Assistance Act, **1974:** 328; **1975:** 32, 64, 209
Emergency Livestock Credit Act
Amendments, **1975:** 332
Extension, **1976–77:** 905
Emergency livestock feed assistance, **1976–77:** 1029
Emergency Petroleum Allocation Act of 1975, **1975:** 594
Emergency Unemployment Compensation Act, **1974:** 328; **1975:** 32, 64, 209
Employee Retirement Income Security Act of 1974, **1974:** 45, 46
Employee Stock Ownership Plan, **1976–77:** 1044
Employees, Federal
Ethnic personnel, **1976–77:** 283
Hatch Act, **1976–77:** 293 [6]
Employees Pay Council, Federal, **1976–77:** 844
Employment Appropriations Act, Public Works, **1976–77:** 652, 653, 683, 686, 845
Employment and Training Act, Comprehensive, **1974:** 67
Employment and unemployment
Administration policy, **1975:** 138 [10]
Agricultural jobs, **1976–77:** 287 [7]
Budget news briefing, **1976–77:** 23 (p. 50)
Campaign debate remarks, **1976–77:** 803, 947
Campaign issue, **1975:** 72 [3], 354 [6]
Chamber of Commerce of the United States, **1976–77:** 365
College graduate opportunities, **1976–77:** 352 [6], 580 [1]
Concord, N.H., budget briefing, **1976–77:** 64
Construction industry, **1974:** 234; **1975:** 309
Economic impact, **1975:** 72 [16], 496 [3]
Economic Report of the President, **1976–77:** 31
Effect on cities, **1975:** 72 [6]
Ex-convicts, **1975:** 341
Federal assistance, **1974:** 72, 240, 262, 271 [13, 20], 290, 328; **1975:** 32, 64, 70, 72 [6], 109 [9], 125 [12], 169, 209, 288, 366, 369, 372, 511 [2, 7], 512, 554 [8], 573 [5], 616 [4, 7], 678 [8]
Federal employment, equal opportunity, **1975:** 124
Federal summer youth employment program, **1976–77:** 310–313
Florida budget briefing, **1976–77:** 89
Foreign boycott practices, **1975:** 689, 690
Handicapped persons, **1975:** 156, 174
Highway construction, **1975:** 85 [3], 309
Illegal aliens, **1975:** 109 [18]
Inflation, impact, **1974:** 67
Insurance benefits, **1974:** 72, 121, 328

Employment and unemployment—*continued*
Interview remarks, **1976–77:** 778
Job Corps, **1975:** 52
Job creation, **1975:** 502 [6, 7], 508, 579, 580, 623, 631; **1976–77:** 68 [8], 95
Job security, **1974:** 72
Legislation, **1976–77:** 685
Manpower Report of the President, **1975:** 209
Mentally retarded, **1974:** 136
Migrant workers, **1974:** 179 [4], 205, 240, 286
Minority groups, **1975:** 124, 141, 142, 243 [11], 282, 410, 496 [5], 502 [7], 602 [9, 10], 616 [7, 8, 10]
Mortgage payment relief, **1975:** 351
National Alliance of Businessmen, **1976–77:** 306
News conference remarks, **1974:** 127 [2], 236 [23]; **1976–77:** 86 [9], 107 [12], 212 [9–11], 282 [3], 387 [23], 418 [6, 16, 19], 763 [11, 12]
Newsweek magazine interview, **1974:** Appendix D
Northeast Republican Conference, **1976–77:** 62
Pension plans, **1974:** 45, 46
Pittsburgh Economic Club, remarks, **1976–77:** 967
President's assessment, **1975:** 36 [19], 54, 68, 85 [5, 18], 90 [2, 4], 125 [12], 243 [11], 316 [6], 354 [6, 17], 396 [6], 479 [1, 2], 501 [1, 2], 502 [4], 508, 510, 511 [2, 4], 514, 526, 527 [3], 531, 557, 622 [23], 650, 666 [23], 750 [10]; **1976–77:** 49, 65, 118, 195, 209 [16], 308
Public service employment, **1974:** 39 [3], 108, 121
Public works, **1975:** 479 [2], 602 [15], 616 [6, 12], 622 [21], 662, 666 [13], 678 [8]; **1976–77:** 83, 113, 138 [4], 311, 313, 356 [4]
Radio-Television News Directors Association, **1976–77:** 48 [4]
Retirement programs, **1976–77:** 189 [12]
Safety and health programs, **1975:** 65, 363, 682
Social security benefits, **1976–77:** 362 [3], 385 [1]
Statistics, **1976–77:** 284, 555
Trade reform, impact, **1974:** 274
Unemployment benefits, **1975:** 32, 64, 209, 366, 501 [2], 508, 666 [13]; **1976–77:** 138 [10], 207 [3]
Unemployment trend, **1976–77:** 116, 293 [8], 333 [14]
University of Michigan, remarks, **1976–77:** 784
Veterans, **1974:** 192; **1975:** 156, 174, 502 [7]
Vocational education, **1975:** 71, 234, 496 [9], 554 [8], 602 [11], 616 [4, 7]
Women, **1975:** 124, 185, 209
Youth, **1974:** 47; **1975:** 172, 174, 178, 243 [11], 333, 511 [7], 544 [8], 602 [9], 617 [7]; **1976–77:** 95, 138 [9], 266 [18], 293 [4], 310–313
See also Federal employees.

Energy
Administration policy, **1975:** 26, 28, 32, 36 [1, 8], 82, 85 [2, 6], 90 [1], 108, 283, 318, 321, 395; **1976–77:** 333 [10], 373 [2, 5]
Agency reorganization, **1975:** 29
Agricultural requirements, **1975:** 84, 502 [17]
Alternate sources, **1976–77:** 284 [3]
Budget news briefing, **1976–77:** 23 (p. 74, 75)
Campaign debate remarks, **1976–77:** 803
Campaign issue, **1975:** 488 [8]
Coastal zone management, **1975:** 274
Concord, N.H., budget briefing, **1976–77:** 64
Congressional action, **1974:** 131; **1975:** 42, 45 [1], 54, 69, 72 [5], 82, 84, 90 [1], 91, 99, 108, 109 [4, 20], 115, 120, 121, 135, 149, 167, 225, 283, 356, 402, 418, 420, 460 [5], 488 [1], 511 [1], 512, 517, 526, 528, 530, 537, 538, 542, 548, 571, 573 [6], 592, 594, 602 [1], 622 [16], 678 [13]
Conservation, **1974:** 138, 146, 150, 165, 166, 233, 271 [15]; **1975:** 26, 28, 41, 46, 64, 69, 70, 85 [3, 7], 120, 149, 354 [15], 364, 421, 488 [1, 3], 600 [14], 616 [1], 741, 742; **1976–77:** 116
Economic impact, **1975:** 537, 538
Economic Report of the President, **1976–77:** 1070
Efficiency labeling, **1975:** 742
Emergency contingency plans, **1976–77:** 1083
Environmental impact, **1974:** 292, 320; **1975:** 28, 70, 496 [2], 615 [10], 616 [11]
Federal reorganization proposals, **1976–77:** 1055
Foreign sources, **1976–77:** 385 [5]
Funding, **1976–77:** 22
Geothermal, **1974:** 138; **1975:** 108, 169
Home insulation standards, **1975:** 28
Hydroelectric, **1974:** 172, 202; **1975:** 498
Independence, **1976–77:** 210 [16], 1078
International interdependence, **1974:** 81, 94; **1975:** 54, 179, 498
International organization, **1975:** 64, 179, 460 [17], 498, 552 [8]
Joint statements
France, **1974:** 302
Japan, **1974:** 249
Land use, **1975:** 488 [5, 9]
Legislation, **1974:** 326; **1975:** 60, 270, 666 [15], 739 [3]; **1976–77:** 101, 139, 140, 685
Legislative priorities, messages to Congress, **1974:** 72, 240
Mandatory fuel allocation program, **1976–77:** 356 [5]
Message to Congress, **1976–77:** 1045
National Energy Outlook Report, **1976–77:** 177
New England situation, **1975:** 510, 511 [2], 548
News conference remarks, **1976–77:** 67 [16], 86 [2, 4], 535 [4]
Newsweek magazine interview, **1974:** Appendix D

Energy—*continued*
Northeast Republican Conference, **1976–77:** 62
Offshore oil and gas development, **1974:** 233, 262
Powerplants, **1975:** 28
President's assessment, **1975:** 488 [1], 509, 512, 526, 557, 612, 666 [9], 670; **1976–77:** 49, 272
Prices, **1975:** 70
Project Independence, **1974:** 6, 39 [14], 42, 94, 127 [6]; **1975:** 488 [13]; **1976–77:** 284 [3]
Public utilities, **1975:** 28, 60, 321, 326, 395, 554 [13], 615 [23]
Research and development, **1974:** 138; **1975:** 28, 29, 46, 60, 64, 69, 70, 71, 82, 85 [6, 19], 90 [5], 108, 152, 488 [2, 5, 12], 562, 580, 581 [1], 582 [10], 600 [7], 616 [1], 620 [4], 621, 622 [13], 663, 741, 742; **1976–77:** 68 [5], 71, 189 [6], 195, 417, 461, 1045
Resources, **1976–77:** 116, 209 [3], 362 [7], 401 [8]
Solar, **1974:** 138; **1975:** 108, 488 [9]; **1976–77:** 86 [2], 118, 356 [9]
State and local production, **1974:** 176, 202
State of the Union Address, **1975:** 28; **1976–77:** 1057
Surface mining, legislation, **1974:** 326; **1975:** 270
Taxation, **1975:** 28, 36 [25], 60, 90 [2], 121, 582 [9]
Unemployment, impact, **1975:** 538
U.S.-Japanese cooperation, **1975:** 475
See also specific energy resource.
Energy Administration, Federal, **1974:** 165, 166, 195 [1, 20], 196, 228, 236 [24]
Energy Agency, International, **1974:** 284
Energy Conference, Washington, **1974:** 94
Energy Conference, World, **1974:** 94
Energy Conservation Act, Emergency Highway, **1974:** 240
Energy Independence Act of 1975, **1975:** 60, 621
Energy Independence Authority, proposed, **1975:** 580, 581 [1], 582 [10], 600 [7], 616 [1], 620 [4], 621, 622 [13], 663; **1976–77:** 1045
Energy Institute, International, proposed, **1976–77:** 987
Energy Management program, Federal, **1974:** 165
Energy Policy and Conservation Act, **1975:** 741, 742; **1976–77:** 31
Energy Policy Council, **1974:** 72
Energy Reorganization Act of 1974, **1974:** 137, 138
Energy Research and Development Administration
Administrator, **1974:** 195 [1]; **1975:** 488 [9]; **1976–77:** 23 (p. 75), 980
Automotive transport research and development bill, veto, **1976–77:** 811
Defense-related programs, **1976–77:** 459
Deferrals and rescissions, **1976–77:** 1069
Electric and hybrid vehicle research, development, and demonstration bill, veto, **1976–77:** 777
Establishment, **1974:** 72, 94, 137, 138; **1975:** 29, 64
Energy R & D Administration—*continued*
Legislation, proposed, **1974:** 72; **1975:** 358, 359
News conference remarks, **1976–77:** 86 [2]
Nuclear energy, **1976–77:** 987, 1045
Research and development programs, **1976–77:** 803
Solar energy, **1975:** 488 [9]
Energy Resources Council
Activation of, **1974:** 121 [1ftn.]
Chairman, **1974:** 165, 166; **1975:** 227; **1976–77:** 177
Establishment, **1974:** 138
Executive Director, **1975:** 92; **1976–77:** 177
Federal energy activities, reorganization, **1976–77:** 1045
Natural gas shortages, **1975:** 661
Energy Supply and Environmental Coordination Act, **1975:** 28
Engineers, U.S. Corps of, **1976–77:** 583, 802
England.
See United Kingdom.
Environment
Administration policy, **1975:** 72 [15], 373; **1976–77:** 68 [15]
Agricultural production, **1975:** 15
Campaign debate remarks, **1976–77:** 947
Campaign issue, **1975:** 488 [8]
Clean Air Act, **1974:** 685; **1975:** 28, 64, 70, 72 [15], 364, 527 [15], 616 [11]; **1976–77:** 685
Coal, **1975:** 28, 152
Concord, N.H., budget briefing, **1976–77:** 64
Economic tradeoff, **1975:** 527 [9]
Energy
Conservation, **1974:** 138, 146, 150, 292
Impact, **1975:** 28, 70, 496 [2], 615 [10], 616 [11]
Message to Congress, **1976–77:** 1045
Federal pollution standards, **1975:** 527 [15]
Flood control, **1974:** 307
Forest and rangeland renewal, **1974:** 13
Industrial pollution, **1976–77:** 882
National parks, **1974:** 185
News conference remarks, **1976–77:** 418 [17]
"No growth" policy, **1976–77:** 383
Nuclear powerplant siting, **1975:** 488 [6]
Offshore oil and gas development, **1974:** 233, 262
Pollution
Air, **1974:** 121, 131; **1975:** 26, 28, 32, 64, 70, 72 [15], 108, 364, 445, 446, 527 [15], 616 [11]; **1976–77:** 352 [7]
Federal standards, **1976–77:** 373 [9], 558
Noise standards, **1976–77:** 934, 941, 959
Oil, pollution control legislation, **1975:** 388
Waste disposal, **1976–77:** 923
Water standards, **1976–77:** 240 [4]
President's assessment, **1976–77:** 144
Reclamation projects, **1974:** 202
Remarks at Springfield, Ill., farm forum, **1976–77:** 181
Research, **1975:** 373

Environment—*continued*
Surface mining, legislation, **1974:** 121, 131, 240, 326; **1975:** 75, 270, 615 [10], 616 [16]
Tennessee Valley Authority, legislation, **1974:** 320
United Nations Conference on the Human Environment, **1975:** 310
Waste disposal and treatment, **1974:** 89; **1976–77:** 923, 938
Water and sewage programs, **1975:** 622 [21]; **1976–77:** 192 [8]
Water supplies, **1974:** 305
Wilderness areas, **1974:** 276, 277
World Environment Day, **1975:** 310: **1976–77:** 556
World Weather Program, **1975:** 317
Environmental Assistance program, Rural, **1974:** 318
Environmental Protection Agency
Administrator, **1975:** 20, 92, 364, 496 [2]
Budget restraint, **1974:** 262
Catalytic converters, testing, **1976–77:** 352 [7]
Legislative priorities, **1974:** 240
News conference remarks, **1976–77:** 418 [17]
Regulations, **1976–77:** 327 [2]
Safe Drinking Water Act, **1974:** 305
Small business regulations, **1976–77:** 558
Environmental Quality, Council on, **1974:** 233, 292; **1976–77:** 220, 838
Environmental Research Center, National, **1975:** 373
EPA.
See Environmental Protection Agency.
Epilepsy Month, National, **1975:** 638
Epizootics, International Office of, **1974:** 270
Equal Credit Opportunity Act Amendments of 1976, **1976–77:** 249, 250
Equal Employment Opportunity Commission, **1975:** 141, 142, 282, 496, [5], 602, [10], 616 [8, 10]
Equal employment opportunity program, **1975:** 124
Equal rights amendment, **1975:** 24, 185, 307, 396 [14], 578 [2], 616 [21]; **1976–77:** 406, 634
Equal time provision, **1975:** 615 [11]
ERA.
See Equal rights amendment.
ERDA.
See Energy Research and Development Administration.
Erlenborn, Repr. John N., **1974:** 191
Esch amendment, **1975:** 565 [7], 573 [10], 578 [9], 622 [17]; **1976–77:** 510
Estate taxes, **1976–77:** 579, 685, 735, 784, 793, 847, 848
Estonia, **1975:** 430
Ethiopia
Haile Selassie, **1975:** 505
Security assistance programs, **1975:** 649
Ethnic organizations, Milwaukee, Wis., **1976–77:** 283
Ethnicity and Neighborhood Revitalization, Conference on, **1976–77:** 426
Eucharistic Congress, International, **1976–77:** 720
Europe
Administration policy, **1974:** 6
Balance of payments, **1974:** 20, 242
Commission of the European Communities, **1975:** 290n.
Communism, **1976–77:** 402 [1]
Conference on Security and Cooperation in Europe, **1975:** 289, 290 [8], 316 [5], 354 [11], 430, 439, 450, 459, 460 [13, 14, 15], 463, 472, 479 [7], 581 [8]; **1976–77:** 283
East-West relations, **1975:** 430, 459, 479 [7]
Economy, **1975:** 460 [12]
Mutual and balanced force reductions, **1974:** 129, 258, 271 [8], 284; **1975:** 64, 119, 440, 450, 459, 460 [3], 479 [7]
President's visits.
See specific country.
U.S. Armed Forces, deployment, **1975:** 101, 186, 281
U.S. relations, **1975:** 276 [2, 4, 8]
See also specific country
Europe, Conference on Security and Cooperation in, **1974:** 129, 258, 284, 302
European Communities, **1974:** 105
European Economic Community, **1974:** 302; **1975:** 276 [8], 668, 718; **1976–77:** 621
European journalists, interview, **1975:** 276
Evansville, Ind., **1976–77:** 355–357
Everett McKinley Dirksen Congressional Leadership Research Center, **1975:** 495
Everett McKinley Dirksen Honorary Chair of Government and Public Affairs, Bradley University at Peoria, Ill., **1976–77:** 185
Evert, Chris, **1976–77:** 163
Exchange Club, National, **1976–77:** 663
Exchange Stabilization Fund, **1975:** 312
Executive, Legislative, and Judicial Salaries, Commission on, **1976–77:** 1068
Executive Boards, Federal, **1976–77:** 660
Executive branch activities under the Privacy Act of 1974, **1976–77:** 681
Executive clemency
Draft evaders and military deserters
Clemency statements, **1974:** 266, 329; **1975:** 243 [5]
News conference remarks, **1974:** 39 [2], 80 [10], 236 [13]; **1975:** 36 [14]
Presidential Clemency Board, **1975:** 566, 573 [12]
Return program
Extension, **1975:** 58, 113
Proclamation, **1974:** 77, 78
Termination, **1976–77:** 68 [20]

Executive clemency—*continued*
Draft evaders—*continued*
Veterans of Foreign Wars convention, **1974:** 16
Hart, Mrs. Philip A., letter, **1976–77:** 1077
Hunt, E. Howard, petition for pardon, **1976–77:** 333 [5]
News conference remarks, **1976–77:** 325 [3]
Nixon, Richard, pardon
House Judiciary subcommittee testimony, **1974:** 112, 155
News conference remarks, **1974:** 39 [1], 80 [1, 3, 6, 9], 127 [10], 195 [22], 236 [13]; **1975:** 396 [5]
Newsweek magazine interview, **1974:** Appendix D
Proclamation, **1974:** 60, 61
Question-and-answer sessions, remarks, **1976–77:** 116, 185 [4], 209 [13], 210 [10]
Policy statement, **1974:** 68
Remarks, **1976–77:** 1039
Vietnam war era selective service discharges, **1976–77:** 1076
Watergate figures, **1975:** 109 [13]
Executive Office of the President
Appropriations, **1975:** 160
Budget, **1975:** 72 [19]
See also White House staff.
Executive Orders
Commission on CIA Activities Within the United States, establishment, **1975:** 19
Energy Research and Development Administration, activation, **1975:** 29
Federal labor-management relations in the Federal service, **1975:** 76
Income tax returns, inspection of, **1974:** 80 [7]
Japanese-American internment, World War II, **1976–77:** 111
National Commission on the Observance of International Women's Year, 1975, establishment, **1975:** 24
Nuclear Regulatory Commission, activation, **1975:** 29
Presidential Clemency Board, termination, **1975:** 566
President's Advisory Committee on Refugees, establishment, **1975:** 267
President's Commission on Olympic Sports, establishment, **1975:** 338
See also Appendix B, 1974, 1975, 1976–77.
Executive privilege, **1975:** 685
Executive Protective Service, **1975:** 701
Executive reorganization authority, **1975:** 175
Exhibits, special international, **1974:** 8
Eximbank.
See Export-Import Bank of the United States.
Explorer Presidents' Congress, National, **1975:** 177
"Expo 81," **1976–77:** 1034
Export Administration Act of 1969, **1976–77:** 327 [7]
Export-Import Bank of the United States, **1974:** 72, 130, 240; **1975:** 569
Exports
Agricultural commodities, **1975:** 85 [9], 502 [3], 554
American Conference on Trade, **1974:** 274
Dairy products, **1975:** 502 [3]
Enriched uranium, **1975:** 357, 358
Farm commodities control, **1974:** 153
Grain, **1974:** 210; **1975:** 78, 396 [13], 460 [10], 490, 497 [1, 4], 511 [3, 12], 528, 539, 548, 552 [8], 554 [2], 571, 581 [6], 582 [8], 598, 600 [1, 6], 602 [1, 5, 7, 13], 616 [5], 620 [7], 622 [1], 636, 650, 750 [7]
Nuclear materials, **1975:** 241, 276 [6], 357, 358
See also International commerce.
Extradition treaties
Australia, **1974:** 28
Canada, **1974:** 74

F. Edward Hébert Library, **1975:** 206
F-15 aircraft, **1974:** 235
F-16 aircraft, **1975:** 565 [2], 578 [5]
FAA.
See Federal Aviation Administration.
Fabiola, Queen, **1975:** 287
"Face the Nation" interview, **1976–77:** 560
Fahey, Charles J., **1976–77:** 932
Fair trade laws, **1975:** 192, 196, 220, 723, 724
Fairbanks, Alaska, **1975:** 703
Fairfax, Va., **1974:** 59
Faisal Ibn Abdul Aziz, **1975:** 155
Family farms, **1976–77:** 287 [11, 14], 389
Far East trip.
See specific country.
Farm Credit Directors, National, **1976–77:** 793
Farm Family of the Year, National, **1975:** 409
Farm forums
Fond du Lac, Wis., **1976–77:** 288
Omaha, Nebr., **1976–77:** 422
Rockford, Ill., **1976–77:** 203
Springfield, Ill., **1976–77:** 181
Farm Labor Contractor Registration Act Amendments of 1974, **1974:** 205, 240, 286
Farmer cooperatives, **1976–77:** 181
Farmers of America, Future, **1974:** 150
Farmers Home Administration, **1975:** 409; **1976–77:** 558
Farms and farming
Livestock prices, protest, **1974:** 152, 153
Migrant workers, **1974:** 179 [4], 205, 286
See also Agriculture and agricultural programs.
Father-Son/Mother-Daughter events, **1976–77:** 657 [15]

FBI.
See Federal Bureau of Investigation.
FCC.
See Federal Communications Commission.
FEA.
See Federal Energy Administration.
Federal Advisory Committees, **1975:** 162
Federal-Aid Highway Act of 1976, **1976–77:** 428, 429
Federal-Aid Highway Amendments of 1974, **1975:** 11
Federal Aviation Administration
Administrator, **1976–77:** 661, 941, 959, 1072
Budget deferral, **1976–77:** 739
Noise standards for commercial aircraft, **1976–77:** 934
Federal Bureau of Investigation
Director, **1975:** 648 [8]; **1976–77:** 763 [18, 24], 925 [3]
Information on citizens, **1975:** 72 [2, 10]
Investigatory files, **1975:** 45 [5]
J. Edgar Hoover F.B.I. Building, dedication, **1975:** 596
La Guardia Airport, bombing incident, investigation, **1975:** 749
Lee Harvey Oswald letter, **1975:** 558ftn.
Martin Luther King, Jr., actions concerning, **1975:** 695 [10]
News conference remarks, **1976–77:** 107 [13]
Personnel changes, **1976–77:** 674 [35]
See also Intelligence activities.
Federal Bureau of Prisons, **1975:** 341
Federal coal leasing amendments bill, veto, **1976–77:** 640
Federal Columbia River Transmission System Act, **1974:** 176
Federal Communications Commission, **1975:** 392; **1976–77:** 314
Federal cost reduction campaign, **1975:** 244, 245, 722
Federal Council on the Aging, **1975:** 424; **1976–77:** 708, 932
Federal Council on the Arts and Humanities, **1975:** 740
Federal Criminal Code, **1975:** 341, 532; **1976–77:** 685, 803, 818, 827
Federal Crop Insurance Corporation, **1976–77:** 685
Federal departments and agencies
Budget cuts, **1975:** 626
Cabinet members, relations with Congress, **1975:** 750 [18]
Consumer representation plans, **1975:** 527 [12], 658
Data collection, **1976–77:** 173
Energy conservation efforts, **1974:** 165, 166
Energy message, **1976–77:** 1045
Federal Advisory Committees, **1975:** 162
Freedom of Information Act amendments, **1974:** 125, 160, 236 [1]
Federal departments—*continued*
Government programs, consolidation, **1975:** 750 [19]
Government in the Sunshine Act, **1976–77:** 772, 773
Inflation impact statements, **1974:** 121
Information disclosure, **1975:** 1
Paperwork reduction, **1975:** 500, 595, 602 [2], 631
Political philosophy of Presidential appointees, **1975:** 615 [7]
Privacy Act of 1974, implementation, **1975:** 595
Regulations, Congressional review, **1975:** 487
Reorganization, **1975:** 175, 678 [9]; **1976–77:** 192 [1]
See also Memorandums to Federal officials and agencies; *specific department or agency.*
Federal Disaster Assistance Administration, **1976–77:** 583, 1029
Federal Drug Enforcement Administration, **1975:** 341
Federal Election Campaign Act Amendments of 1974, **1974:** 148, 149
Federal Election campaign Act Amendments of 1976, **1976–77:** 457
Federal Election Commission
Congressional action, **1976–77:** 102, 103, 123, 145, 231, 370, 420 [6]
Establishment, **1974:** 149
Extension, **1976–77:** 378 [8]
Federal election law, **1975:** 527 [4]
Members, swearing in, **1975:** 184; **1976–77:** 500
News conference remarks, **1976–77:** 418 [4]
Presidential travel expenses, **1975:** 565 [13]
President's assessment, **1976–77:** 321 [5], 383
Republican National Convention accommodations, **1976–77:** 657 [7]
Federal employees
Budget news briefing, **1976–77:** 23 (p. 59, 60, 62, 70, 71)
Career civil service, **1974:** 91
Citizenship requirements for employment, **1976–77:** 752
Civil service merit system, **1975:** 111
Combined Federal Campaign, **1974:** 103; **1975:** 413, 564, 593
Compensation, **1974:** 63; **1975:** 328
Concord, N.H., budget briefing, **1976–77:** 64
Discriminatory foreign policies, **1975:** 689, 690
District Court judges, **1974:** 72, 240
Employment reduction, **1974:** 43
Equal opportunity, **1975:** 124
Federal cost reduction campaign, **1975:** 244, 245, 722
Federal Summer Intern program, **1975:** 178
Financial disclosure requirements, **1976–77:** 675
General schedule classification, **1976–77:** 539
Handicapped persons, **1975:** 156
Hatch Act amendments, **1976–77:** 334, 335

Federal employees—*continued*
Intergovernmental personnel policy report, **1974:** 101
Labor-management relations, **1975:** 76
Legislation, **1976–77:** 685
Occupational safety and health programs, **1975:** 63, 363, 682
One percent add-on in retirement system, **1976–77:** 254
Pay increase, **1974:** 39 [26], 43, 72, 82, 87, 115, 117, 262; **1975:** 26, 28, 32, 46, 64, 143, 328, 506, 554 [15], 729; **1976–77:** 116, 352 [13], 401 [5], 844
Personnel reduction, **1975:** 500, 501 [4], 502 [1], 737; **1976–77:** 803
Reclassification, **1974:** 205
Reemployment rights, **1974:** 63
Retirement pay, increase, **1975:** 26, 28, 32, 64
Rockefeller Public Service Awards, **1974:** 275
Standards of conduct, **1976–77:** 674 [1]
Strikes, **1975:** 582 [1]
Travel expense allowances, **1975:** 21
U.S. Savings Bonds program, **1975:** 159, 627
White House Fellowship program, **1975:** 269
Women, **1976–77:** 366
Federal Employees Pay Council, **1976–77:** 844
Federal Energy Administration
Administrator, **1974:** 165, 166, 195 [1, 20], 196, 228, 236 [24]; **1975:** 121, 496 [2], 564, 593, 661; **1976–77:** 23 (p. 52)
Alaska's Naval Petroleum Reserve No. 4, **1976–77:** 789
Federal Energy Office, establishment, **1976–77:** 705
National Energy Outlook Report, **1976–77:** 177
Natural gas shortages, interagency task force, **1975:** 661
Oil price controls, **1975:** 225
Regulations, **1976–77:** 189 [5]
Termination date, extension, **1976–77:** 101, 372, 685
Federal Energy Management Program, **1974:** 165; **1976–77:** 1015
Federal Energy Office, **1976–77:** 705
Federal Executive Boards, **1975:** 151; **1976–77:** 660
Federal Fire Prevention and Control Act of 1974, **1974:** 197
Federal fire prevention and control bill, veto, **1976–77:** 655
Federal Government
News conference remarks, **1976–77:** 282 [11]
President's assessment, **1975:** 371, 396 [16]; **1976–77:** 192 [5], 266 [11]
Reform, proposed agenda, **1976–77:** 468
Federal grant and cooperative agreement act, veto, **1976–77:** 944
Federal Highway Administration, **1974:** 50
Federal Home Loan Bank Board, **1975:** 678 [11]; **1976–77:** 626
Federal Housing Administration, **1974:** 30; **1975:** 243 [15]
Federal Incentive Awards program, **1975:** 722
Federal Insecticide, Fungicide, and Rodenticide Act, extension, veto, **1976–77:** 725
Federal Labor Relations Council, **1975:** 76
Federal Law Enforcement Training Center, **1975:** 367
Federal Maritime Commission, **1975:** 392; **1976–77:** 314
Federal Paperwork, Commission on, **1974:** 323
Federal Pay, Advisory Committee on, **1974:** 115, 117
Federal Power Commission, **1974:** 243; **1975:** 127, 392; **1976–77:** 314
Federal Prevailing Rate Advisory Committee, **1976–77:** 751
Federal Regional Councils, **1975:** 616 [19]
Federal Reserve Board
Chairman, **1976–77:** 23 (p. 65), 626, 803
Compensation for officials, **1976–77:** 1074
President's views, **1976–77:** 288
Federal Reserve System
Board of Governors, Chairman, **1974:** 109, 121
Chairman, **1975:** 602 [15]
Member, swearing in, **1975:** 403
Monetary policy, **1975:** 204 [9], 511 [3], 565 [17], 602 [4]
Federal Savings and Loan Insurance Corporation, **1974:** 200
Federal spending
Congressional action, **1975:** 164, 220, 223
Cost reduction campaign, **1975:** 244, 245, 722
Defense spending.
See under Defense and national security.
Deficit spending, **1975:** 3, 26, 28, 32, 36, [12, 24], 39, 46, 54, 62, 63, 64, 70, 72 [8, 16], 85 [17], 89, 90 [1, 7], 125 [14], 164, 166 [5], 167, 169, 171, 187, 195, 223, 252, 288, 318, 354 [17], 436, 478, 511 [3], 527 [2], 565 [17], 602 [14, 18], 626, 647, 707
Grants administration, **1974:** 280
Inflationary impact, **1975:** 232, 496 [1], 511 [3], 554 [12]
Message to Congress, **1974:** 262
1976 campaign issue, **1975:** 166 [9]
President's voting record in Congress, **1974:** 195 [5]
Radio-Television News Directors Association, **1976–77:** 48 [1]
Reduction proposals, **1975:** 379 [1, 2, 10], 527 [2], 614, 615 [1], 616 [1, 2], 617, 620 [3, 13], 622 [5, 16, 18, 25], 623, 626, 629, 630, 631, 650, 666 [15, 26], 695 [20], 731, 732, 735, 737, 750 [10]; **1976–77:** 22, 215 [6]
Research and development, **1976–77:** 266 [3]
State of the Union Address, **1976–77:** 19
See also Appropriations; Budget, Federal; Inflation.

Federal Summer Employment Program for Youth, **1975:** 178; **1976–77:** 310, 311, 312, 313
Federal Summer Intern program, **1975:** 178
Federal Trade Commission
Bureau of Competition, **1976–77:** 836
Chairman, **1976–77:** 314
Regulatory reform, meeting, **1975:** 392
Federal travel, administration actions to control, **1976–77:** 45
Federal unemployment insurance, **1976–77:** 862
Feldman, George, **1976–77:** 853
Feltner, Richard L., **1976–77:** 583
Ferrez, Luis, **1976–77:** 1042
Ferrier, Johan Henri Eliza, **1975:** 693
FHA.
See Federal Housing Administration.
Fiedler, Arthur, **1976–77:** 1052
Fielding, Bruce G., **1975:** 335
Filberts, **1975:** 16
Final Days, The, book about Richard M. Nixon's last days as President, **1976–77:** 333 [2], 362 [13]
Finance Corporation, International, **1974:** 110
Financial institutions.
See Banking and finance.
Financial Institutions Act of 1975, proposed, **1976–77:** 3
Findlay, Ohio, **1976–77:** 579
Findley, Repr. Paul, **1974:** 191
Finland
Conference on Security and Cooperation in Europe, **1975:** 459
President Urho Kekkonen, **1975:** 455, 456n., 459n.; **1976–77:** 707, 711
President's visit, **1975:** 455–457, 459
Prime Minister Keijo Liinamaa, **1975:** 457n.
Finley, Murray H., **1974:** 109
Fire Data Center, National, **1974:** 197
Fire Prevention and Control Act of 1974, Federal, **1974:** 197
Fire Prevention and Control Administration, National, **1974:** 197; **1976–77:** 776
Fire Prevention and Control bill, Federal, veto, **1976–77:** 655
Fire Research Center, **1976–77:** 776
Fisher, Robert Lee, **1976–77:** 309
Fisheries, International Commission for the Northwest Atlantic, **1975:** 584
Fishery Conservation and Management Act of 1976, **1976–77:** 337
Fishing industry
Conservation, **1975:** 30, 584
Fishery agreements
Bulgaria, **1976–77:** 1067
China, Republic of, **1976–77:** 1047
German Democratic Republic, **1976–77:** 1049
Poland, **1976–77:** 785
Romania, **1976–77:** 1048
Fishing industry—*continued*
Union of Soviet Socialist Republics, **1976–77:** 1050
Fishery Conservation and Management Act of 1976, **1976–77:** 337
News conference remarks, **1976–77:** 67 [4], 535 [17]
Shrimp agreement with Brazil, **1975:** 320
Tuna legislation, **1976–77:** 523
200-mile coastal limit, **1975:** 509, 511 [8]
Fitzsimmons, Frank E., **1974:** 109
Fiumicino, Italy, **1975:** 305
Flader, Robert, **1975:** 238
Flanigan, Peter M., **1974:** 237
Flat Tops Wilderness, Colo., **1975:** 726
Fleming, Robben W., **1976–77:** 1028
Fletcher, James C., **1976–77:** 679
Flint, Mich., **1976–77:** 485
Flood control, **1974:** 307
Florida
Budget briefing for local officials, **1976–77:** 89
Governor Reuben Askew, **1975:** 654
News conference remarks, **1976–77:** 86 [8, 10], 107 [6]
Presidential primary, **1975:** 655 [3], 657 [20]; **1976–77:** 198
President's visits, **1975:** 108–110, 653–655; **1976–77:** 86–99, 148–167, 175, 818, 819
Radio-Television News Directors Association, **1976–77:** 48 [3, 7]
Telephone remarks on dedication of the Science and Technology Exposition, Kennedy Space Center, **1976–77:** 591
U.S. phosphate interests, **1974:** 111
Wilderness areas, **1974:** 277
Flory, Paul John, **1975:** 568
Flournoy, Hugh, **1974:** 211, 213
FNLA.
See Angola—National Front for the Liberation of Angola.
Folklife Center, American, **1976–77:** 5
Fond du Lac, Wis., **1976–77:** 288, 289
Fong, Sen. Hiram L., **1976–77:** 810
Food
Exchange for oil imports, **1974:** 236 [8]; **1975:** 548, 552 [8], 582 [8], 616 [5], 620 [7], 622 [12, 14], 636
Exports, **1975:** 554 [2]; **1976–77:** 8
Florida budget briefing, **1976–77:** 89
Foreign assistance, **1974:** 80 [15], 81, 102, 187, 240, 325; **1975:** 78, 137, 161, 273, 396 [13], 554 [2], 600 [5], 649; **1976–77:** 769
Foreign trading, **1976–77:** 392 [5]
Land use, **1975:** 488 [5]
Monopolies, **1976–77:** 116
News conference remarks, **1976–77:** 107 [19]
Prices, **1974:** 121, 150; **1975:** 501 [13]; **1976–77:** 95

Food—*continued*
Production, legislation, **1974:** 121, 240
School lunches and child nutrition programs, **1974:** 210; **1975:** 609, 615 [8], 616 [15], 620 [11]
Supplies and prices, **1974:** 121, 150
U.S.-Japanese joint communique, **1974:** 249
U.S. production, **1975:** 64
Food and Agricultural Development Fund, International, **1976–77:** 545
Food Aid Convention, **1975:** 319
Food Conference, World, **1974:** 80 [15], 81, 86; **1975:** 64, 137, 147, 179; **1976–77:** 904
Food and Drug Administraion, **1976–77:** 911
Food for Peace program, **1974:** 102, 240; **1975:** 78, 137, 396 [13], 600 [5]; **1976–77:** 36
Food Program, World, **1974:** 102
Food stamp program, **1975:** 28, 36 [22], 64, 89, 143, 435, 620 [14], 622 [5, 19], 626, 634, 647; **1976–77:** 19, 122, 327 [9], 420 [9], 685, 721
Food Stamp and Supplemental Security Income Amendments, **1976–77:** 943
Food Stamp Vendor Accountability Act, Emergency, **1976–77:** 650
Football Coaches Association, American, **1975:** 25
Football Foundation and Hall of Fame, National, **1974:** 289
Footwear industry, **1976–77:** 346, 347
Forbes, Malcolm S., **1975:** 235
Ford, Betty, **1974:** 109, 118, 131, 135; **1975:** 460 [11], 501 [10], 530, 552 [12], 578 [2], 602 [6], 615 [12], 695 [14], 739 [12], 750 [15]; **1976–77:** 16, 95, 98, 116, 121, 138 [13], 210 [12], 339 [1], 617, 657 [18], 726, 784, 856, 1014
Ford, Jack, **1975:** 460 [11], 620 [8]; **1976–77:** 95, 726
Ford, Mike, **1976–77:** 95
Ford, Steve, **1976–77:** 95, 726
Ford, Susan, **1976–77:** 95, 726
Ford Committee, Citizens for, **1976–77:** 853
Ford family, campaign participation, **1975:** 615 [12]
Ford Motor Co., **1976–77:** 778
Foreign assistance
Administration policy, **1975:** 137, 138 [6]
Appropriations, **1974:** 72, 240, 325; **1975:** 161; **1976–77:** 270
Authorization legislation, **1975:** 260
Budget news briefing, **1976–77:** 23 (p. 74)
Developing countries, **1975:** 273, 518, 649
Development and disaster assistance programs, **1975:** 649; **1976–77:** 104, 114, 545
Economic assistance, **1975:** 719
Food, **1974:** 80 [15], 81, 102, 187, 240, 325; **1976–77:** 769
Funding, **1975:** 581 [2]
Humanitarian assistance, **1975:** 125 [1, 2, 4, 11], 161, 163, 502 [8]
Legislation, **1974:** 240, 325; **1976–77:** 303, 436, 437

Foreign assistance—*continued*
Military assistance, **1975:** 36 [3], 91, 109 [11], 161, 440, 502 [8], 517, 581 [2], 649; **1976–77:** 20
Cambodia, **1975:** 36 [13], 107, 109 [3, 21], 125 [1, 2, 4, 11], 138 [13], 161, 166 [2]
Chile, **1974:** 325
China, Peoples Republic of, **1975:** 582 [3]
Greece, **1975:** 719
Turkey, **1974:** 120, 135, 144, 145, 147, 156, 164; **1975:** 73, 387, 390, 447
Vietnam, **1975:** 36 [13], 53, 72 [1], 85 [15], 109 [3], 125 [1], 125 [4], 161, 166 [2, 11, 14]
Military credit sales program, **1976–77:** 757
President's assessment, **1976–77:** 116
Security assistance programs, **1975:** 649
See also specific countries and programs.
Foreign Assistance Act of 1974, **1974:** 240, 325
Foreign Assistance and Related Programs Appropriations Act, 1975, **1975:** 161; **1976–77:** 629
Foreign diplomatic missions, **1975:** 701
Foreign exchange students, **1976–77:** 418 [19], 665
Foreign Intelligence Advisory Board, **1976–77:** 199
Foreign Investment Study Act of 1974, **1974:** 193
Foreign leaders, meetings with.
See Meetings with foreign leaders.
Foreign oil depletion allowance, **1974:** 240
Foreign Payments Disclosure Act, proposed, **1976–77:** 709
Foreign policy
Address to Joint Session of Congress, **1975:** 179
Administration policy, **1975:** 64, 137, 179, 189 [1, 4, 8], 198, 204 [3, 13], 243 [7], 276 [2, 3], 459; **1976–77:** 580
Africa, **1976–77:** 372, 378 [7]
Campaign debate remarks, **1976–77:** 854, 947
Campaign issue, **1976–77:** 209 [14], 862
Chicago Council of Foreign Relations, **1976–77:** 208
Conference on Security and Cooperation in Europe, **1975:** 459
Congressional role, **1975:** 36 [20], 91; **1976–77:** 118
Defense treaties, **1975:** 700
Détente, **1975:** 36 [15], 189 [4, 5], 276 [3], 289, 290 [2], 354 [10], 459, 492, 501 [8], 502 [5], 530, 581 [8], 657 [7], 663, 666 [19, 22], 695 [22], 739 [8], 750 [5]; **1976–77:** 138 [4], 283, 287 [4], 362 [2]
Domino theory, **1975:** 166 [2], 750 [23]
Eastern Europe, **1976–77:** 339 [6], 401 [2]
Economic Report of the President, **1976–77:** 1070
Food, instrumental in, **1976–77:** 392 [5]
Food assistance programs, **1975:** 161, 273, 554 [2], 600 [5]
Foreign boycott practices, **1975:** 689, 690
Foreign governments, U.S. intervention, **1975:** 166 [3, 11], 578 [3], 581 [4], 685, 686

Foreign policy—*continued*
Illegal business activities, **1976–77:** 266 [17]
Intelligence activities, **1976–77:** 110
International alliances, U.S. attitude, **1975:** 354 [5]
International cooperation, **1975:** 28; **1976–77:** 109
Middle East, **1976–77:** 401 [4]
NBC News interview, **1976–77:** 6
Negotiations, disclosure to public, **1975:** 502 [14]
News conference remarks, **1976–77:** 86 [12, 17], 212 [16], 325 [16], 535 [12], 674 [4]
North Atlantic Treaty Organization Council, **1975:** 289
Nuclear weapons, use, **1975:** 290 [3]
Pacific Doctrine, **1975:** 716
Panama Canal, **1976–77:** 354 [9], 362 [1], 398 [10], 415 [1]
Pittsburgh Economic Club, remarks, **1976–77:** 967
Policy formulation, **1975:** 204 [3]
President's assessment, **1975:** 109 [16], 166 [15]; **1976–77:** 77, 231 [7], 240 [5], 362 [8], 398 [4]
President's Foreign Intelligence Advisory Board, **1976–77:** 279
President's war powers, **1975:** 36 [4]
Project Independence, **1975:** 488 [13]
Radio-Television News Directors Association, **1976–77:** 48 [1]
Remarks at Springfield, Ill., farm forum, **1976–77:** 181
State of the Union Address, **1976–77:** 1057
University of Michigan, remarks, **1976–77:** 784
U.S. intelligence, **1976–77:** 505
Vietnam conflict, effect, **1975:** 243 [7]
World Affairs Council of Oregon, **1976–77:** 505
See also Joint statements, *specific country*.
Foreign political prisoners, **1976–77:** 283
Foreign Public Documents, Convention Abolishing the Requirement of Legislation for, **1976–77:** 676
Foreign Sovereign Immunities Act, **1976–77:** 937
Foreign Students Service Council, **1975:** 250
Forest Management Act, National, **1976–77:** 946
Forest and Rangeland Renewable Resources Planning Act of 1974, **1974:** 13; **1976–77:** 170, 171
Forest System, National, **1975:** 726
Forrestal, U.S.S., **1976–77:** 647
Fort Benning, Ga., **1975:** 329
Fort Chaffee refugee facility, **1975:** 484
Fort Lauderdale, Fla., **1976–77:** 88, 89
Fort McHenry National Monument and Historic Shrine, **1975:** 379
Fort Myers, Fla., **1976–77:** 95, 96
Fort Smith, Ark., **1975:** 483, 484
Fort Wayne, Ind., **1976–77:** 414–416
Fort Worth, Tex., **1976–77:** 379–381
Fort Worth/Tarrant County Bar Association, **1976–77:** 380
40 Committee, **1974:** 80 [5]; **1975:** 678 [2]; **1976–77:** 107 [10]
Foster, John S., Jr., **1976–77:** 199
Foster Grandparents program, **1975:** 550; **1976–77:** 318
Fountain Valley, Calif., **1976–77:** 954
Fourth of July, **1976–77:** 641
Fowler, William Alfred, **1975:** 568
FPC.
See Federal Power Commission.
France
Bicentennial gift to America, **1976–77:** 499
Economic Summit Meeting, **1975:** 680
Joint statement, **1974:** 302
President Valéry Giscard d'Estaing, **1974:** 297, 300, 301, 302; **1975:** 54, 289n., 457n., 459n., 680; **1976–77:** 489, 494, 495, 499, 1021
President's visit, **1975:** 680
Representative to NATO, **1976–77:** 267
Summit conference in Puerto Rico, **1976–77:** 621
Franco, Francisco, **1975:** 291, 292n., 294, 684
Frank, John E., **1975:** 421
Frankel, Max, **1976–77:** 854
Franz, Bill, **1974:** 184
Franz, Bob, **1974:** 184
Fraser, J. Malcolm, **1975:** 727; **1976–77:** 692, 696, 698
Frederick, Pauline, **1976–77:** 854
Fredrickson, Donald, **1975:** 370
Freedom, President's views on, **1976–77:** 327 [10]
Freedom Bell, **1975:** 421
Freedom Day celebration, **1975:** 271
Freedom Foundation dinner, **1976–77:** 361
Freedom of Information Act amendments, **1974:** 31, 160, 236 [1], 240
Freeland, Mich., **1976–77:** 487
French West Indies, President's visit, **1974:** 297, 300–302
Fresno, Calif., **1974:** 213; **1976–77:** 263, 264
Frey, Repr. Louis, Jr., **1976–77:** 48 [7], 86 [8]
Friendly, Henry J., **1976–77:** 1052
Fromme, Lynette Alice, **1975:** 533n., 655 [2]
FTC.
See Federal Trade Commission.
Fuel
Divestiture of fuel companies, **1976–77:** 1045
Mandatory allocation program, **1976–77:** 356 [5]
Funding Simplification Act of 1974, Joint, **1974:** 280
Fungicide, and Rodenticide Act, Federal Insecticide, **1976–77:** 725
Future Farmers of America, **1974:** 150; **1975:** 419; **1976–77:** 287 [8]
Future Homemakers of America, **1976–77:** 235

Future standards of living, President's views, **1976–77:** 321 [7]
Futures Trading Commission Act of 1974, Commodity, **1974:** 189, 240

Gabon, Generalized System of Preferences, **1975:** 154
Galvin, Robert W., **1976–77:** 199
Gambling, legalized, **1976–77:** 972
Gandhi, Indira, **1976–77:** 68 [17]
Gannon, James, **1976–77:** 803
Garagiola, Joe, **1976–77:** 960
Garcia-Lomas, Miguel Angel, **1975:** 292
Garment, Leonard, **1974:** 283
Garn, Jake, **1974:** 218
Garrett, Ray, Jr., **1975:** 570
Gas, natural
Canadian imports, **1975:** 648 [3]
Deregulation, **1974:** 72, 121, 240; **1975:** 28, 64, 82, 84, 85 [19], 220, 374, 375, 496 [1], 502 [17], 527 [16], 562, 612, 663, 742; **1976–77:** 138 [9], 189 [11], 321 [8], 398 [1]
Economic Report of the President, **1976–77:** 31
Energy message, **1976–77:** 1045
Excise tax, **1975:** 26, 28, 60, 64, 70
Legislation, **1976–77:** 685
Message to Congress, **1976–77:** 140
News conference remarks, **1976–77:** 67 [19], 86 [6], 325 [10], 898 [16]
Offshore development, **1974:** 233, 262
Offshore resources, **1975:** 64
Pipelines, **1975:** 527 [16]; **1976–77:** 657 [21]
Prices, **1975:** 65, 562
Production, **1976–77:** 185 [12]
Radio-Television News Directors Association, **1976–77:** 48 [1]
Shortages, **1975:** 615 [16], 661
Trans-Canada pipeline, possibility, **1976–77:** 657 [21]
Gasoline
Consumption reports, **1974:** 150, 271 [15]
Florida budget briefing, **1976–77:** 89
Independent retail dealers, **1975:** 538, 551
Prices, **1974:** 271 [15]; **1975:** 26, 45 [1], 396 [4], 582 [9]; **1976–77:** 1039
Rationing, **1974:** 127 [5], Appendix D; **1975:** 32, 36 [1, 16, 24], 45 [1], 71, 82, 109 [8]
Tax, **1974:** 121, 127 [5], 152, 153, 154, 210, 236 [9], 271 [17], Appendix D; **1975:** 138 [17], 383, 393, 678 [16]
Gates, Thomas S., Jr., **1976–77:** 229, 340
General Accounting Office, SS *Mayaguez*, report, **1976–77:** 854
General Agreement on Tariffs and Trade, **1974:** 130, 274
General Aviation Manufacturers Association, **1976–77:** 538
General Motors Corporation, **1974:** 5, 23
General revenue sharing, **1974:** 79, 133, 271 [18], 319; **1975:** 28, 32, 64, 69, 70, 90 [1], 102, 138 [16], 169, 214, 215, 216, 393, 554 [14], 578 [8], 678 [8]; **1976–77:** 19, 38, 49, 57, 62, 64, 65, 89, 95, 126, 185 [3], 209 [1], 210 [1], 215 [4], 216, 231 [1], 284 [5], 321, 352 [11], 354, [2], 373, 415 [5], 417, 551, 552, 561, 566, 586, 685, 782, 835, 890, 947
General Services Administration
Administrator, **1974:** 165, 166, 195 [19], 313; **1975:** 458
Budget deferrals, **1976–77:** 1046
Consumer representation plans, memorandum, **1976–77:** 820
Stockpiles, disposal, **1974:** 240
Generalized System of Preferences, **1975:** 154, 226, 668; **1976–77:** 141, 780, 1086
Geneva Conference, **1974:** 271 [3, 12]; **1975:** 45 [2], 179, 204 [7]
Geneva Protocol of 1925, **1975:** 37, 38
George C. Marshall Memorial Corridor, **1976–77:** 348
George Washington Masonic National Memorial, **1975:** 95
Georgia
Freedom Foundation dinner, Atlanta, **1976–77:** 361
Military Order of World Wars, Atlanta, **1976–77:** 359
News conference remarks, **1976–77:** 418 [20]
President Ford Committee, reception, **1976–77:** 360
President's arrival, **1976–77:** 358
President's visits, **1975:** 69, 71, 72, 329, 678, 679; **1976–77:** 358–362
Primary results, **1976–77:** 427
Public forum, Atlanta, **1976–77:** 362
Georgine, Robert A., **1975:** 35
Geothermal energy, **1974:** 138; **1975:** 108, 169
Gerald R. Ford Health and Physical Education Building, Grand Rapids Junior College, **1976–77:** 1010
German Democratic Republic, **1974:** 284; **1976–77:** 1049
Germany, Federal Republic of
Chancellor Helmut Schmidt, **1974:** 279, 282, 284; **1975:** 54, 289n., 440, 441, 444, 457n., 680n.; **1976–77:** 668, 669, 671
Deployment of U.S. Armed Forces, **1974:** 20, 242
John J. McCloy Fund for German-American Exchanges, **1975:** 331
Joint statement, **1974:** 284
President Walter Scheel, **1975:** 330, 331, 334, 443
President's visit, **1975:** 440–444
Summit conference in Puerto Rico, **1976–77:** 621
U.S. troops, deployment, **1975:** 281
Gerstenberg, Richard C., **1974:** 109

GI bill, **1975:** 554 [4]
G.I. Forum, American, **1975:** 410
Gibson, Andrew E., **1974:** 195 [1], 228, 236 [24], Appendix D
Gibson, Kenneth, **1976–77:** 561
Gierek, Edward, **1974:** 119, 123, 128, 129, 130, 143; **1975:** 448, 449, 450, 451, 454
Girls Nation, **1975:** 414; **1976–77:** 714
Giscard d'Estaing, Valéry, **1974:** 297, 300, 301, 302; **1975:** 54, 289n., 457n., 459n., 680; **1976–77:** 489, 494, 495, 499, 621, 1021
Glendale, Calif., **1976–77:** 864, 865
Global Atmospheric Research Program, **1976–77:** 824
Goblaskas, Dave, **1975:** 548
Goddard Memorial Trophy, Robert H., **1975:** 180
Gödel, Kurt, **1975:** 568
Godwin, Gov. Mills E., Jr., **1976–77:** 52, 948
Goebel, Paul, Jr., **1974:** 208, 209
Golden Helmet Award, **1976–77:** 920
Goldwater, Sen. Barry, **1975:** 622 [20]; **1976–77:** 418 [15]
Golf Hall of Fame, World, **1974:** 70, 71
Conçalves, Vasco, **1975:** 289n., 290 [5]
Goodpaster, Gen. Andrew J., **1974:** 80 [12], 312
Gorch Fock, **1976–77:** 671
Government, Federal
  Public confidence, **1976–77:** 354 [10], 674 [21], 675, 803
  Reduction of bureaucracy, **1976–77:** 354 [5], 406
  State of the Union Address, **1976–77:** 1057
Government employees.
  Federal Executive Boards, **1975:** 151
  Intergovernmental personnel policy, report, **1974:** 101
  Strikes, **1975:** 502 [10], 554 [11], 582 [1]
  See also Federal employees.
Government National Mortgage Association, **1974:** 162; **1975:** 372
Government in the Sunshine Act, **1976–77:** 772, 773
Governors
  Offshore oil and gas development, meeting, **1974:** 233
  Telegram on inflation-fighting efforts, **1974:** 146, 151, 232
  White House dinner, **1975:** 102
Governors' Conference, National, **1976–77:** 126, 131
Graham, Martha, **1976–77:** 900
Grain
  Exchange for oil, **1975:** 548, 552 [8], 582 [8], 616 [5], 620 [7], 622 [12, 14], 636
  Exports, **1975:** 78, 396 [13], 460 [10], 490, 497 [1, 4], 511 [3, 12], 528, 539, 548, 552 [8], 554 [2], 571, 581 [6], 582 [8], 598, 600 [1, 6], 602 [1, 5, 7, 13], 616 [5], 620 [7], 622 [1], 636, 650, 750 [7]; **1976–77:** 8, 192 [2], 288, 333 [17], 854
Grain—*continued*
  Farm forum remarks
    Fond du Lac, Wis., **1976–77:** 288
    Omaha, Nebr., **1976–77:** 442
    Rockford, Ill., **1976–77:** 203
    Springfield, Ill., **1976–77:** 181
  Inspection, **1976–77:** 372
  Insurance, **1976–77:** 189 [9]
  International Wheat Agreement, 1971, **1975:** 319
  News conference remarks, **1976–77:** 898 [3]
  Prices, **1975:** 396 [13], 497 [2, 3]
  Radio-Television News Directors Association, **1976–77:** 48 [13]
  Texas Grain and Feed Association, remarks, **1976–77:** 327 [1, 5]
Grain Standards Act, United States, **1976–77:** 939
Grand Junction, Colo., **1974:** 219
Grand Lodge of the District of Columbia Masons, **1976–77:** 243
Grand Rapids, Mich., **1974:** 207–209; **1975:** 17; **1976–77:** 221, 486, 1009, 1013
Grandparent program, Foster, **1975:** 550
Grants, Federal
  Categorical programs, **1976–77:** 116, 209 [11]
  Consolidation, **1975:** 750 [19]
  Florida budget briefing, **1976–77:** 89
  National Governors' Conference, **1976–77:** 126
  See also General revenue sharing; *specific programs.*
Grassley, Charley, **1974:** 188
Gray, Gordon, **1976–77:** 199
Great Britain.
  See United Kingdom.
Great Falls National Historic Site, N.J., **1976–77:** 562
Great Lakes, military cargo, **1975:** 502 [20]
Great Lakes Basin Commission, **1975:** 425; **1976–77:** 594
Greater Houston Builders and Contractors Associations, **1976–77:** 383
Greece
  Administration policy, **1975:** 179
  American Hellenic Educational Progressive Association, **1976–77:** 302
  CIA officer, slaying, **1975:** 745
  Cyprus conflict, **1974:** 120, 135, 144, 145, 151, 195 [21], 236 [21]; **1975:** 390, 479 [10], 608, 718; **1976–77:** 60, 68 [9], 118, 283, 315, 582, 717, 850, 1051
  NATO participation, **1975:** 290 [7]
  Prime Minister Constantine Caramanlis, **1975:** 289n., 456n.
  Security assistance programs, **1975:** 649, 719
Green, Edith, **1976–77:** 853, 959, 975
Green Bay, Wis., **1976–77:** 290–293
Green Bay Packers, **1976–77:** 291
Greener, William, **1976–77:** 740
Greensboro, N.C., **1974:** 174; **1976–77:** 212

Greenspan, Alan, **1974:** 39 [13], 52, 109; **1975:** 54, 626; **1976–77:** 23 (p. 74), 30, 118, 120
Greenville, S.C., **1974:** 173
Greenville, U.S.S., **1975:** 426
Griffin, Sen. Robert P., **1974:** 135; **1976–77:** 617, 732, 784
Griswold, Erwin N., **1975:** 19
Gross, Repr. H. R., **1974:** 188
GSA.
 See General Services Administration.
Guatemala
 Disaster assistance, **1976–77:** 114
 U.S. disaster assistance, **1976–77:** 104
Guilford, N.C., **1976–77:** 213
Guinea-Bissau, independence, **1974:** 4
Gulfport, Miss., **1976–77:** 814
Gun control, **1975:** 243 [14], 341, 582 [2], 615 [13], 622 [6]; **1976–77:** 287 [1], 352 [3], 401 [6], 947
Gunfiring incident at Soviet Mission to United Nations, **1976–77:** 286
Guyer, Repr. Tennyson, **1974:** 184; **1976–77:** 578
Gyorgy, Paul, **1976–77:** 557, 914

Haig, Gen. Alexander M., Jr., **1974:** 80 [12], 155
Haile Selassie, **1975:** 505
Hall, Paul, **1974:** 109
Hallgrímsson, Geir, **1975:** 290n.
Hammond, Charles J., Jr., **1975:** 591
Hampton, Robert E., **1974:** 115
Handicapped
 Education, **1975:** 707
 Employment, **1975:** 156, 174
 Federal aid, **1976–77:** 293 [7], 415 [6]
 March of Dimes Birth Defects Prevention Month, **1975:** 734
 National Epilepsy Month, **1975:** 638
 Teachers of children with impaired hearing, **1976–77:** 182
 Vocational rehabilitation programs, **1974:** 206
 White House Conference, **1975:** 691; **1976–77:** 242
Handicapped American of the Year, **1975:** 229; **1976–77:** 369
Handicapped Awareness Week, National, **1976–77:** 490
Handlowy Bank, **1974:** 130
Hanley, Repr. James M., **1976–77:** 810
Hanrahan, Repr. Robert P., **1974:** 191
Harald, Crown Prince, **1976–77:** 636
Hardware Manufacturers Association, American, **1975:** 500
Harmer, John, **1974:** 211
Harmon International Aviation Trophies, **1975:** 235
Harmsen, Stephen, **1974:** 218
Harper, John D., **1974:** 109
Harper's Acre Retirement Home, **1976–77:** 117
Harris, Thomas, **1975:** 184
Harry S Truman Memorial Scholarship Act, **1975:** 6
Harsha, Repr. William H., **1974:** 184
Hart, Jane (Mrs. Philip A.), **1976–77:** 1039, 1077
Hart, Sen. Philip A., **1976–77:** 1038
Hart-Scott-Rodino Antitrust Improvements Act, **1976–77:** 836
Hartford, Conn., **1975:** 629, 630; **1976–77:** 672
Hastie, William H., **1976–77:** 344
Hatch Act, **1976–77:** 293 [6], 334, 335
Hathaway, Stanley K., **1975:** 327, 431
Hauppage, N.Y., **1976–77:** 1000
Hawaii
 President's visit, **1975:** 715, 716
 Wilderness area, **1974:** 277
Hawaii, University of, **1975:** 716
Hawk missiles, **1975:** 573 [4]
Hawthorne, Calif., **1976–77:** 858
Hays, Brooks, **1976–77:** 595
Hays, Repr. Wayne L., **1976–77:** 581
Headstart, Economic Opportunity, and Community Partnership Act of 1974, **1975:** 12
Headstart program, **1974:** 39 [21]
Health, Education, and Welfare, Department of
 Appropriations, **1974:** 72, 240, 285; **1975:** 59, 201, 681, 737
 Appropriations Act, 1977, veto, **1976–77:** 830
 Assistant Secretary of Health, **1975:** 370
 Budget deferrals and rescissions, **1974:** 89; **1975:** 59, 201, 437, 541, 607 635, 681; **1976–77:** 227, 364, 697, 822, 1046
 Budget news briefing, **1976–77:** 23 (p. 62–64, 66, 67)
 Child support program, reporting standards, **1975:** 487
 Commissioner of Education, **1976–77:** 915
 Community services, **1975:** 12, 502 [18]
 Deferrals and rescissions, **1976–77:** 1017
 Education, consolidation of programs, **1975:** 602 [3], 648 [3]
 Equality in school athletic programs, **1976–77:** 356 [8]
 Father-Son/Mother-Daughter events, decision, **1976–77:** 657 [15]
 Indochina refugees, **1975:** 415
 National Institute of General Medical Sciences, **1974:** 197
 Office of Consumer Affairs, **1976–77:** 820
 Office of Education, Commissioner, **1976–77:** 792
 Office of the Inspector General, establishment, **1976–77:** 901
 Recombinant DNA experiments, **1976–77:** 801
 Secretary, **1974:** 42, 72, 109, 132, 197, 206, 291; **1975:** 20, 92, 126, 360, 480; **1976–77:** 23 (p. 62–64, 66, 67), 626, 674 [20], 688, 708, 715, 723

HEW—*continued*
Student assistance programs, **1974:** 263
Swine flu vaccine, **1976–77:** 257, 258
Vocational Rehabilitation Act amendments, **1974:** 206, 240
See also specific constituent agencies.
Health, Education, and Welfare Appropriation Act, 1975, Departments of Labor and, **1974:** 285
Health, Education, and Welfare Appropriation Act, 1977, veto, Departments of Labor and, **1976–77:** 830
Health Care Act, Veterans Omnibus, **1976–77:** 940
Health Care Improvement Act, Indian, **1976–77:** 840
Health Maintenance Organization Amendments of 1976, **1976–77:** 873
Health and medical care
Birth defects, **1975:** 734
Black lung program, **1974:** 205
Budget news briefing, **1976–77:** 23 (p. 62, 63)
Burn treatment program, **1974:** 197
Cigarette tar and nicotine content, Federal regulation, **1974:** 169, 186
Concord, N.H., budget briefing, **1976–77:** 64
Cooley's anemia programs, **1975:** 545; **1976–77:** 823
Economic Report of the President, **1976–77:** 1070
Education, financial assistance, **1975:** 602 [12], 616 [9]; **1976–77:** 889
Elderly persons, **1975:** 424; **1976–77:** 24, 39, 70, 92, 533
Emergency medical services, **1976–77:** 420 [2]
Federal health programs, **1975:** 64, 65, 622 [5], 626; **1976–77:** 68 [1], 135, 136, 288
Florida budget briefing, **1976–77:** 89
Grant programs, **1976–77:** 209 [10]
Health revenue sharing and health services funding, **1974:** 319
Heart and lung diseases, reports, **1975:** 259, 361; **1976–77:** 491, 496
Legislation, **1974:** 72; **1976–77:** 685
Malpractice insurance, Federal role, **1976–77:** 189, [4], 207 [5]
Medical and diagnostics devices, **1976–77:** 542
Medical profession, President's assessment, **1976–77:** 293 [5]
Medicare, **1975:** 126; **1976–77:** 512
Mental retardation, **1974:** 136
National Cancer Program, **1976–77:** 296
National Epilepsy Month, **1975:** 638
National health insurance programs, **1974:** 6, 240; **1975:** 36 [11], 64, 527 [11], 750 [19]; **1976–77:** 207 [5], 327 [9], 333 [4], 362 [15], 406, 420 [7]
National Health Service Corps, **1975:** 436
Nationalized medical system, **1976–77:** 266 [1]
Health and medical care—*continued*
News conference remarks, **1976–77:** 86 [3]
Nurses, training, **1975:** 3, 436; **1976–77:** 385 [3]
Occupational health programs, **1975:** 65, 363, 682
Public health services bill, veto, **1975:** 436
Radiation control, **1975:** 362
Radio-Television News Directors Association, **1976–77:** 48 [12]
Research and development
Cancer, **1974:** 186, 222
Funding, **1975:** 259; **1976–77:** 333 [13], 505
Heart and lung disease, **1974:** 97
St. Edward Mercy Medical Center, **1975:** 483
Sickle cell anemia, **1975:** 77, 530; **1976–77:** 425
State of the Union Address, **1976–77:** 19
Swine flu immunization program, **1976–77:** 257, 258, 280, 341, 342, 674 [20], 688, 715, 718, 723
Uniformed Services University of Health Sciences, **1975:** 394
United States-Japan Cooperative Medical Science Program, **1975:** 384
University of Michigan, remarks, **1976–77:** 784
Veterans
Hospitals, **1974:** 16; **1976–77:** 94, 95, 456, 940, 961
Medical benefits, **1976–77:** 897
Health Professions Educational Assistance Act of 1976, **1976–77:** 889
Health Services Administration, **1976–77:** 823
Hearing-impaired, visual television aids, **1976–77:** 929
Heart disease, **1975:** 259, 361
Heart and Lung Council, National, **1976–77:** 496; **1975:** 259
Heart and Lung Institute, National, **1974:** 97; **1975:** 361; **1976–77:** 491
Hébert, Repr. F. Edward, **1975:** 206
Helsinki, Finland, **1975:** 455, 456, 457, 459
Helsinki Conference.
See Conference on Security and Cooperation in Europe.
Hempstead, N.Y., **1976–77:** 1001, 1002
Henderson, Repr. David N., **1976–77:** 810
Hendricks, Sterling Brown, **1976–77:** 557, 914
Heppner, Oreg., **1974:** 307
Herman, George, **1976–77:** 560
Hernández-Colón, Gov. Rafael, **1976–77:** 618
Heroin.
See Drugs.
Hesburgh, Theodore M., **1975:** 138 [1]
Hester, Camilla A., **1976–77:** 884
HEW.
See Health, Education, and Welfare, Department of.
Hickory, N.C., **1976–77:** 240
Highland, Fla., **1976–77:** 158

Highway Administration, Federal, **1974:** 50
Highway Energy Conservation Act, Emergency, **1974:** 240
Highway Traffic Safety Administration, National, **1974:** 50
Highway Trust Fund, **1974:** 65; **1975:** 64, 72 [9], 84, 108, 383, 393
Highways
  Budget deferral, **1974:** 89
  Carpooling, **1974:** 240; **1975:** 11
  Construction, **1975:** 11, 64, 72 [9], 84, 85 [3], 108, 309, 367, 382, 383, 393, 622 [21]; **1976–77:** 95, 189 [2], 373 [1]
  Federal-Aid Highway Act of 1976, **1976–77:** 428, 429
  Gasoline tax, **1975:** 678 [16]
  Interstate trucking, **1974:** 240
  Safety, **1974:** 50, 194; **1975:** 613; **1976–77:** 616, 753
  Speed limit, nationwide, **1974:** 194, 240; **1975:** 11, 128
  Trucks, allowable weights, **1975:** 11
Hillis, Repr. Elwood, **1974:** 154
Hills, Carla A., **1975:** 131, 678 [18], 695 [14]; **1976–77:** 16, 23 (p. 68, 69), 89, 626, 712, 925 [14], 930, 931, 947
Hills, Roderick M., **1976–77:** 314
Hirohito, Emperor of Japan, **1974:** 245, 249, 250; **1975:** 603, 606, 610
Hirschfelder, Joseph O., **1976–77:** 557, 914
Hispanic Assembly, Republican National, **1976–77:** 702
Hispanic Heritage Week, National, **1974:** 48, 49; **1976–77:** 768, 788
Historic Preservation Fund, National, **1976–77:** 826
Hoffa, Jimmy, **1975:** 622 [7]
Hoffman, Paul G., **1974:** 122
Hogan, Jack, **1974:** 76
Hogan, Repr. Lawrence, J., **1974:** 155
Holidays.
  See Days of observance.
Holland, Harry, **1976–77:** 932
Hollywood, Fla., **1975:** 108, 109
Hollywood-Burbank Airport, **1976–77:** 862
Holm, Jeanne, **1976–77:** 193
Holshouser, Gov. James E., Jr., **1976–77:** 212 [2], 369, 771
Holton-Arms School, **1975:** 307
Holtzman, Repr. Elizabeth, **1974:** 155
Home Mortgage Disclosure Act of 1975, **1976–77:** 3
Home Purchase Assistance Act of 1974, Emergency, **1974:** 161, 162, 234
Homosexuals, **1976–77:** 185 [10], 318
Honduras, hurricane disaster, **1974:** 95
Hong Kong, Generalized System of Preferences, **1975:** 668
Honolulu, Hawaii, **1975:** 715, 716
Honor America Program, **1976–77:** 642
Hooper, James, F., III, **1975:** 615 [4], 616 [13], 678 [17]
Hoover, Herbert, memorial legislation, **1975:** 6
Hoover, J. Edgar, **1975:** 596
Hoover F.B.I. Building, J. Edgar, **1975:** 596
Hoover Institution on War, Revolution, and Peace, **1975:** 6
Hope, Bob, **1974:** 289; **1975:** 87; **1976–77:** 98
Hopkinton, R.I., **1975:** 591
Horse Protection Act Amendments, **1976–77:** 666
House of Representatives.
  See under Congress.
Housing
  Administration policy, **1976–77:** 339 [12, 13], 356 [2]
  Budget news briefing, **1976–77:** 23 (p. 68, 69)
  Congressional action, **1975:** 354 [1]
  Construction, **1974:** 127 [11], 237; **1975:** 351; **1976–77:** 118
  Credit, **1976–77:** 3
  Federal assistance, **1975:** 350, 351, 354 [1], 372, 496 [3], 622 [11], 678 [11]
  Financial reform, **1975:** 144
  Florida budget briefing, **1976–77:** 89
  Greater Houston Builders and Contractors Associations, **1976–77:** 383
  Housing and Community Development Act of 1974, **1974:** 29, 30
  Insulation standards, **1975:** 28, 46, 60
  Legislation, **1976–77:** 685
  Mortgage interest rates, **1975:** 243 [15]
  Mortgage purchasing assistance, **1974:** 30, 121, 161, 162
  National Association of Realtors, **1974:** 234
  President's assessment, **1975:** 629
  Prices, **1975:** 243 [15]
  Relocation assistance, **1975:** 49
  Rental, **1974:** 234, 240
  Section 8 program, **1976–77:** 333 [15]
  Starts and permits, **1976–77:** 790, 969
  State of the Union Address, **1976–77:** 19
Housing Administration, Federal, **1974:** 30
Housing Authority, National Capital, **1974:** 231
Housing Authorization Act, **1976–77:** 712
Housing and Community Development Act of 1974, **1974:** 29, 30, 72
Housing and Urban Development, Department of
  Assistant Secretary of Housing Management, resignation, **1976–77:** 35
  Community Development Block Grant Assistance program, **1975:** 167
  Secretary, **1974:** 29, 109, 132, 291; **1975:** 20, 92, 131, 350, 351; **1976–77:** 16, 23 (p. 68, 69), 89, 625, 626, 712, 925 [14], 930, 931, 947
  Under Secretary, **1974:** 29
  See also specific constituent agencies.

Houston, Tex., **1975:** 82; **1976–77:** 382–386, 388, 994
Houston Music Theatre, **1976–77:** 995
HUD.
See Housing and Urban Development, Department of.
Hudnut, Repr. William H., III, **1974:** 154
Hughes, Howard R., **1976–77:** 339 [9]
Human rights, **1976–77:** 283, 842
Humanities, and Cultural Affairs Act of 1976, Arts, **1976–77:** 875
Humanities, Federal Council on the Arts and the, **1975:** 740
Humanities, National Endowment for the, **1975:** 325
Humphrey, Sen. Hubert H., **1975:** 655 [11], 750 [16]; **1976–77:** 118, 120, 159, 262, 935
Humphrey-Hawkins bill, **1976–77:** 580 [2], 803
Hungary, József Cardinal Mindszenty, **1975:** 242
Hungate, Repr. William L., **1974:** 112, 155
Hunt, E. Howard, **1975:** 582 [7]; **1976–77:** 333 [5]
Hunt Commission, **1976–77:** 189 [10]
Hurricane disaster, Honduras, **1974:** 95
Hussein I, King of Jordan, **1974:** 12, 14; **1975:** 222; **1976–77:** 271, 274
Hutar, Patricia, **1976–77:** 791
Hutchison, Ray, **1976–77:** 742
Hydroelectric power, **1974:** 176, 202; **1975:** 498

ICC.
See Interstate Commerce Commission.
Iceland
Prime Minister Geir Hallgrímsson, **1975:** 290n.
Taxation convention with United States, **1975:** 385
Idaho, wilderness areas, **1974:** 276, 277
IEA.
See International Energy Agency.
Illinois
Lincoln Home National Visitor's Center, **1976–77:** 180
Presidential primary, **1976–77:** 189
President's visits, **1974:** 15, 190, 191; **1975:** 395–397, 495, 496, 499, 500, 598; **1976–77:** 180–192, 202–211, 907, 968–970
Republican Party campaign, **1975:** 138 [7], 396 [2]
United Republican Fund, **1974:** 191
Wilderness area, **1974:** 276, 277
Immigration
Illegal aliens, **1975:** 20, 109 [18]; **1976–77:** 64, 373 [8]
Indochina refugees, **1976–77:** 1053
Legislation on illegal, **1974:** 72
Naturalization ceremony, Miami, Fla., **1976–77:** 148
Immigration—*continued*
News conference remarks, **1976–77:** 325 [1], 418 [19]
Skinner, Jonty, **1976–77:** 420 [10]
Vietnamese refugees, **1975:** 163, 166 [1, 7], 167, 169, 179, 181, 189 [12], 204 [2], 224, 231, 243 [3, 10], 260, 262, 267, 347, 415, 484, 530, 746
Immigration and Nationality Act Amendments, **1976–77:** 927
Immigration and Naturalization Service, **1976–77:** 148
Immunities Act, Foreign Sovereign, **1976–77:** 937
Impact Aid program, **1975:** 433; **1976–77:** 373 [10]
Imports
Agricultural products, **1975:** 490
Automobiles, **1976–77:** 401 [1]
Chrome, **1976–77:** 420 [5]
Coffee, **1975:** 188; **1976–77:** 295
Dairy products, **1974:** 152, 153, 210, 219; **1975:** 232, 502 [3]; **1976–77:** 268, 288
Earthenware industry, **1976–77:** 409
Filberts, **1975:** 16
Fish, **1975:** 30
Meat, **1974:** 210, 219; **1975:** 232; **1976–77:** 376
Oil, **1974:** 121, 195 [15], 274; **1975:** 8, 26, 28, 32, 36 [1, 17], 41, 42, 45 [1], 54, 60, 64, 90 [1], 99, 108, 120, 121, 225, 270, 276 [5], 283, 418, 420, 485, 488 [1], 498, 537, 542, 562, 594, 636, 648 [3]; **1976–77:** 541
Shoes, **1976–77:** 284 [1], 347
Stainless steel flatware industry, **1976–77:** 410, 412
Sugar, **1974:** 241; **1976–77:** 795, 796
Zinc, tariff legislation, veto, **1974:** 264
See also International commerce.
Impoundment Control Act of 1974, Congressional Budget and, **1974:** 40, 72, 89, 262, 318; **1975:** 59, 62, 64, 166 [5], 167, 171, 367, 437
Income tax.
See under Taxation.
Independence, Mo., **1976–77:** 447
Independence Day, **1975:** 377
India, **1976–77:** 68 [17]
Indian Affairs, Bureau of, **1975:** 10, 488 [4]; **1976–77:** 808
Indian Claims Commission, **1974:** 198
Indian Health Care Improvement Act, **1976–77:** 840
Indian Health Service, **1976–77:** 808
Indian Ocean, U.S. military presence, **1976–77:** 266 [5]
Indian Self-Determination and Education Assistance Act, **1975:** 10
Indiana
Butler University, **1976–77:** 352
General revenue sharing, briefing for Indianapolis officials, **1976–77:** 417

Indiana—*continued*
President Ford Committee, **1976–77:** 353, 357, 416
Presidential primary, **1976–77:** 418 [1], 427
President's visits, **1974:** 154; **1975:** 137, 138; **1976–77:** 351, 355, 414, 609, 610, 979
Public forums, **1976–77:** 352, 354, 356, 415
Indiana Broadcasters Association, **1976–77:** 354
Indiana Dunes National Seashore, **1976–77:** 919
Indianapolis, Ind., **1974:** 154; **1976–77:** 351, 353, 417, 979
Indian, American
Education, **1975:** 10
Federal assistance, **1975:** 10
Land use for energy, **1975:** 488 [4]
Leaders, meeting with the President, **1976–77:** 670
Native American Awareness Week, **1976–77:** 867
Voting rights, **1975:** 477
Indochina
Administration policy, **1974:** 6
Foreign assistance, **1974:** 325
Refugees
Interagency Task Force, **1975:** 415, 746
Status report, transmittals, **1976–77:** 247, 611, 797, 1053
U.S.-French joint communique, **1974:** 302
See also Southeast Asia; *specific country*.
Indonesia
Administration policy, **1975:** 716
Grant assistance programs, **1975:** 649
Joint communique, **1975:** 710
Military sales credits, **1975:** 649
President Suharto, **1975:** 381, 709, 710
President's visit, **1975:** 709, 710
World Bank, loan, **1976–77:** 181
Inflation
Budget news briefing, **1976–77:** 23 (p. 50)
Campaign issue, **1974:** 79, 154, 170, 172, 173, 174, 175, 182, 188, 191, 209, 211, 215, 218; **1976–77:** 95
Congress, addresses to Joint Session, **1974:** 6, 121; **1976–77:** 19
Economic Report of the President, **1976–77:** 31, 1070
General Motors, prices, **1974:** 5, 23
Inflation impact statements, **1975:** 196, 392
Legislation affecting, **1974:** 9, 32, 33, 34, 40, 47, 62, 197, 202, 240, 261, 263, 285, 317, 318, 319, 326, 328
Monitoring agency, **1974:** 19, 32, 33, 72; **1975:** 31, 176, 328, 438, 486, 687
News conference responses, **1974:** 39 [9, 25], 127 [2, 11], 195 [2, 13], 271 [13]
Newsweek magazine interview, **1974:** Appendix D
President's assessment, **1975:** 26, 28, 36 [26, 27], 64, 68, 69, 70, 72 [13], 138 [9], 147, 166 [5],
Inflation—*continued*
President's assessment—*continued*
189 [10], 204 [8], 354 [17], 479 [1, 2], 496 [1], 501 [1], 511 [3], 527 [2], 554 [12], 571, 573 [5], 602 [1, 4, 8, 14], 731, 732
Public suggestions, **1974:** 150, 170, 171
Question-and-answer sessions, remarks
Dallas, Tex., **1976–77:** 321
Dover, N.H., **1976–77:** 118
Indianapolis, Ind., **1976–77:** 352 [13]
Marion, Ill., **1976–77:** 192
Radio address, **1976–77:** 957
Republican conferences, remarks, **1976–77:** 49, 62
Telegram to State and local officials, **1974:** 146, 151
White House Conference on Domestic and Economic Affairs, **1974:** 214
WIN program, **1974:** 121, 127 [1, 4], 150, 170, 171, 172, 195 [2], 214, 232, 290
Inflation, Citizen's Action Committee to Fight, **1974:** 109, 121, 146, 150, 232
Inflation, Conference on, **1974:** 6, 54, 56, 67, 106, 109, 121, 150, 236 [21]
Inflation Impact Statements program, **1976–77:** 1043
Information, public, document declassification, **1974:** 31, 160, 236 [1], 240
Information Agency, United States, **1976–77:** 1046
Inhofe, James M., **1974:** 182, 183
Inkley, Ronald W., **1974:** 218
Inland Daily Press Association, **1976–77:** 138
Insecticide, Fungicide, and Rodenticide Act, Federal, **1976–77:** 725
Inspector General, Office of the, **1976–77:** 901
Institute of Education, National, **1975:** 253
Institute of General Medical Sciences, National, **1974:** 197
Institute of Occupational Safety and Health, National, **1975:** 363
Insurance
Health, **1974:** 240
Unemployment benefits, **1974:** 121, 328
Insurance Corporation, Federal Savings and Loan, **1974:** 200
Intelligence activities
Administration policy, **1975:** 204 [6]
Campaign debate remarks, **1976–77:** 803
Congressional investigations, **1975:** 125 [3], 138 [15], 179, 316 [1, 4], 551, 565 [5], 573 [8], 581 [9], 600 [4], 615 [5], 657 [8], 659, 663, 678 [2], 685, 686, 750 [9]; **1976–77:** 40, 192 [5]
Covert operations, **1975:** 125 [3], 138 [4, 12], 204 [6], 243 [8], 316 [1, 2, 4, 8], 565 [3], 582 [7], 695 [21]
Document classification, **1974:** 60, 160, 236 [1]; **1975:** 341

Intelligence activities—*continued*
Domestic surveillance, **1975:** 45 [5]
Electronic surveillance, proposed legislation, **1976–77:** 252
Federal violations, **1975:** 316 [4]
Florida budget briefing, **1976–77:** 89
Foreign Intelligence Advisory Board, **1976–77:** 199
Foreign involvement, **1974:** 80 [5, 16]
Foreign policy, **1976–77:** 505
Identity of agents, **1976–77:** 283
Justice Department review, **1975:** 316 [1, 2, 4], 323
Legislation, **1976–77:** 685
News conference remarks, **1976–77:** 86 [14, 15], 107 [1, 2, 4, 7, 13, 16], 387 [28]
President's assessment, **1975:** 492; **1976–77:** 118
President's Foreign Intelligence Advisory Board, **1976–77:** 279
Reform of intelligence community, **1976–77:** 110, 231 [8], 685
Reorganization of intelligence community, **1976–77:** 207 [6]
Report, **1975:** 324
U.S.-Soviet capabilities, **1975:** 354 [16]
See also Central Intelligence Agency; Federal Bureau of Investigation.
Intelligence Oversight Board, **1976–77:** 107 [10, 14], 124
Intelligence Review Board, **1976–77:** 207 [6]
Interagency Task Force for Indochina Refugees, **1975:** 415, 746
Inter-American Convention on the Granting of Political Rights to Women, **1976–77:** 241
Inter-American Treaty of Reciprocal Assistance (Rio Treaty), **1975:** 700
Interdepartmental Committee for the Voluntary Payroll Savings Plan for the Purchase of United States Savings Bonds, **1975:** 159, 627
Interest rates, **1974:** 199
Intergovernmental Maritime Consultative Organization, **1974:** 157; **1975:** 391
Intergovernmental Personnel Policy, Advisory Council on, **1974:** 101
Interior, Department of the
Assistant Secretary, **1976–77:** 702
Budget rescissions, **1975:** 437; **1976–77:** 802
Georgia reclamation project, **1976–77:** 418 [20]
Predator control reorganization, **1976–77:** 1082
Reclamation Authorization Act of 1975, **1976–77:** 201
Rescissions and deferrals, **1976–77:** 336
Secretary, **1974:** 72, 109, 121, 132, 138, 185, 233, 276, 277, 291, 324; **1975:** 20, 92, 327, 431, 633; **1976–77:** 13, 583, 670, 789
Teton Dam collapse, **1976–77:** 583, 587
See also specific constituent agencies.
Interlochen, Mich., **1975:** 399
Interlochen Arts Academy, **1975:** 399
Internal Revenue Service
Corporate payments abroad, **1976–77:** 709
Drug trafficking, **1976–77:** 818
Income tax returns, access to, **1974:** 127 [14]
International Association of Chiefs of Police, **1974:** 96; **1976–77:** 818
International Atomic Energy Agency, **1975:** 520; **1976–77:** 987
International Bank for Reconstruction and Development, **1974:** 110; **1975:** 518; **1976–77:** 181, 685
International Chamber of Commerce, **1976–77:** 86 [1]
International Civil Aviation Conference, **1976–77:** 959
International Civil Aviation Organization, **1974:** 86
International Clergy Week, **1976–77:** 43
International Coffee Agreement of 1968, **1975:** 188
International Coffee Agreement of 1976, **1976–77:** 295
International commerce
American Conference on Trade, **1974:** 274
Balance of payments, **1975:** 602 [8], 650
China, People's Republic of
Discussions, **1975:** 622 [14]
U.S.-China agreement, **1976–77:** 674 [17]
Commodity futures, **1974:** 189, 240
Corporate payments abroad, **1976–77:** 709
Developing countries, **1974:** 72; **1975:** 2, 147, 154, 226, 273, 668
Domestic International Sales Corporation, **1975:** 554 [7]
Exchange of food and oil, **1974:** 236 [8]; **1975:** 548, 552 [8], 582 [8], 616 [5], 620 [7], 622 [12, 14], 636
Export administration legislation, **1974:** 72
Fair trade laws, **1975:** 192, 196, 220, 723, 724
Farm forum remarks, Rockford, Ill., **1976–77:** 203
Foreign boycott practices, **1975:** 689, 690
Foreign grain sales, **1976–77:** 192 [3], 333 [17], 422, 576
Generalized System of Preferences, **1976–77:** 141, 780, 1086
Hazardous materials, transportation, **1975:** 9
International Coffee Agreement, 1976, **1976–77:** 295
International Economic Report of the President, **1976–77:** 1071
International relations, **1975:** 64, 226
Japan, relations with United States, **1975:** 475
Joint statements
Germany, Federal Republic of, **1974:** 284
Japan, **1974:** 249
Poland, **1974:** 129, 130
Legislation, **1976–77:** 685

International commerce—*continued*
Limitations of exports, **1976–77:** 181
Metric system conversion, **1975:** 744
Mexico, relations with United States, **1974:** 179 [3]
Multilateral trade negotiations, **1976–77:** 11
Oil prices, **1976–77:** 541
Radio-Television News Directors Association, **1976–77:** 48 [13]
Reform legislation, **1974:** 72, 240, 271 [13], 274, 299
Romania
Agreement with United States, **1975:** 210, 211, 668
Waiver authority extension, **1976–77:** 548
Soviet agreement, **1975:** 36 [15], 91, 179, 226
Summit conference in Puerto Rico, remarks, **1976–77:** 619–621
Tariffs, **1975:** 16, 226
Textiles, **1975:** 311
Trade Act of 1974, **1975:** 2, 64, 226
Trade Agreements program, **1975:** 226; **1976–77:** 189 [1]
United Nations activities, **1976–77:** 842
U.S. footwear industry, **1976–77:** 284 [1], 347
U.S. oil tanker preference legislation, **1974:** 240, 327
U.S. shipping, **1975:** 207, 527 [8]
U.S. vessels, transport of oil, **1974:** 240, 327
See also Exports; Imports.
International Commission for the Northwest Atlantic Fisheries, **1975:** 584
International Conference on Air Law, **1974:** 86
International Conference on Urban Transportation, **1974:** 65
International Convention for the Safety of Life at Sea, 1960, amendments, **1974:** 157
International Convention for the Safety of Life at Sea, 1974, **1976–77:** 748
International Council on Shopping Centers, **1976–77:** 516
International Development, Agency for, **1974:** 95; **1976–77:** 104, 493, 545, 1037
International Development Association, **1974:** 110; **1975:** 518
International development and food assistance act of 1975, proposed, **1975:** 649
International Economic Policy, Council on, **1974:** 109, 321
International Economic Report of the President, **1975:** 147; **1976–77:** 223
International Energy Agency, **1974:** 284; **1975:** 64, 179, 460 [17], 498, 552 [8]
International Energy Institute, proposed, **1976–77:** 987
International Eucharistic Congress, **1976–77:** 720
International exhibitions, special, **1974:** 8; **1976–77:** 492
International Finance Corporation, **1974:** 110; **1975:** 518
International Food and Agricultural Development Fund, **1976–77:** 545
International Fund for Agricultural Development, **1976–77:** 1037
International Labor Organizations, **1976–77:** 26, 842
International Monetary Fund, **1974:** 110, 284, 302; **1975:** 147, 518; **1976–77:** 621, 685, 986, 1071
International Navigational Rules Act of 1976, **1976–77:** 874
International Office of Epizootics, **1974:** 270
International Olympic Committee, **1976–77:** 657 [9], 902
International organizations, U.S. assistance, **1975:** 161
International Red Cross, **1974:** 83
International Security Assistance and Arms Export Control Act, **1976–77:** 630
International Star Class Yacht Racing Association, **1975:** 499
International Telecommunication Convention, **1974:** 158
International terrorism, prevention, **1976–77:** 876
International Tin Agreement, **1976–77:** 612
International Trade Commission, United States.
See United States International Trade Commission.
International Whaling Commission, **1975:** 30; **1976–77:** 910
International Wheat Agreement, 1971, **1975:** 319; **1976–77:** 605
International Wheat Council, **1976–77:** 769
International Women's Year, 1975, National Commission on the Observance of, **1975:** 24, 185
Interstate Commerce Commission, **1975:** 392
Interstate and Defense Highways, National System of, **1975:** 64, 382, 383, 393
Interviews.
See under News media.
Investment Study Act of 1974, Foreign, **1974:** 193
Iowa
President's visits, **1974:** 187, 188, 210; **1975:** 490, 491; **1976–77:** 904
Wilderness area, **1974:** 276, 277
Iowa Development Commission, **1975:** 490
Iowa State University, **1976–77:** 904
Iran
Military arms, sales, **1976–77:** 854
Shah Mohammad Reza Pahlavi, **1975:** 258, 261, 263, 276 [5]
Ireland
Joint communique, **1976–77:** 226
President Eamon de Valera, **1975:** 507
Prime Minister Liam M. Cosgrave, **1976–77:** 222, 225, 226

Irving (Tex.) Bar Association Law Day, dinner, **1976–77:** 323
Israel
American Jewish Committee, **1976–77:** 473
B'nai B'rith Biennial Convention, remarks, **1976–77:** 766
B'nai B'rith International Bicentennial Convention, **1976–77:** 196
Campaign debate remarks, **1976–77:** 854
Capital city, **1974:** 39 [22]
Generalized System of Preferences, **1975:** 668
Lebanon, involvement, **1976–77:** 505
Middle East peace negotiations, **1974:** 195 [8], 236 [20], 271 [3, 12]
News conference remarks, **1976–77:** 325 [4], **898** [3], **925** [13]
Newsweek magazine, interview, **1974:** Appendix D
North Atlantic Treaty Organization, membership, **1975:** 125 [10]
Prime Minister Yitzhak Rabin, **1974:** 66, 75; **1975:** 204 [7], 243 [2], 316 [9], 322, 516, 522; **1976–77:** 32, 34, 41, 560 [8], 854
Rescue of hostages in Uganda, **1976–77:** 648, 657 [4, 10]
Security assistance programs, **1975:** 649
Senate letter of support, **1975:** 299
Syria, disengagement of forces, **1975:** 648 [7]
Terrorist attack, **1975:** 123, 125 [10]
Troop disengagement agreement with Egypt, **1975:** 515, 516, 517, 522, 530, 552 [7], 600 [8], 625
United Nations
Membership, **1975:** 552 [9], 581 [10]
Zionism resolution, **1975:** 640, 655 [6], 669, 678 [12]
United States-Israel Convention on Income Tax, **1976–77:** 78
U.S. Ambassador, **1975:** 239
U.S. assistance, **1975:** 45 [2], 552 [7], 565 [2, 4, 11, 15], 573 [4], 578 [5], 581 [2], 582 [3], 600 [17]; **1976–77:** 68 [14], 210 [2], 420, 885
See also Middle East.
Italian Americans, **1976–77:** 787, 806
Italy
Earthquake, U.S. disaster assistance, **1976–77:** 545, 787
Joint statement, **1974:** 105
News conference remarks, **1976–77:** 674 [14, 19]
President Giovanni Leone, **1974:** 100, 104, 105; **1975:** 301, 302, 305
President's visit, **1975:** 301, 302, 304, 305
Prime Minister Aldo Moro, **1975:** 302, 459n., 680n.
Prime Minister Giulio Andreotti, **1976–77:** 1023, 1024
Summit conference in Puerto Rico, **1976–77:** 621
U.S. disaster assistance, **1976–77:** 453, 493, 545, 787

J. Edgar Hoover F.B.I. Building, **1975:** 596
Jack, R. V., **1975:** 272
Jackie Gleason Inverrary Classic, **1975:** 110
Jackson, Philip C., Jr., **1975:** 403
Jackson, Miss., **1976–77:** 703, 704
Jacksonville, Fla., **1975:** 654, 655
Jacksonville Naval Air Station, Fla., **1975:** 653
James, Lt. Gen. Daniel L., "Chappie," **1976–77:** 362 [5]
James, Frances, **1976–77:** 30
Japan
Administration policy, **1974:** 6; **1975:** 179, 475, 650, 716
Bicentennial gift to U.S., **1976–77:** 623
Diet, **1974:** 247
Emperor Hirohito, **1974:** 245, 249, 250; **1975:** 603, 606, 610
Joint announcement, **1975:** 475
Joint communique, **1974:** 249
Joint statement, **1975:** 476
Medical science program with the United States, **1975:** 384
News conference remarks, **1974:** 271 [1]
Non-proliferation of nuclear weapons, **1976–77:** 514
President's intention to visit, **1974:** 195 [8]
President's visit, **1974:** 238, 244–251, 259
Prime Minister Eisaku Sato, **1975:** 303
Prime Minister Kakuei Tanaka, **1974:** 244, 249
Prime Minister Takeo Miki, **1975:** 474, 475, 476, 680n.; **1976–77:** 624
Summit conference in Puerto Rico, **1976–77:** 621
Whaling operations, **1975:** 30
Japan Press Club, **1974:** 246
Japan-United States Friendship Act, **1975:** 637
Japan-United States Friendship Commission, **1975:** 637
Japanese Americans, **1976–77:** 111
Jarman, Repr. John, **1975:** 44
Jaroszewicz, Piotr, **1975:** 453n.
Jaszi, George, **1974:** 275
Jaworski, Leon, **1974:** 39 [6], 80 [2, 11], 155; **1975:** 479 [5]
Jaycees, United States, **1975:** 540; **1976–77:** 610, 790
Jefferson, Thomas, **1976–77:** 338
Jeffords, James, M., **1974:** 118
Jerusalem, Israel, **1974:** 39 [22]
Jewish High Holy Days
Messages, **1974:** 55; **1975:** 521
News conference remarks, **1974:** 80
Statement, **1976–77:** 809
Jewish influence, comments by Chairman, Joint Chiefs of Staff, **1974:** 236 [7]
Job Corps, **1975:** 52
Job security assistance program, **1974:** 72, 121
Jobs and Unemployment Assistance Act, Emergency, **1974:** 328

John F. Kennedy Center for the Performing Arts, **1976–77:** 623
John F. Kennedy International Airport, **1976–77:** 934
John F. Kennedy Space Center, **1976–77:** 591
John J. McCloy Fund for German-American Exchanges, **1975:** 331
Johnson, Repr. Albert W., **1976–77:** 810
Johnson, Repr. James P., **1974:** 219
Johnson, Lady Bird, **1976–77:** 304, 1052
Johnson, Lyndon Baines, memorial, **1974:** 107
Johnson City, Tenn., **1976–77:** 476
Johnson Memorial Grove, Lyndon Baines, **1976–77:** 304
Joint Chiefs of Staff, **1976–77:** 925 [3], 947
Joint communiques.
  See Joint statements.
Joint Funding Simplification Act of 1974, **1974:** 280
Joint statements
  Australia, **1976–77:** 698
  Colombia, **1975:** 589
  France, **1974:** 302
  Germany, Federal Republic of, **1974:** 284
  Indonesia, **1975:** 710
  Ireland, **1976–77:** 226
  Italy, **1974:** 105
  Japan, **1974:** 249; **1975:** 475, 476
  Jordan, **1974:** 14
  Korea, Republic of, **1974:** 255
  Pakistan, **1975:** 78
  Philippines, **1975:** 713
  Poland, **1974:** 128, 129, 130, 143; **1975:** 450, 454
  Portugal, **1974:** 168
  Romania, **1975:** 465
  Summit conference in Puerto Rico, **1976–77:** 621
  Union of Soviet Socialist Republics, **1974:** 257, 258
  Yugoslavia, **1975:** 146, 471
Joint United States-Polish Trade Commission, **1974:** 129, 130, 143; **1975:** 450
Joliet, Ill., **1976–77:** 907
Jones, Reginald H., **1974:** 109
Jordan
  Joint statement, **1974:** 14
  King Hussein I, **1974:** 12, 14; **1975:** 222; **1976–77:** 271, 274
  Security assistance programs, **1975:** 649
  U.S. military assistance, **1975:** 573 [4]
Jordan-United States Joint Commission, **1974:** 14
Jørgenson, Anker, **1975:** 289n.
Juan Carlos
  As King of Spain, **1976–77:** 547, 549, 553
  As Prince of Spain, **1975:** 293n., 684n.
Justice, Department of
  Antitrust Division, **1976–77:** 836
  Antitrust investigations, **1974:** 121, 271 [19], 317
  Appropriations, **1974:** 72
Justice, Department of—*continued*
  Assistant Attorney General, Criminal Division, **1974:** 224
  Attorney General, **1974:** 77, 78, 80 [2ftn.], 132, 155, 291, 295, 313; **1975:** 20, 79, 92, 323, 324, 479 [6], 566; **1976–77:** 116, 497, 543, 560 [6], 626, 709, 763 [18], 972, 1076
  Career Criminal Impact program, **1974:** 96
  Deputy Attorney General, **1975:** 132
  Drug abuse message, **1976–77:** 368
  Foreign boycott practices, investigation, **1975:** 689
  La Guardia Airport, bombing incident, investigation, **1975:** 749
  Major Violators Unit, **1974:** 96
  News conference remarks, **1976–77:** 535 [10]
  Office of Professional Responsibility, proposed, **1976–77:** 675
  Office of Special Prosecutor, proposed, **1976–77:** 675
  Pardon Attorney, **1974:** 155
  Reorganization legislation, **1976–77:** 685
  Solicitor General, **1975:** 485n.
  Watergate Special Prosecution Force
    Deputy Director, **1974:** 155
    Director, **1974:** 155
    Presidential documents and recordings, **1974:** 80 [2, 4], 195 [19], 313
  See also specific constituent agencies.
Juvenile Justice and Delinquency Prevention Act of 1974, **1974:** 62, 181

Kalamazoo, Mich., **1975:** 337; **1976–77:** 485
Kansas
  President's visits, **1974:** 220; **1975:** 83–85, 556; **1976–77:** 735
  Republican Party, **1975:** 85 [13]
  State legislature, address, **1975:** 84
Kansas City, Mo., **1974:** 150, 151; **1975:** 555, 557; **1976–77:** 726–734
Kastenmeier, Repr. Robert W., **1974:** 155
Kaunda, Kenneth D., **1975:** 200
Kay, Emmet James, **1974:** 83
Kaye, Nathan, **1975:** 591
Keating, Kenneth B., **1975:** 239
Keen, Ralph, **1974:** 183
Keene, N.H., **1975:** 547; **1976–77:** 115–117
Kehoe, John T., **1974:** 211
Kekkonen, Urho, **1975:** 455, 459n., 465n.; **1976–77:** 707, 711
Kelley, Clarence M., **1975:** 648 [8]; **1976–77:** 674 [35], 763 [18], 763 [24], 925 [3]
Kennedy, Cornelia, **1975:** 695 [14]
Kennedy, David Douglas, **1974:** 203
Kennedy, Sen. Edward M., **1974:** 31; **1975:** 655 [11]
Kennedy, John F., **1975:** 166 [13], 243 [8], 558, 695 [19]

Kennedy, Walter L., **1974:** 118
Kennedy, Commission To Report on the Assassination of President John F., **1975:** 166 [13], 243 [8], 558
Kennedy Center for the Performing Arts, John F., **1976–77:** 623
Kennedy International Airport, John F., **1976–77:** 934
Kennedy Space Center, Fla., John F., **1976–77:** 591
Kent County, Mich., Republican Committee, **1976–77:** 831
Kentucky
  Armed Forces Day, dinner, **1976–77:** 484
  Bill signings, remarks, **1976–77:** 483
  President Ford Committee, reception, **1976–77:** 482
  Presidential primaries, **1976–77:** 523
  President's visits, **1974:** 175; **1975:** 620 [5]; **1976–77:** 481, 980
  Wilderness area, **1974:** 276, 277
Kerwin, Capt. Joseph, **1975:** 235
Kidnapping, mandatory prison terms, **1975:** 341
Killanin, Lord Michael, **1976–77:** 902
Kimball, Spencer W., **1976–77:** 637
Kincheloe Air Force Base, Mich., **1975:** 401
King, Billie Jean, **1975:** 417
King, Coretta Scott, **1976–77:** 17
King, Martin Luther, Jr., **1975:** 27, 695 [10]; **1976–77:** 17
Kingsley, Daniel T., **1974:** 243
Kirchgoens, Federal Republic of Germany, **1975:** 442
Kirkland, Joseph Lane, **1974:** 109; **1975:** 19
Kiser, Bill, **1976–77:** 369
Kissinger, Henry A., **1974:** 22, 79, 80 [5], 81, 109, 124, 127 [7, 18], 195 [14], 215, 226, 236 [10], 259, Appendix D; **1975:** 36 [10], 45 [2], 72 [19], 109 [2, 17], 153, 204 [3, 5], 354 [5], 479 [9], 489, 516, 523, 531, 600 [17], 657 [1, 3, 15, 19, 28, 29], 662, 666 [7], 678 [2], 685, 695 [18, 22], 718, 750 [18]; **1976–77:** 16, 60, 133, 159, 207 [1], 209 [14], 212 [16, 17], 215 [1], 287 [9], 293 [2], 308, 325 [20], 339 [3], 352 [2], 362 [8], 396, 406, 418 [15], 523 [3], 560 [12], 599, 763 [1], 770, 778, 784, 850, 854, 856, 939, 1061
Kleppe, Thomas S., **1975:** 633; **1976–77:** 13, 583, 670, 789
Kluczynski, Repr. John C., **1975:** 51
Knauer, Virginia H., **1974:** 41; **1975:** 230
Knowles, Warren P., **1976–77:** 307
Knoxville, Tenn., **1975:** 615, 616
Kobelinski, Mitchell P., **1976–77:** 81, 82, 805
Koby, Chester "Buddy," **1976–77:** 565
Kohler, Gov. Walter J., **1976–77:** 284
Kompfner, Rudolf, **1975:** 568
Korea, Republic of
  Administrative policy, **1975:** 716
  Campaign debate remarks, **1976–77:** 854
Korea, Republic of—*continued*
  Joint communique, **1974:** 255
  National Assemblymen, **1975:** 353
  News conference remarks, **1974:** 271 [1]; **1976–77:** 418 [5]
  President Park Chung Hee, **1974:** 252, 254, 255
  President's visit, **1974:** 238, 252–255, 259
  Security assistance programs, **1975:** 649
  Taxation and fiscal evasion convention with, U.S., **1976–77:** 754
  United Nations membership, **1975:** 552 [9]
  U.S. military involvement, **1975:** 316 [7], 354 [9]
Korologos, Tom C., **1974:** 309
Kovacevic, Zivorad, **1975:** 470n.
Kraft, Joseph, **1976–77:** 947
Kraków, Poland, **1975:** 452, 453
Kreisky, Bruno, **1974:** 227, 229; **1975:** 296, 298
Kubasov, Valery N., **1975:** 412
Kuras, Henry, **1975:** 272
Kyoto, Japan, **1974:** 251

La Crosse, Wis., **1976–77:** 265, 266
La Guardia Airport, New York City, **1975:** 749
La Mesa, Calif., **1976–77:** 955
Labor
  Blue collar support for the President, **1976–77:** 354 [3]
  Collective bargaining, **1975:** 134; **1976–77:** 312 [12]
  Common situs picketing legislation, **1975:** 501 [3], 554 [16], 739 [4, 12], 743
  Demonstrations, **1975:** 85 [20]
  Federal involvement, **1975:** 76, 97, 326, 378, 600 [2], 602 [10]
  Georgine, Robert A., dinner honoring, **1975:** 35
  Labor-management legislation, **1976–77:** 293 [3], 398 [5]
  Longshoremen's strike, **1975:** 497 [1, 3], 539
  National Center for Productivity and Quality of Working Life, **1975:** 721
  Pay increases, **1975:** 64
  Pension funds, **1975:** 80, 622 [8], 648 [1]
  Public employee strikes, **1975:** 502 [10], 554 [11], 582 [1]
  Seniority provision in labor contracts, **1975:** 602 [10]
  Taft-Hartley Act, **1976–77:** 287 [3]
  Trucking industry contract negotiations, **1976–77:** 294
  Unions
    Antitrust laws, **1976–77:** 398 [7]
    Investigations, **1975:** 622 [8]
  United Mine Workers of America, **1975:** 47
  Wage controls, **1975:** 36 [26], 72 [17], 565 [17]
  Worker productivity, **1975:** 602 [8]

Labor, Department of
Appropriation act, 1977, veto, **1976–77:** 830
Appropriations, **1974:** 72, 240, 285; **1975:** 59, 737
Budget deferrals and rescissions, **1975:** 59; **1976–77:** 227, 651, 1022
Dedication of new building, **1974:** 163
Employment figures, **1976–77:** 284
Farm labor contractor registration, **1974:** 286
Hearing officer position reclassifications, **1974:** 205
Secretary, **1974:** 41, 42, 67, 72, 109, 132, 291, 328; **1975:** 20, 80, 92, 140, 311, 328, 600 [2], 689, 739 [13], 743; **1976–77:** 15, 75, 626
Under Secretary, **1975:** 311
See also specific constituent agencies.
Labor Contractor Registration Act Amendments of 1974, Farm, **1974:** 205, 240, 286
Labor Day, **1974:** 44; **1975:** 513, 514; **1976–77:** 755
Labor and Health, Education, and Welfare Appropriation Act, 1975, Departments of, **1974:** 285
Labor and Health, Education, and Welfare Appropriation Act, 1977, veto, Departments, of, **1976–77:** 830
Labor-Management Committee, President's, **1974:** 109
Labor Organization, International, **1976–77:** 842
Laguna Hills, Calif., **1976–77:** 512
Laird, Melvin, **1976–77:** 199
Lake Worth, Fla., **1976–77:** 152
Land, Edwin H., **1976–77:** 199
Land Heritage program, Bicentennial, **1976–77:** 743, 745, 746
Land and Water Conservation Fund bill, **1976–77:** 825, 826
Landgrebe, Repr. Earl F., **1974:** 154
Langhorne, Pa., **1976–77:** 996
Lansing, Mich., **1976–77:** 485
Lantana, Fla., **1976–77:** 153
Laos
American prisoner, release, **1974:** 83
General System of Preferences, withdrawal, **1976–77:** 141
Larry, R. Heath, **1974:** 109
Las Vegas, Nev., **1974:** 234; **1975:** 171; **1976–77:** 515–517
Latin America
Administration policy, **1975:** 251
Coffee exports, **1975:** 188
Inter-American Treaty of Reciprocal Assistance (Rio Treaty), protocol, **1975:** 700
Panama Canal, negotiations, **1975:** 251, 589, 615 [9]
Security assistance programs, **1975:** 649
U.S. trade relations, **1975:** 179
See also specific country.
Latin American Citizens, League of United, **1975:** 410
Latta, Repr. Delbert L., **1974:** 184
Latter-day Saints, Church of Jesus Christ of, **1976–77:** 637
Latvia, **1975:** 430
Lauderhill, Fla., **1975:** 110
Lausche, Frank, **1976–77:** 1005
Law, World Conference on, **1975:** 632
Law Enforcement Assistance Act, **1975:** 166 [10]
Law Enforcement Assistance Administration, **1974:** 96; **1975:** 341, 400, 532, 554 [5, 10], 590; **1976–77:** 664, 685, 818
Law enforcement and crime
Administration policy, **1975:** 166 [10], 217, 340, 341, 532; **1976–77:** 406
American violence, **1975:** 578 [6]
Antitrust activities, **1974:** 121, 271 [19], 317; **1975:** 392
Campaign debate remarks, **1976–77:** 803, 947
Capital punishment, **1976–77:** 215 [12], 513
Career Criminal Impact program, **1974:** 96; **1975:** 341, 590
Compensation of victims, **1975:** 341
Conviction rates, **1975:** 341
Corrections system reform, **1975:** 341
Crime message
Federal offenses, sentencing standards, **1975:** 341
Remarks at briefing, **1975:** 340
Special message to Congress, **1975:** 341
Crime rates, **1975:** 341
Customs inspection, **1974:** 201
Diplomats, protection, **1974:** 86, 230
Drug abuse, **1976–77:** 128, 129, 323, 368
Drug Law Enforcement, Cabinet Committee for, **1976–77:** 464
Drug trafficking, **1975:** 341, 655 [10], 720, 748; **1976–77:** 323, 685
Electronic surveillance, **1976–77:** 252
Extradition treaties, **1974:** 28, 74
Federal Criminal Code, **1975:** 341, 532
Foreign diplomatic missions, protection, **1975:** 701
Fort Worth/Tarrant County Bar Association, **1976–77:** 380
Gun control, **1975:** 243 [14], 341, 582 [2], 615 [13], 622 [6]; **1976–77:** 68 [2], 287 [1], 352 [3]
International Association of Chiefs of Police, **1974:** 96; **1976–77:** 818
International cooperation, **1976–77:** 109
Investigatory files, disclosure, **1974:** 31, 160, 236 [1]
Justice in America, remarks, **1975:** 45 [6]
Legislation, **1976–77:** 685, 742
Mandatory prison sentences, **1975:** 341, 532, 600 [16], 615 [13], 622 [6]; **1976–77:** 685
President's views, **1976–77:** 513
Prison reform, **1975:** 341

Law enforcement and crime—*continued*
Prosecution standards, **1975:** 341
Radio address, **1976–77:** 988
Rehabilitation programs, **1975:** 341
Remarks at South Florida Chapter Bar Association dinner, **1976–77:** 97
State of the Union Address, **1976–77:** 19
Undercover operations, District of Columbia, **1976–77:** 664
University of Michigan, remarks, **1976–77:** 784
U.S. citizens' legal rights abroad, **1976–77:** 325 [19]
Youth, **1974:** 62, 181; **1975:** 341, 532; **1976–77:** 685
Law Enforcement Training Center, Federal, **1975:** 367
Law of the Sea Conference, **1975:** 450, 511 [8], 527 [5]; **1976–77:** 67 [4], 337
Lawton, Okla., **1976–77:** 866
Laxalt, Sen. Paul, **1976–77:** 732
LBJ memorial, **1974:** 107
Leach, Jim, **1974:** 188
Lead, stockpile disposal, **1974:** 240
League of United Latin American Citizens, **1975:** 410
League of Women Voters, **1976–77:** 750
Lebanon
Administration policy, **1976–77:** 505
Assassination of U.S. embassy officials, **1976–77:** 599, 606
Evacuation of American citizens, **1975:** 655 [5]; **1976–77:** 604, 607, 608
News conference remarks, **1976–77:** 282 [5], 325 [4]
Syrian intervention, **1976–77:** 560 [8]
Terrorist abduction, **1975:** 396 [1, 7]
Lee, Robert E., **1975:** 473
Lee, Stewart M., **1975:** 230
Lee Kuan Yew, **1975:** 249
Legal profession, opportunities, **1975:** 578 [7]
Legal Services Corporation, **1974:** 39 [21]; **1976–77:** 699
Legislation, disapproved.
See Veto remarks, messages, and memorandums of disapproval.
Legislation, remarks and statements on approval
Airport and Airway Development Act Amendments, remarks and statement, **1976–77:** 661, 662
Alaska Natural Gas Transportation Act, statement, **1976–77:** 945
Alcohol and Drug Abuse Education Act Amendments of 1974, statement, **1974:** 93
Allied wartime veterans medical benefits, remarks, **1976–77:** 897
American Folklife Preservation Act, statement, **1976–77:** 5
Amtrak Improvement Act of 1974, statement, **1974:** 201

Legislation, approved—*continued*
Amtrak Improvement Act of 1975, statement, **1975:** 279
Antitrust Procedures and Penalties Act, statement, **1974:** 317
Armed Forces Reserves Bill, remarks, **1976–77:** 483
Arthritis, Diabetes, and Digestive Diseases Amendments, statement, **1976–77:** 924
Arts, Humanities, and Cultural Affairs Act of 1976, statement, **1976–77:** 875
Arts and Artifacts Indemnity Act, statement, **1975:** 740
Bretton Woods Agreement Act Amendments, statement, **1976–77:** 926
Budget rescission legislation, statements, **1974:** 318; **1975:** 173; **1976–77:** 269
Child Day Care Bill, remarks and statement, **1976–77:** 759, 760
Coastal Zone Management Act Amendments, remarks and statement, **1976–77:** 690, 691
Commission on Federal Paperwork, establishment, statement, **1974:** 323
Commodity Futures Trading Commission Act of 1974, statement, **1974:** 189
Comprehensive Alcohol Abuse and Alcoholism Prevention, Treatment, and Rehabilitation Act Amendments, statement, **1976–77:** 693
Congaree Swamp, S.C., designation as a national monument, statement, **1976–77:** 918
Consumer Goods Pricing Act of 1975, remarks and statement, **1975:** 723, 724
Consumer Leasing Act of 1976, remarks, **1976–77:** 249
Consumer Product Safety Commission Improvements Act of 1976, statement, **1976–77:** 458
Continuing appropriations resolution, statement, **1974:** 164
Council on Wage and Price Stability Act, remarks, and statement, **1974:** 32, 33
Council on Wage and Price Stability Act Amendments of 1975, statement, **1975:** 486
Cuyahoga Valley National Recreation Area in Ohio, establishment, statement, **1974:** 324
Deepwater Port Act of 1974, statement, **1975:** 8
Defense Production Act Amendments of 1974, statement, **1974:** 114
Delta Queen, exemption from certain vessel laws, statement, **1976–77:** 912
Department of Defense Appropriations Act, 1975, statement, **1974:** 126
Department of Defense Appropriations Act, 1976, statement, **1976–77:** 73
Department of Defense Appropriations Act, 1977, remarks, **1976–77:** 800

Legislation, approved—*continued*
Department of Defense Appropriations Authorization Act, 1977, statement, **1976–77:** 667
Departments of Labor, and Health, Education, and Welfare Appropriation Act, 1975, statement, **1974:** 285
District of Columbia Criminal Code, prohibition of revision, statement, **1976–77:** 761
Drug Abuse Office and Treatment Act Amendments, statement, **1976–77:** 232
Education for All Handicapped Children Act of 1975, statement, **1975:** 707
Education Amendments of 1974, remarks and statement, **1974:** 24, 25
Education Amendments of 1976, statement, **1976–77:** 888
Emergency Compensation and Special Unemployment Assistance Extension Act of 1975, **1975:** 366
Emergency Food Stamp Vendor Accountability Act, statement, **1976–77:** 650
Emergency Home Purchase Assistance Act of 1974, remarks and statement, **1974:** 161, 162
Emergency Housing Act of 1975, **1975:** 372
Emergency Jobs and Unemployment Assistance Act, statement, **1974:** 328
Emergency Livestock Credit Act, extensions, remarks, **1975:** 332; **1976–77:** 905
Emergency Petroleum Allocation Act of 1975, remarks, **1975:** 594
Emergency Unemployment Compensation Act, statement, **1974:** 328
Employee Retirement Income Security Act of 1974, remarks and statement, **1974:** 45, 46
Energy Policy and Conservation Act, remarks and statement, **1975:** 741, 742
Energy Reorganization Act of 1974, remarks and statement, **1974:** 137, 138
Equal Credit Opportunity Act Amendments of 1976, remarks and statement, **1976–77:** 249, 250
Eugene O'Neill's home and property, designation as historical site, statement, **1976–77:** 917
Evidentiary rules, bill establishing, statement, **1975:** 5
Farm Labor Contractor Registration Act Amendments of 1974, statement, **1974:** 286
Federal-Aid Highway Act of 1976, remarks and statement, **1976–77:** 428, 429
Federal-Aid Highway Amendments of 1974, **1975:** 11
Federal-aid highway funds, statements, **1975:** 309
Federal Columbia River Transmission System Act, statement, **1974:** 176

Legislation, approved—*continued*
Federal deposit insurance increase, statement, **1974:** 200
Federal Election Campaign Act Amendments of 1974, remarks and statement, **1974:** 148, 149
Federal Election Campaign Act Amendments of 1976, statement, **1976–77:** 457
Federal employees' compensation benefits, statement, **1974:** 63
Federal Fire Prevention and Control Act of 1974, statement, **1974:** 197
Financial institutions, electronic fund transfers, and home mortgage disclosure, statement, **1976–77:** 3
Fishery Conservation and Management Act of 1976, statement, **1976–77:** 337
Flat Tops Wilderness, Colo., inclusion in National Wilderness Preservation System, statement, **1975:** 726
Food stamp program, bill prohibiting changes in, statement, **1975:** 89
Food Stamp and Supplemental Security Income Amendments, statement, **1976–77:** 943
Foreign Assistance Act of 1974, statement, **1974:** 325
Foreign Assistance and Related Programs Appropriations Act, 1975, statement, **1975:** 161
Foreign Assistance and Related Programs Appropriations Act, 1976, statement, **1976–77:** 629
Foreign Investment Study Act of 1974, statement, **1974:** 193
Foreign Sovereign Immunities Act, statement, **1976–77:** 937
Forest and Rangeland Renewable Resources Planning Act of 1974, statement, **1974:** 13
Government in the Sunshine Act, remarks and statement, **1976–77:** 772, 773
Harry S Truman Memorial Scholarship Act, statement, **1975:** 6
Hart-Scott-Rodino Antitrust Improvements Act, statement, **1976–77:** 836
Headstart, Economic Opportunity, and Community Partnership Act of 1974, statement, **1975:** 12
Health Maintenance Organization Amendments of 1976, statement, **1976–77:** 873
Health Professions Educational Assistance Act of 1976, statement, **1976–77:** 889
Herbert Hoover, memorial bill, statement, **1975:** 6
Horse Protection Act Amendments of 1976, statement, **1976–77:** 666
Housing Authorization Act, statement, **1976–77:** 712
Housing and Community Development Act of 1974, remarks and statement, **1974:** 29, 30

Legislation, approved—*continued*
Immigration and Nationality Act Amendments of 1976, statement, **1976–77:** 927
Income tax reduction, extension bill, remarks, **1976–77:** 628
Indian Claims Commission appropriations, statement, **1974:** 198
Indian Health Care Improvement Act, statement, **1976–77:** 840
Indian Self-Determination and Education Assistance Act, statement, **1975:** 10
Indiana Dunes National Seashore, expansion, statement, **1976–77:** 919
Interest rate regulation, statement, **1974:** 199
International Security Assistance and Arms Export Control Act, statement, **1976–77:** 630
International terrorism prevention, statement, **1976–77:** 876
Japan-United States Friendship Act, statement, **1975:** 637
Jefferson, Thomas, commemoration of birth, remarks, **1976–77:** 338
Joint Funding Simplification Act of 1974, statement, **1974:** 280
Juvenile Justice and Delinquency Prevention Act of 1974, statement, **1974:** 62
Land and Water Conservation Fund, remarks and statement, **1976–77:** 825, 826
Lee, General Robert E., restoration of rights of citizenship, remarks, **1975:** 473
Legislative Branch Appropriation Act, 1977, statement, **1976–77:** 841
Lowell Historic Canal District Commission, establishment, statement, **1975:** 13
Medical Device Amendments of 1976, statement, **1976–77:** 542
Medicare extension, statement, **1976–77:** 673
Metric Conversion Act of 1975, statement, **1975:** 744
Mid-decade population census, statement, **1976–77:** 913
Military Construction Authorization Act, 1977, statement, **1976–77:** 834
Motor Vehicle and Schoolbus Safety Amendments of 1974, statement, **1974:** 194
National Emergencies Act, statement, **1976–77:** 781
National Fire Prevention and Control Administration and Fire Research Center, appropriations, statement, **1976–77:** 776
National Forest Management Act, statement, **1976–77:** 946
National Mass Transportation Assistance Act of 1974, remarks, **1974:** 261
National Science and Technology Policy, Organization, and Priorities Act of 1976, remarks and statement, **1976–77:** 451, 452

Legislation, approved—*continued*
National swine flu immunization program, remarks and statement, **1976–77:** 341, 342, 723
Naval Petroleum Reserves Production Act of 1976, remarks and statement, **1976–77:** 298, 299
New River, N.C., remarks, **1976–77:** 771
Northern Mariana Islands, covenant establishing commonwealth status, remarks and statement, **1976–77:** 255, 256
Office of the Inspector General, Department of Health, Education, and Welfare, statement, **1976–77:** 901
Older American Amendments of 1975, statement, **1975:** 698
Olson, Dr. Frank, relief of survivors, statement, **1976–77:** 883
Olympic Winter Games Authorization Act, statement, **1976–77:** 829
Packers and Stockyards Act of 1921, amendments, remarks and statement, **1976–77:** 774, 775
Point Reyes National Seashore, Calif., statement, **1976–77:** 916
Postal Reorganization Act Amendments, statement, **1976–77:** 810
Presidential Recordings and Materials Preservation Act, statement, **1974:** 313
Privacy Act of 1974, statement, **1975:** 1
Public Broadcasting Financing Act of 1975, statement, **1976–77:** 2
Public Safety Officers' Benefits Act of 1976, remarks and statement, **1976–77:** 827, 828
Public Works and Economic Development Act of 1965, extension, statement, **1974:** 108
Public Works Employment Appropriations Act, statement, **1976–77:** 845
Public Works for Water and Power Development and Atomic Energy Commission Appropriation Act, 1975, statement, **1974:** 40
Railroad Revitalization and Regulatory Reform Act, remarks and statement, **1976–77:** 58, 59
Reclamation Authorization Act of 1975, statement, **1976–77:** 201
Reclamation Development Act of 1974, statement, **1974:** 202
Resource Conservation and Recovery Act, statement, **1976–77:** 938
Rural Electrification Administration Technical Amendments Act, statement, **1976–77:** 928
Rural research and development activities, remarks, **1976–77:** 301
Safe Drinking Water Act, statement, **1974:** 305

Legislation, approved—*continued*
Sea Grant Program Improvement Act of 1976, statement, **1976–77:** 874
Second Supplemental Appropriations Act, remarks, **1976–77:** 545
Securities Acts Amendments of 1975, statement, **1975:** 308
Sinai Pennisula early warning system, U.S. participation, remarks, **1975:** 625
Small Business Amendments of 1974, statement, **1974:** 34
Small Business Omnibus Bill, statement, **1976–77:** 558
Smithsonian Institution, museum support facilities, statement, **1975:** 576
Social Security Act, child support amendments, statement, **1975:** 487
Social Services Amendments of 1974, statement, **1975:** 14
Spanish Americans, publication of economic and social statistics, remarks and statement, **1976–77:** 596, 597
Speedy Trial Act of 1974, statement, **1975:** 7
State and Local Fiscal Assistance Amendments of 1976, remarks, **1976–77:** 890
Summer youth employment appropriations, remarks, **1975:** 333
Supplementary Security Income Bill, statement, **1976–77:** 721
Tax Reduction Act of 1975, remarks, **1975:** 164
Tax Reform Act of 1976, remarks and statement, **1976–77:** 847, 848
Teton Dam disaster assistance, remarks, **1976–77:** 758
Tourism programs appropriations, remarks, **1975:** 389
Toxic Substances Control Act, statement, **1976–77:** 882
Trade Act of 1974, remarks, **1975:** 2
Transportation Safety Act of 1974, statement, **1975:** 9
Turkey, U.S. military assistance restriction, statement, **1974:** 164
United States Grain Standards Act, statement, **1976–77:** 939
Valley Forge National Historical Park, Pa., establishment, remarks, **1976–77:** 644
Valley Forge State Park, display of flag, statement, **1975:** 380
Veterans benefits, remarks and statements, **1976–77:** 832, 833, 903, 940
Veterans Day, bill redesignating observance date, statement, **1975:** 575
Veterans Disability Compensation and Survivor Benefits Act of 1975, statement, **1975:** 478
Voting Rights Act of 1965, extension, remarks, **1975:** 477

Legislation, approved—*continued*
Waste water treatment plants, loan guarantees for construction, statement, **1976–77:** 923
Wetlands Loan Extension Act of 1976, statement, **1976–77:** 106
Whale Conservation and Protection Study Act, statement, **1976–77:** 910
Youth Conservation Corps, statement, **1974:** 47
Legislative Branch Appropriation Act, 1977, **1976–77:** 841
Legislative Council of the National Retired Teachers Association, **1976–77:** 24
Lemnitzer, Gen. Lyman L., **1975:** 19n.; **1976–77:** 199
Lenoir Rhyne College, **1976–77:** 240
Leonard, Will E., Jr., **1976–77:** 780, 796
Leone, Giovanni, **1974:** 100, 104, 105; **1975:** 301, 302, 305
Leonov, Col. Aleksei, **1975:** 412, 624
Letters, messages, telegrams
American National Red Cross, letter accepting honorary chairmanship, **1974:** 11
Apollo-Soyuz Test Project crews, message prior to launch of mission, **1975:** 405
Beame, Mayor Abraham D., letter on New York City's financial assistance request, **1975:** 254
Benny, Jack, death, telegram to Mrs. Jack Benny, **1974:** 322
Black History Month, **1976–77:** 74
Burch, Dean, letter authorizing establishment of President Ford Committee, **1975:** 343
Caplin, Mortimer M., letter on civil service merit system, **1975:** 111
Carter, Jimmy, telegram, **1976–77:** 908, 1014
Chinese New Year, message, **1976–77:** 42
Cigarette tar and nicotine regulation, letter to National Cancer Advisory Board chairman, **1974:** 169
Data collection by the Federal Government, letter to heads of departments and agencies, **1976–77:** 173
District of Columbia city council chairman, message disapproving shopbook rule bill, **1976–77:** 146
Egan, John Patrick, death, telegram to Mrs. Egan, **1975:** 118
Federal cost reduction campaign, message to Federal civilian and military personnel, **1975:** 245
Ferrier, President Johan Henri Eliza, letter on U.S. recognition of Surinam, **1975:** 693
Flanigan, Peter M., letter accepting withdrawal of nomination to be U.S. Ambassador to Spain, **1974:** 237
Fraser, Malcolm, letter on his election as Australian Prime Minister, **1975:** 727

Letters, messages, telegrams—*continued*
Generalized System of Preferences, removal of products from duty-free treatment, letter to United States International Trade Commission Chairman, **1976–77:** 780
Gibson, Andrew E., letter accepting withdrawal of candidacy for Federal Energy Administrator, **1974:** 228
Hart, Mrs. Philip A., letter on clemency program, **1976–77:** 1077
Inflation, telegram to State and local officials, **1974:** 146
International Clergy Week, **1976–77:** 43
International Commission for the Northwest Atlantic Fisheries, message to special meeting, **1975:** 584
International Olympic Committee, letter to President Killanin, **1976–77:** 902
International Trade Commission, Chairman, Imports of dry milk mixtures and other imports, letter, **1976–77:** 268
Israeli rescue of hostages in Uganda, letter to Israeli Prime Minister Yitzhak Rabin, **1976–77:** 648
Kingsley, Daniel T., letter accepting withdrawal of nomination to be a Federal Power Commissioner, **1974:** 243
Lopez Arellano, President Oswaldo, letter about Honduran hurricane disaster, **1974:** 95
Machel, President Samora Moises, letter on U.S. recognition of Mozambique, **1975:** 355
Malraux, André, death, message to French President Giscard d'Estaing, **1976–77:** 1021
McCabe, Edward A., election of directors of the Student Loan Marketing Association, **1975:** 55
Miller, Arnold R., telegram on 85th anniversary of the United Mine Workers of America, **1975:** 47
National Conference of Catholic Bishops, letter to Archbishop Joseph L. Bernardin, **1976–77:** 769
National Handicapped Awareness, Week, message, **1976–77:** 490
National Newspaper Carrier Day, message, **1976–77:** 878
National Newspaper Week, message, **1976–77:** 879
Naval Petroleum Reserves Production Act, letter to Secretary of the Interior, Federal Energy Administrator, and Secretary of the Navy, **1976–77:** 789
Pereira, President Aristides, letter on U.S. recognition of the Republic of Cape Verde, **1975:** 404
President's papers, donation to Government, letter to Archivist of U.S. and president of University of Michigan, **1976–77:** 1028

Letters, messages, telegrams—*continued*
Ramadan, message, **1976–77:** 821
Republican Vice-Presidential candidate selection, letter to Convention delegates, **1976–77:** 706
Rockefeller, Nelson A., letter on President's Panel on Federal Compensation, **1975:** 729
Silberman, Laurence H., letter on United States participation in the International Labor Organization, **1976–77:** 26
Sugar imports, letter to United States International Trade Commission Chairman, **1976–77:** 796
See also Congress, communications to; Days of observance; Memorandums to Federal officials and agencies; Resignations and retirements.
Levey, Jeanne, **1976–77:** 98
Levi, Edward H., **1975:** 79, 479 [6], 678 [18]; **1976–77:** 116, 497, 560 [6], 626, 709, 763 [18], 972, 1079
Lewis, Drew, **1974:** 131
Lexington, Mass., **1975:** 199
Libby, Mont., **1975:** 498
Libby Dam, **1975:** 498
Liberia, President William R. Tolbert, Jr., **1976–77:** 794, 798
Library of Congress
American Folklife Center, **1976–77:** 5
Librarian, **1975:** 672
Library and Information Services, White House Conference on, **1976–77:** 266 [6], 678
Libya, news conference remarks, **1976–77:** 674 [11, 12]
Liinamaa, Keijo, **1975:** 457n.
Lilly Endowment Continuing Conference for the Liberal Arts, **1974:** 281
Lima, Ohio, **1976–77:** 578
Lincoln, Abraham, **1975:** 86; **1976–77:** 80
Lincoln, George A., **1975:** 284
Lincoln, Ill., **1976–77:** 907
Lincoln, Nebr., **1974:** 153; **1976–77:** 445, 446
Lincoln Day Dinner, **1976–77:** 221
Lincoln Home National Visitor's Center, **1976–77:** 180
Lindbergh, Charles A., **1974:** 37
Linz, Federal Republic of Germany, **1975:** 444
Lippmann, Walter, **1974:** 298
Lisagor, Peter, **1976–77:** 1027
Lithuania, **1975:** 430
Little, Franklin Rockefeller, **1975:** 205
Little Beaver Creek, Ohio, **1976–77:** 72
Little League World Series, **1974:** 36
Litton, Repr. Jerry, **1976–77:** 713
Livestock Credit Act, Emergency
Amendments, **1975:** 332
Extension, **1976–77:** 905

Livestock feed assistance, emergency, **1976–77:** 1029
Livestock industry, **1976–77:** 422
Livonia, Mich., **1976–77:** 1008
Loans
  Billing revisions, **1974:** 200
  Disaster, **1974:** 34, 265
  Discrimination, **1974:** 30, 200; **1976–77:** 3
  Interest rate regulation, **1974:** 199
  Rural electric and telephone program, deferrals and rescissions, **1974:** 89
  Small business, **1974:** 34
  State usury laws, exemptions, **1974:** 199
  See also Mortgages.
Local governments.
  See State and local governments.
Locks and Dam, **1976–77:** 26, 181, 203, 738
Logan Community College, John A., **1976–77:** 192
Long Beach, Calif., **1974:** 212
Longview, Tex., **1976–77:** 376
Lopez Arellano, Oswaldo, **1974:** 95
Lopez Michelsen, Alfonso, **1975:** 586, 587, 589
Los Angeles, Calif., **1974:** 211; **1975:** 573, 647, 648; **1976–77:** 262, 863
Los Angeles Press Club, **1976–77:** 523
Louisiana
  Bossier City Ambassador's Club, **1976–77:** 374
  Meeting with State officials, **1976–77:** 373
  President's visits, **1975:** 206–208; **1976–77:** 371–374, 812
  U.S. district judge, **1976–77:** 372, 373 [6]
  Wilderness area, **1974:** 277
Louisiana National Guard Military Ball, **1976–77:** 375
Louisville, Ky., **1974:** 175; **1975:** 552 [10], 554 [3], 620 [5]; **1976–77:** 481–484
Low, George M., **1974:** 275
Lowell Historic Canal District Commission, **1975:** 13
Low-income persons
  Administration programs, **1975:** 554 [9]
  Economic opportunities report, **1975:** 544
  Federal assistance, **1975:** 138 [5], 698; **1976–77:** 64
  Food stamp program, **1975:** 28, 36 [22], 64, 89, 143, 435, 620 [14], 622 [5, 19], 626, 634, 647; **1976–77:** 122
  Health care programs, **1976–77:** 136
  School lunch and child nutrition programs, **1975:** 609, 615 [8], 616 [15], 620 [11]
  Social services, **1976–77:** 126
  Tax reduction, effect, **1975:** 622 [22]
Loy Norris High School, **1975:** 337
Lozano, Ignatio, **1976–77:** 702
Lubavitch, American Friends of, **1975:** 265
Lubbock, Tex., **1976–77:** 400–404
Luce, Claire Boothe, **1976–77:** 199
Lugar, Richard G., **1974:** 154
Lujan, Repr. Manuel, Jr., **1976–77:** 702
Lukash, Rear Adm. William M., **1974:** 80 [1], 155
Luke Air Force Base, Ariz., **1974:** 235
Lumber industry, Greater Houston Builders and Contractors Association, **1976–77:** 383
Lung disease, **1974:** 97, 205; **1975:** 259, 361; **1976–77:** 491, 496
Lung Institute, National Heart and, **1974:** 97
Lunney, Glynn S., **1975:** 482
Luns, Joseph M.A.H., **1975:** 287, 290 [1]
Lutcher, La., **1976–77:** 812
Lutheran Church, American, **1974:** 134
Luxembourg
  Ambassador to U.S., **1975:** 674
  Prime Minister Gaston Thorn, **1975:** 289n., 674
Lyndon Baines Johnson Memorial Grove, **1976–77:** 304
Lynn, James T., **1974:** 29, 109, 214; **1975:** 81, 626; **1976–77:** 23 (p. 59, 65, 66), 315, 687

MacAvoy, Paul W., **1976–77:** 30, 315, 964
Machel, Samora Moises, **1975:** 355
Mack, Bill, **1974:** 184
Mackin, Catherine, **1976–77:** 778
Mackinac Island, Mich., **1975:** 400
MacLeish, Archibald, **1976–77:** 1052
MacNeil, Robert, **1975:** 276
Madigan, Repr. Edward R., **1974:** 191
Madrid, Spain, **1975:** 291, 292, 293, 294
Magna Carta delegation, **1976–77:** 554
Mahon, Repr. George H., **1974:** 287; **1975:** 347; **1976–77:** 611, 796
Maine, President's visit, **1975:** 508, 509
Major Violators Unit, **1974:** 96
Malaysia
  Military sales credit, **1975:** 649
  Prime Minister Tun Abdul Razak, **1976–77:** 18
Malibu, Calif., **1975:** 574
Malkiel, Burton, **1976–77:** 30
Mallary, Repr. Richard W., **1974:** 118
Malraux, André, **1976–77:** 1021
Man of the Year award, **1975:** 103
Management and Budget, Office of
  Alternative energy sources study, **1976–77:** 1045
  Consumer representation plans, **1976–77:** 820
  Deputy Director, **1976–77:** 23 (p. 66), 64
  Director, **1974:** 41, 109, 115, 117, 303; **1975:** 20, 81, 92, 311, 328, 626; **1976–77:** 23 (p. 59, 65, 66), 45, 315, 626, 687, 844, 1043
  Federal civilian positions, reduction, **1974:** 43
  Federal grant programs, **1976–77:** 944
  Letter to Congressional Committee Chairmen on Federal Compensation, **1976–77:** 1074
  National Security and International Affairs, Associate Director, **1976–77:** 23 (p. 59)
  Privacy legislation, **1974:** 125

Manchester, N.H., **1975:** 193; **1976–77:** 63
Manila, Philippines, **1975:** 711, 712, 714
Mann, Repr. James, R., **1974:** 155
Manpower Report of the President, **1975:** 209
Mansfield, Sen. Mike, **1974:** 21, 135
Mao Tse-tung, **1975:** 706n.; **1976–77:** 767
March of Dimes Birth Defects Prevention Month, January 1976, **1975:** 734
March of Dimes National Poster Child, **1975:** 734
Marcos, Ferdinand E., **1975:** 711, 712, 713, 714
Marijuana, **1975:** 565 [19], 615 [12], 620 [8]; **1976–77:** 68 [3], 215 [15], 266 [8], 325 [8]
Marine Corps, U.S., **1975:** 204 [1], 667; **1976–77:** 378 [4]
Marine Mammal Protection Act of 1972, **1975:** 730
Marion, Ill., **1976–77:** 191, 192
Maritime Administration, **1974:** 327; **1975:** 18
Maritime Consultative Organization, Inter-Governmental, **1974:** 157; **1975:** 391
Maritime industry.
  See under Shipping.
Markley, Rodney W., Jr., **1976–77:** 831
Marriott, J. Willard, Sr., **1976–77:** 642
Marrs, Theodore C., **1976–77:** 670
Marsh, John O., Jr., **1974:** 155
Marshals, Deputy U.S., **1974:** 7
Martin, Graham, **1975:** 243 [10]
Martin, Repr. James G., **1974:** 174; **1976–77:** 234
Martin, James S., Jr., **1976–77:** 679
Martin, John B., **1976–77:** 932
Martinez, Samuel R., **1976–77:** 343, 702
Martinique, French West Indies, **1974:** 297, 300, 301
Maryland
  President's visits, **1975:** 307, 379, 394, 516, 517, 523, 702; **1976–77:** 671
  Primary results, **1976–77:** 497
  Wilderness areas, **1974:** 276, 277
Masonic National Memorial, George Washington, **1975:** 95
Mass transit, **1974:** 65, 127 [17]; **1975:** 85 [3], 128, 383, 393
Mass Transportation Administration, Urban, **1974:** 65
Mass Transportation Assistance Act of 1974, National, **1974:** 240, 261
Massachusetts
  Boston school desegregation, **1974:** 127 [20], 142
  Lowell Historic Canal District, **1975:** 13
  Oilspill, **1976–77:** 1036
  President's visits, **1975:** 197–199, 662–665
  Wilderness area, **1974:** 277
Mastics, George, **1974:** 184
Mathews, David, **1975:** 480; **1976–77:** 23 (p. 62), 626, 674 [20], 688, 708, 715, 723
Mathias, Sen. Charles McC., Jr., **1975:** 695 [11]
Mathias, Repr. Robert B., **1974:** 213
Matia, Paul, **1974:** 184
Mayaguez, SS, **1975:** 256, 257, 276 [2], 426; **1976–77:** 287 [10], 356 [10], 852, 854
Mayer, Jean, **1975:** 230
Maynard, Robert, **1976–77:** 947
Mayne, Repr. Wiley, **1974:** 155, 188, 210
Mayors, telegram on inflation-fighting efforts, **1974:** 146, 151
Mayors, U.S. Conference of, **1976–77:** 38
MBFR.
  See Mutual and balanced force reductions.
McCabe, Edward A., **1975:** 55
McClellan, Sen. John L., **1975:** 347; **1976–77:** 611, 797
McClory, Repr. Robert, **1974:** 191
McCloy, John J., **1975:** 331
McCollister, John Y., **1974:** 153
McCormack, John W., **1976–77:** 1026
McGee, Sen. Gale W., **1976–77:** 810
McLucas, John L., **1976–77:** 661, 941
Meany, George, **1974:** 109; **1975:** 85 [5], 539; **1976–77:** 23 (p. 65), 288
Meat imports, **1974:** 210, 219
Medal for Distinguished Public Service, Department of Defense, **1976–77:** 267
Medford, Oreg., **1976–77:** 501, 502
Medicaid, **1974:** 319
Medical care.
  See Health and medical care.
Medical Device Amendments of 1976, **1976–77:** 542
Medical malpractice insurance, **1976–77:** 95, 189 [4], 207 [5]
Medical Sciences, National Institute of General, **1974:** 197
Medicare, **1974:** 319; **1975:** 126; **1976–77:** 19, 23 (p. 57, 58, 62, 63, 66), 24, 69, 70, 89, 92, 207 [5], 512, 673, 685
"Meet the Press" interview, **1975:** 666
Meetings with agency and department heads, Drug Enforcement Administration, exchange of remarks with Administrator, **1976–77:** 129
Meetings with Foreign Leaders
  Australia, Prime Minister J. Malcolm Fraser, **1976–77:** 692, 696
  Austria, Chancellor Bruno Kreisky, **1974:** 227, 229; **1975:** 296n., 298
  Belgium
    King Baudouin, **1975:** 287, 289n.
    Prime Minister Leo Tindemans, **1975:** 287
  Canada, Prime Minister Pierre Elliott Trudeau, **1974:** 278; **1975:** 290n.; **1976–77:** 600
  China, People's Republic of
    Chairman Mao Tse-tung, **1975:** 706n.
    Prime Minister Lee Kuan Yew, **1975:** 249
    Vice-Premier Teng Hsiao-ping, **1975:** 706, 708
  Colombia, President Alfonso Lopez Michelsen, **1975:** 586, 587, 589

Meetings with Foreign Leaders—*continued*
Commission of the European Communities, President François-Xavier Ortoli, **1975:** 290n.
Conference on Security and Cooperation in Europe, **1975:** 459
Denmark
Prime Minister Anker Jørgenson, **1975:** 289n.
Queen Margrethe, **1976–77:** 455
Economic Summit Meeting, **1975:** 680
Egypt, President Anwar el-Sadat, **1975:** 297, 298, 299, 300, 642–644, 654
Finland, President Urho Kekkonen, **1975:** 455n., 456n., 459n.; **1976–77:** 707, 711
France, President Valéry Giscard d'Estaing, **1974:** 297, 300–302; **1975:** 289n., 457n., 459n., 680; **1976–77:** 489, 494, 495, 499
Germany, Federal Republic of
Chancellor Helmut Schmidt, **1974:** 279, 282, 284; **1975:** 289n., 440, 441, 444, 457n., 680n.; **1976–77:** 668, 669, 671
President Walter Scheel, **1975:** 330, 331, 334, 443
Greece, Prime Minister Constantine Caramalis, **1975:** 289n., 456n.
Iceland, Prime Minister Geir Hallgrímsson, **1975:** 290n.
Indonesia, President Suharto, **1975:** 381, 709, 710
Iran, Shah Mohammad Reza Pahlavi, **1975:** 258, 261, 263
Ireland, Prime Minister Liam M. Cosgrave, **1976–77:** 222, 225, 226
Israel, Prime Minister Yitzhak Rabin, **1974:** 66, 75; **1975:** 322; **1976–77:** 32, 34, 41
Italy
President Giovanni Leone, **1974:** 100, 104, 105; **1975:** 301, 302, 305, 459n.
Prime Minister Aldo Moro, **1975:** 302, 680n.
Prime Minister Giulio Andreotti, **1976–77:** 1023, 1024
Japan
Emperor Hirohito, **1974:** 245, 249, 250; **1975:** 603, 606, 610
Prime Minister Kakuei Tanaka, **1974:** 244, 249
Prime Minister Takeo Miki, **1975:** 474–476, 680n.; **1976–77:** 623, 624
Jordan, King Hussein I, **1974:** 12, 14; **1975:** 222; **1976–77:** 271, 274
Korea, Republic of, President Park Chung Hee, **1974:** 252, 254, 255
Liberia, President William R. Tolbert, Jr., **1976–77:** 794, 798
Luxembourg, Prime Minister Gaston Thorn, **1975:** 289n., 674
Mexico, President Luis Echeverría Alvarez, **1974:** 177–180
Netherlands, Prime Minister Johannes den Uyl, **1975:** 255

Meetings with Foreign Leaders—*continued*
North Atlantic Treaty Organization Council, **1975:** 289
Norway, Prime Minister Trygve Bratteli, **1975:** 290n.
Pakistan, Prime Minister Zulfikar Ali Bhutto, **1975:** 74, 78
Philippines, President Ferdinand E. Marcos, **1975:** 711–14
Poland, First Secretary Edward Gierek, **1974:** 119, 123, 128–30, 143; **1975:** 448–451, 454
Portugal
President Francisco da Costa Gomes, **1974:** 168
Prime Minister Vasco Gonçalves, **1975:** 289n.
Romania, President Nicolae Ceausescu, **1975:** 461–65
Spain
Generalissimo Francisco Franco, **1975:** 291, 292n., 294
Juan Carlos (as King), **1976–77:** 547, 549, 553
Juan Carlos (as Prince), **1975:** 293n.
President of Government Carlos Arias Navarro, **1975:** 292n., 293, 459n.
Tunisia, Prime Minister Hedi Nouira, **1975:** 233
Turkey, Prime Minister Süleyman Demirel, **1975:** 289n., 457
Union of Soviet Socialist Republics, General Secretary L. I. Brezhnev, **1974:** 256–58; **1975:** 456, 460 [1]
United Kingdom
Prime Minister Harold Wilson, **1975:** 57, 61, 290n., 456n., 457n., 680n.
Queen Elizabeth II, **1976–77:** 654, 656
Vatican, Pope Paul VI, **1975:** 304n.
Yugoslavia
President Josip Broz Tito, **1975:** 466–469, 471
Prime Minister Dzemal Bijedic, **1975:** 145, 146, 468n.
Zambia, President Kenneth D. Kaunda, **1975:** 200
Meir, Golda, **1976–77:** 497
Meisch, Adrien, **1975:** 674
Meloy, Francis E., Jr., **1976–77:** 599, 604, 606
Melvin, Ill., **1974:** 190
Memorandums of disapproval.
See Veto messages and memorandums of disapproval.
Memorandum to Federal officials, employees, and agencies
Agricultural Policy Committee, establishment, **1976–77:** 200
Airline safety, **1975:** 725
Arab boycotts of American businesses, **1976–77:** 859
Budgets cuts, Fiscal Year 1975, **1974:** 132
Budget deferrals and rescissions, **1974:** 90; **1975:** 133

Memorandum to Federal officials—*continued*
Career civil service, **1974:** 91
Combined Federal Campaign, **1974:** 103; **1975:** 413, 564; **1976–77:** 449, 450, 590
Commission on CIA Activities Within the United States, **1975:** 323, 324
Consumer representation plans, **1976–77:** 820
Domestic Council, **1975:** 92
Domestic Council Committee on Illegal Aliens, establishment, **1975:** 20
Drug Abuse Prevention, Treatment, and Rehabilitation, Cabinet Committee on, **1976–77:** 465
Drug Law Enforcement, Cabinet Committee for, **1976–77:** 464
Federal cost reduction campaign, **1975:** 244, 722
Federal employment, equal opportunity, **1975:** 124
Federal energy conservation, **1974:** 165
Federal Energy Management Program, establishment, **1976–77:** 1015
Federal Executive Boards, annual reports, **1975:** 151; **1976–77:** 660
Federal Summer Employment Program for Youth, **1975:** 178; **1976–77:** 310, 312
Foreign boycott practices, **1975:** 690
General schedule classification, **1976–77:** 539
Handicapped persons, Federal employment, **1975:** 156
Interdepartmental Savings Bond Committee, Chairman, **1975:** 159, 627; **1976–77:** 13
Minority banks, Federal deposits, **1975:** 639
Minority business development program, **1974:** 291
Natural gas shortages, **1975:** 661
Noise standards for commercial aircraft, memorandum for Federal Aviation Administrator, **1976–77:** 941
Occupational safety and health programs, **1975:** 65
President's Committee on Urban Development and Neighborhood Revitalization, **1976–77:** 626
President's Panel on Federal Compensation, establishment, **1975:** 328
Recombinant DNA experiments, **1976–77:** 801
Red Cross Month, **1975:** 104; **1976–77:** 134
Special Assistant for Indian Affairs, designation, **1976–77:** 741
Special Representative for Trade Negotiations
Footwear industry, **1976–77:** 346
Import relief for earthenware industry, **1976–77:** 409
Stainless steel flatware industry, **1976–77:** 410
Swine flu immunization program, **1976–77:** 280
Task Force on Questionable Corporate Payments Abroad, establishment, **1976–77:** 275

Memorandum to Federal officials—*continued*
Textile Trade Policy Group, establishment, **1975:** 311
Transition of the Presidency, **1974:** 3
U.S. Savings Bond program, **1975:** 159
Vietnam war era selective service discharges, Service Secretaries, Commandant of the Coast Guard, and Attorney General, **1976–77:** 1076
See also Appendix B, 1974.
Memorial Day, **1975:** 278; **1976–77:** 544
Memphis, Tenn., **1976–77:** 477–480
Mental Retardation, President's Committee on, **1974:** 136
Merchant marine, **1975:** 207
Metric Board, United States, **1975:** 744
Metric Conversion Act of 1975, **1975:** 744
Mexico
Drug abuse message, **1976–77:** 368
Drug trafficking, illicit, **1975:** 748
Illegal aliens, **1976–77:** 64
Migrant farmworkers, **1974:** 179 [4]
News conference remarks, **1976–77:** 325 [1, 13]
Oil deposits, **1974:** 179 [2, 6]
President Luis Echeverría Alvarez, **1974:** 127 [1], 177, 178, 179, 180; **1976–77:** 137
President's intention to visit, **1974:** 127 [1]
President's visit, **1974:** 177
Mexico-United States Interparliamentary Conference, **1976–77:** 137
MIA's.
See Missing in action.
Michel, Repr. Robert H., **1974:** 191
Michigan
Gov. William G. Milliken, **1975:** 622 [2]
Kalamazoo high school students, **1975:** 337
President's visits, **1974:** 94, 134, 135, 207–209; **1975:** 398–401, 622, 623; **1976–77:** 49, 460–463, 485–488, 783, 784, 1007–1010, 1013, 1033
Republican State Convention, **1974:** 35
Michigan Club, University of, **1975:** 122
Mid-America Committee for International Business and Government Cooperation, **1975:** 395
Middendorf, J. William, II, **1975:** 693n.
Middle East
Administration policy, **1974:** 6; **1975:** 276 [7], 354 [3], 581 [7], 649, 650; **1976–77:** 401 [4], 461
Arab boycott of American businesses, **1976–77:** 854, 859, 925 [5], 925 [8]
Arab investment in the United States, **1975:** 72 [11]
B'nai B'rith Convention, remarks, **1976–77:** 766
Campaign debate remarks, **1976–77:** 854
Civilian technicians in U.N. zone, **1975:** 501 [6], 510, 517, 522, 526, 528, 530, 552 [7], 565 [9], 573 [4], 581 [2], 600 [8], 620 [1], 625, 649, 655 [5]

Middle East—*continued*
Early warning system in the Sinai Peninsula, **1975:** 501 [6], 522, 523, 526, 597, 625
Egyptian-Israeli troop disengagement agreement, **1975:** 515, 516, 517, 522, 523, 530, 552 [7], 600 [8], 625
Geneva Conference, **1974:** 271 [3, 12]
Kissinger, Secretary of State Henry A., visits, **1975:** 153, 523
NATO involvement, **1975:** 276 [7]
Nuclear capability for Middle East nations, **1975:** 578 [5]
Palestine Liberation Organization, **1975:** 204 [7], 695 [23]
Palestinian situation, **1975:** 655 [1]
Peace negotiations, **1974:** 124, 195 [8], 226, 236 [20, 21], 271 [3, 12], Appendix D; **1975:** 45 [2], 85 [1], 153, 179, 204 [7], 243 [2], 290 [10], 297, 299, 316 [9, 11], 322, 460 [9], 479 [8], 489, 501 [6], 502 [16], 517, 597, 625, 642, 648 [7], 695 [23]; **1976–77:** 560 [8], 569
President's visit, possibility, **1975:** 717
Soviet involvement, **1975:** 45 [2], 204 [7], 276 [7], 479 [8]; **1976–77:** 402 [2]
State of the Union Address, **1976–77:** 1057
United Nations involvement, **1974:** 86; **1975:** 276 [7], 517, 526, 648 [7], 655 [5]; **1976–77:** 842
U.S. military aid, **1975:** 36 [3], 260; **1976–77:** 68 [11], 210 [2], 420 [3, 4]
U.S. military intervention, **1975:** 36 [10], 45 [2], 109 [2], 204 [7], 276 [5], 502 [16], 581 [7]
U.S. Sinai Support Mission, **1976–77:** 411
U.S.-Soviet joint communique, **1974:** 258
See also specific country.
Middletown, Ohio, **1976–77:** 574
Midland, Tex., **1975:** 561, 562
Migrant farmworkers, **1974:** 179 [4], 205, 286
Migratory waterfowl, **1976–77:** 106
Miki, Takeo, **1975:** 474, 475, 476, 680n.; **1976–77:** 621, 623, 624
Military, U.S.
See Armed Forces, U.S.
Military assistance.
See Foreign assistance.
Military Assistance Program, **1975:** 161
Military Construction Authorization Act, 1977, **1976–77:** 834
Military construction bill, veto, **1976–77:** 638
Military deserters and draft evaders, **1974:** 16, 77, 78, 80 [10], 236 [13], 266, 329; **1975:** 36 [14], 58, 113, 243 [5], 566, 573 [12]; **1976–77:** 68 [20], 585, 803
Military Justice, Uniform Code of, **1974:** 78; **1975:** 58
Military Order of World Wars, Atlanta Chapter, **1976–77:** 359
Military Selective Service Act, **1974:** 78; **1975:** 58
Milk.
See Dairy products.
Miller, Arnold R., **1974:** 109; **1975:** 47
Miller, Capt. Charles T., **1975:** 426; **1976–77:** 854
Miller, Repr. Clarence E., **1974:** 184
Miller, Herbert J., **1974:** 155
Milliken, Gov. William G., **1974:** 35, 135, 209; **1975:** 622 [2]; **1976–77:** 726
Milonowski, John, **1976–77:** 805
Miltich, Paul A., **1974:** 2
Milwaukee, Wis., **1975:** 501, 502, 503, 651, 652; **1976–77:** 282–85, 989, 990
Mindszenty, József Cardinal, **1975:** 242
Mineral interests, **1974:** 111
Mines and mining
Black lung legislation, **1974:** 205; **1976–77:** 192 [7]
Coal industry, White House meeting, **1975:** 152
Coal miners, education and health concerns, **1975:** 616 [9]
Development, **1975:** 488 [11]
Health programs, **1975:** 682
Surface mining legislation, **1974:** 72, 121, 131, 240, 326; **1975:** 28, 64, 75, 152, 270, 488 [9], 615 [10], 616 [16]; **1976–77:** 209 [12]
United Mine Workers of America, **1975:** 47
Minneapolis, Minn., **1975:** 492, 493, 494
Minnesota
President's visit, **1975:** 492–494
Wilderness areas, **1974:** 276, 277
Minorities
Banks, Federal deposits, **1975:** 639
Black History Month, **1976–77:** 74
Business
Development programs, **1974:** 291; **1975:** 369, 502 [9]
Office of Minority Business, legislation, **1976–77:** 321 [3]
Campaign debate remarks, **1976–77:** 947
Civil rights enforcement, **1975:** 496 [5]
Federal employment, **1975:** 124
General revenue sharing, **1975:** 214
Hispanic Heritage Week, National, proclamation, **1974:** 48, 49
Job training, **1975:** 71
News conference remarks, **1976–77:** 387 [23], 925 [12]
Unemployment, **1975:** 243 [11], 502 [7], 602 [9], 616 [7]
Voting rights, **1975:** 27, 43, 48, 410, 422, 427, 477
See also specific groups.
Minority Business Enterprise, Office of, **1974:** 291
Minuteman III, **1976–77:** 387 [33]
MIRV's, **1976–77:** 854
Missiles
Antiballistic missiles, **1974:** 85; **1975:** 119
Hawk missiles, **1975:** 573 [4]
Intercontinental ballistic missiles, **1974:** 257, 271 [1]

Missiles—*continued*
Multiple independently targetable reentry vehicles, **1974:** 257, 271 [1, 4, 5, 7, 10], Appendix D
Pershing missiles, **1975:** 565 [2, 11], 573 [4], 578 [5], 582 [3], 600 [17]
See also Arms and weapons; Strategic arms limitation.
Missing in action, **1974:** 83, 192; **1975:** 411, 552 [9], 600 [13], 716; **1976–77:** 240 [3], 354 [7], 546, 689, 762, 854
Mission Viejo, Calif., **1976–77:** 511
Mississippi
President's visit, **1976–77:** 703, 704, 813–816
Wilderness area, **1974:** 277
Mississippi River, Locks and Dam, **1976–77:** 26, 738
Mississippi River Basin Commission, Upper, **1975:** 425
Missouri
Harry S Truman statue, **1976–77:** 447
President's visits, **1974:** 150, 151; **1975:** 551–555, 557; **1976–77:** 7, 8, 588, 589, 726–734, 909, 991, 993
Missouri River Basin Commission, **1975:** 425; **1976–77:** 594
Mitchell, James L., **1974:** 29
Mitchell, Mr. and Mrs. Steven K., **1975:** 272
Mizell, Repr. Wilmer, **1974:** 174
Mizer, George, Jr., **1974:** 183
Mobile, Ala., **1976–77:** 817
Model Cities program, **1974:** 29, 30, 39 [21]
Moghrabi, Zohair, **1976–77:** 606
Mohammed Shrine Temple, Peoria, Ill., **1976–77:** 186
Moley, Raymond, **1975:** 98
Monetary Fund, International, **1974:** 110, 284, 302; **1976–77:** 621, 986
Monopolies, **1976–77:** 321 [12]
Monroe, Bill, **1975:** 666
Montana
President's visit, **1975:** 498
Wilderness areas, **1974:** 276, 277
Monterey, U.S.S., **1975:** 277
Monticello, Va., **1976–77:** 649
Mood of country, **1975:** 502 [15]
Moody, Rush, Jr., **1975:** 127
Moore, Sara Jane, **1975:** 583 ftn.
Moorhead, Repr. William S., **1974:** 31
Morality in United States, President's assessment, **1976–77:** 283
Morgan, Col. Ernest R., **1975:** 396 [1, 7]
Morgan, Repr. Thomas E., **1975:** 347, 387; **1976–77:** 611, 797
Morhouse, L. Judson, **1974:** 127 [16]
Moro, Aldo, **1975:** 302, 459n., 680n.; **1976–77:** 621
Mortgages
Credit availability, **1974:** 200, 234, 240; **1976–77:** 3
Mortgages—*continued*
Discrimination, **1974:** 30, 200; **1976–77:** 3
Federal assistance, **1975:** 350, 351, 354 [1], 372; **1974:** 30, 234
Federal deposit insurance legislation, **1974:** 200
Housing, **1974:** 30, 131, 162; **1976–77:** 3
Interest rates, **1975:** 243 [15]
Tax credit, **1975:** 144
Morton, Rogers C. B., **1974:** 109, 121, 127 [6], 135, 165, 166, 195 [1, 10, 20], 233, 236 [9], Appendix D; **1975:** 227, 627, 657 [1], 678 [1]; **1976–77:** 273, 726, 740, 742
Mosher, Repr. Charles A., **1974:** 184
Motor carrier industry, **1975:** 675, 678 [6]; **1976–77:** 685
Motor Vehicle and Schoolbus Safety Amendments of 1974, **1974:** 194
Motor vehicles
Automotive transport research and development bill, veto, **1976–77:** 811
Electric and hybrid vehicle research, development, and demonstration bill, veto, **1976–77:** 777
Emission standards, **1975:** 26, 28, 32, 72 [15], 108, 364, 445, 446; **1976–77:** 947
Fuel efficiency, **1974:** 121; **1975:** 36 [7], 128, 600 [14], 622 [3], 623, 650
General Motors, prices, **1974:** 5, 23
Imports, **1976–77:** 401 [1]
International Conference on Urban Transportation, **1974:** 65
News conference remarks, **1976–77:** 763 [15]
Production, **1976–77:** 118
Safety programs, **1974:** 50; **1975:** 613
Moynihan, Daniel P., **1975:** 365; **1976–77:** 54, 86 [5], 89, 133, 138 [5]
Mozambique
Generalized System of Preferences beneficiary, **1975:** 668
U.S. recognition, **1975:** 355
MPLA.
See Angola—Popular Movement for the Liberation of Angola.
Mullen, Mary, **1976–77:** 24
Multinational corporations, **1976–77:** 1071
Multiple Sclerosis Mother and Father of the Year award, **1976–77:** 454
Multiple Sclerosis Society, National, **1975:** 238
Municipal Assistance Corporation, **1975:** 620 [9], 645, 648
Murchison, Ruby, **1976–77:** 219
Murphy, Betty Southard, **1975:** 97; **1976–77:** 16
Murphy, Robert, **1976–77:** 107 [1, 10], 124, 199
Mutual and balanced force reductions, **1974:** 129, 258, 271 [8], 284; **1975:** 64, 119, 440, 450, 459, 460 [3], 479 [7]; **1976–77:** 701
Myers, George E., **1975:** 230
Myers, Repr. John T., **1974:** 154

Nagako, Empress of Japan, **1974:** 245, 249, 250
Namibia, **1976–77:** 778, 784
Narcotics.
See Drugs and narcotics.
NASA.
See National Aeronautics and Space Administration.
Nash, Col. Edward J., **1975:** 235
Nashua, N.H., **1976–77:** 65
Natchez, SS, **1976–77:** 812
National Advisory Council on Economic Opportunity, **1975:** 544
National Advisory Council on Extension and Continuing Education, **1974:** 133; **1975:** 336
National Aeronautics and Space Administration, **1975:** 180, 482; **1976–77:** 356 [9], 679
National Air and Space Museum, **1976–77:** 631
National Alcoholic Beverage Control Association, **1976–77:** 64
National Alliance of Businessmen, **1974:** 192; **1975:** 174; **1976–77:** 306
National Archives and Records Service, **1976–77:** 639, 1028
National Association for the Advancement of Colored People, **1975:** 369
National Association of Broadcasters, **1975:** 171; **1976–77:** 964
National Association of Evangelicals, **1976–77:** 125
National Association of Food Chains, **1975:** 631
National Association for Foreign Students Affairs, **1975:** 250
National Association of Life Underwriters, **1975:** 579
National Association of Realtors, **1974:** 234
National Association of Secondary School Principals, **1976–77:** 105
National Aviation Experimental Center, **1976–77:** 972
National Baptist Convention, **1975:** 553
National Bicentennial Conference, **1975:** 105
National Cancer Act Amendments of 1974, **1974:** 222
National Cancer Advisory Board, **1974:** 169, 186
National Cancer Institute, **1974:** 186, 222
National Cancer Program, **1974:** 222; **1976–77:** 296
National Capital Housing Authority, **1974:** 231
National Center for Productivity and Quality of Working Life, **1975:** 721
National Civil Service League, **1975:** 111
National Collegiate Athletic Association, **1975:** 22
National Commission on Electronic Fund Transfers, **1976–77:** 3
National Commission on the Observance of International Women's Year, 1975, **1975:** 24, 185; **1976–77:** 634, 651
National Commission on Productivity and Work Quality, **1974:** 121; **1975:** 616 [18]
National Commission on Regulatory Reform, **1974:** 121, 240
National Commission on Supplies and Shortages, **1974:** 114
National Community Christmas Tree, **1974:** 306; **1975:** 736; **1976–77:** 1030
National Conference of Catholic Bishops, **1976–77:** 769
National Conference of Christians and Jews, **1976–77:** 569
National Conference of State Legislatures, **1975:** 216
National Council on the Arts, **1974:** 53; **1975:** 346; **1976–77:** 744
National Council on Crime and Delinquency, **1974:** 181
National Council on Educational Research, **1975:** 253
National defense.
See Defense and national security.
National Defense University, **1976–77:** 1075
National Education Association
Bicentennial commemorative plaque, **1976–77:** 14
Members of the Board, remarks to, **1975:** 234
National Emergencies Act, **1976–77:** 781
National Endowment for the Arts, **1975:** 346, 554 [18]; **1976–77:** 744
National Endowment for the Humanities, **1975:** 325; **1976–77:** 1079
National Energy Outlook Report, **1976–77:** 177
National Entertainment Conference, **1975:** 87
National Environmental Research Center, **1975:** 373
National Epilepsy Month, **1975:** 638
National Exchange Club, **1976–77:** 663
National Explorer Presidents' Congress, **1975:** 177
National Farm Credit Bureau, Directors, **1976–77:** 793
National Farm Family of the Year, **1975:** 409
National Federation of Business and Professional Women's Clubs, **1976–77:** 179
National Federation of Independent Business, **1975:** 335
National Federation of Republican Women, **1975:** 559; **1976–77:** 791
National Fire Data Center, **1974:** 197
National Fire Prevention and Control Administration, **1974:** 197; **1976–77:** 776
National Food Stamp Reform Act of 1975, **1975:** 634
National Football Foundation and Hall of Fame, **1974:** 289
National Forest Management Act, **1976–77:** 946
National Forest System, **1975:** 726
National Governors' Conference, **1976–77:** 126, 131
National Guard Association, **1976–77:** 749

National health insurance programs, **1976–77:** 327 [9], 333 [4], 362 [15], 406, 420 [7]
National Health Service Corps, **1975:** 436
National Heart, Blood Vessel, Lung, and Blood Act of 1972, **1975:** 361
National Heart and Lung Advisory Council, **1975:** 259; **1976–77:** 496
National Heart and Lung Institute, **1974:** 97; **1975:** 361; **1976–77:** 491
National Highway Traffic Safety Administration, **1974:** 50
National Hispanic Heritage Week, **1974:** 48, 49; **1976–77:** 768, 788
National Historic Preservation Fund, **1976–77:** 826
National Industrial Council, **1975:** 318
National Institute of Education, **1974:** 281; **1975:** 253
National Institute of General Medical Sciences, **1974:** 197
National Institute of Occupational Safety and Health, **1975:** 363
National Institutes of Health, **1975:** 370; **1976–77:** 23 (p. 62), 823
National Labor Relations Act, **1975:** 378
National Labor Relations Board
Chairman, **1975:** 97; **1976–77:** 16
Equal Employment Opportunity Commission, conflict, **1975:** 602 [10]
National League of Families of American Prisoners and Missing in Southeast Asia, **1975:** 411; **1976–77:** 689
National Mass Transportation Assistance Act of 1974, **1974:** 240, 261
National Medal of Science, **1975:** 345, 568; **1976–77:** 557, 914
National Multiple Sclerosis Society, **1975:** 238
National Network on Aging, **1976–77:** 70
National Newspaper Association, **1975:** 135; **1976–77:** 231
National Newspaper Carrier Day, **1976–77:** 878
National Newspaper Publishers Association, **1975:** 43
National Newspaper Week, **1976–77:** 879
National Oceanic and Atmospheric Administration, World Weather Program, **1976–77:** 824
National Parkinson Institute, **1976–77:** 98
National Parks System, **1976–77:** 746, 1084
National Prayer Breakfast, **1975:** 56; **1976–77:** 37
National Press Club, **1975:** 645
National Red Cross, American, **1974:** 11
National Religious Broadcasters, **1975:** 50; **1976–77:** 125
National Republican Club of Capitol Hill, **1975:** 213, 543
National Republican Heritage Groups Council, **1975:** 262
National Rural Electric Cooperative Association, **1975:** 321
National Saint Elizabeth Seton Day, **1975:** 546
National School Lunch Act and Child Nutrition Act of 1966 Amendments of 1975, **1975:** 609, 615 [8], 616 [15], 620 [11]
National School Lunch program, **1974:** 210
National Science Board, **1975:** 150; **1976–77:** 130, 839
National Science Foundation, **1975:** 114, 568; **1976–77:** 246
National Science and Technology Policy, Organization, and Priorities Act of 1976, **1976–77:** 451, 452
National security.
See Defense and national security.
National Security Act of 1947, veto of amendments, **1976–77:** 1
National Security Affairs, Assistant to the President, **1975:** 311, 657 [11]
National Security Council, **1975:** 204 [5], 539; **1976–77:** 1
National Space Club, **1975:** 180
National System of Interstate and Defense Highways,**1975:** 64, 382, 383, 393
National Teacher of the Year, **1976–77:** 219
National Teenage Republican Leadership Conference, **1975:** 339; **1976–77:** 603
National Traffic and Motor Vehicle Safety Act of 1966, **1974:** 194
National Transportation Safety Board, **1975:** 9
National Wild and Scenic Rivers system, **1976–77:** 72
National Wilderness Preservation System, **1974:** 276,277; **1975:** 726; **1976–77:** 916
National Wildlife Refuge System, **1976–77:** 746, 1084
National Wildlife Refuge System Administration Act of 1966, **1974:** 185
National YMCA Youth Governors Conference, **1975:** 356
Nationality Act Amendments, Immigration and, **1976–77:** 927
Native American Awareness Week, **1976–77:** 867
NATO.
See North Atlantic Treaty Organization.
Natural gas.
See Gas, natural.
Natural Gas Transportation Act, Alaska, **1976–77:** 945
Natural resources
Forest and rangeland renewal, **1974:** 13
Wilderness areas, **1974:** 176, 177
Naval petroleum reserves, **1974:** 72, 121, 240; **1975:** 28, 64, 189 [11], 742
Naval Petroleum Reserves Production Act of 1976, **1976–77:** 298, 299, 789
Navigational Rules Act of 1976, International, **1976–77:** 877
Navy Department of the, Secretary, **1976–77:** 789, 1076

Navy, U.S.
Administration policy, **1975:** 207
Bicentennial ceremony, **1975:** 619
Disciplining of submarine commander, **1975:** 565 [16]
Indian Ocean fleet, **1974:** 39 [17], 240
Nimitz, U.S.S., commissioning, **1975:** 236
Nuclear power, **1976–77:** 84
President's assessment, **1976–77:** 118
Secretary, **1975:** 693n.; **1976–77:** 789, 1079
Shipbuilding program, **1976–77:** 68 [13], 519
Navy League of the United States, **1975:** 207
NBC News interview, **1975:** 45; **1976–77:** 6
Nebraska
Bergan-Mercy Hospital, groundbreaking ceremonies, **1976–77:** 440
National Educational Secretaries Association, **1976–77:** 445
Omaha farm forum, **1976–77:** 442
President Ford Committees, **1976–77:** 441, 443, 446
President's arrival, **1976–77:** 439
President's visits, **1974:** 153; **1975:** 599, 600, 602; **1976–77:** 439–446
University of Nebraska, **1976–77:** 444
Wilderness area, **1974:** 277
Neel, James Van Gundia, **1975:** 568
Neighborhood Revitalization, Conference on Ethnicity and, **1976–77:** 426
Neighborhood Revitalization, President's Committee on Urban Development and, **1976–77:** 625, 626, 787, 805, 846, 925 [14], 930, 931, 947
Nelson, Jack, **1976–77:** 947
Nessen, Ronald H., **1974:** 92; **1976–77:** 566
Netherlands, Prime Minister Johannes den Uyl, **1975:** 255
Nevada
International Council on Shopping Centers, **1976–77:** 516
President Ford Committee, reception, **1976–77:** 517
President's arrival, **1976–77:** 515
President's visits, **1974:** 234; **1975:** 171; **1976–77:** 515–517
Wilderness areas, **1974:** 276, 277
New Coalition, **1976–77:** 551, 552
New England, energy shortages, **1975:** 510, 548
New England Council, **1975:** 663
New England River Basins Commission, **1975:** 425; **1976–77:** 594
New Hampshire
Democratic primary, **1976–77:** 138 [8]
General Court, address, **1975:** 195
Governor, **1976–77:** 67 [2, 6]
News conference remarks, **1976–77:** 67 [1, 14], 107 [6]
People's Bicentennial Commission, **1976–77:** 68
New Hampshire—*continued*
Presidential primary, **1975:** 657 [24] **1976–77:** 116, 138 [1], 159
President's visits, **1975:** 193–196, 547–549; **1976–77:** 63–66, 68, 115–121
Senatorial election, **1975:** 195, 511 [9], 547, 548, 549, 573 [2]
New Haven, Conn., **1975:** 217
New Jersey
President Ford Committee, **1976–77:** 895
President's visits, **1975:** 612; **1976–77:** 561–565, 894, 972–974
Republican convention delegates, meeting with the President, **1976–77:** 674 [37]
New Jersey School Boards Association, **1976–77:** 974
New Mexico, wilderness area, **1974:** 277
New Orleans, La., **1975:** 206, 207, 208; **1976–77:** 181, 812
New River, N.C., **1976–77:** 771
New Year's Day, **1975:** 751
New York
Financial assistance to New York City, **1975:** 622 [15]
Operation Sail, **1976–77:** 647
President's visits, **1974:** 289; **1975:** 90, 91, 306; **1976–77:** 658, 659, 886, 934, 935, 997–1002
Republican Convention State delegation, **1976–77:** 729
Republican Party reception, Buffalo, **1976–77:** 998
Yeshiva High School, **1976–77:** 885
New York City
Federal assistance, **1975:** 620 [2, 9], 626, 645, 695 [1, 2, 4, 8, 12]; **1976–77:** 266 [14], 373 [4], 398 [6]
Financial situation, **1975:** 254, 602 [17], 616 [20], 622 [15], 645, 648 [1], 655 [8], 657 [20], 666 [13, 15], 678 [3], 683, 695 [1, 4, 25], 750 [4]
La Guardia Airport, bombing incident, **1975:** 749
Municipal bankruptcy legislation, **1975:** 646, 648 [1], 655 [8], 683, 695 [1]
President's visits, **1974:** 289; **1975:** 90, 91; **1976–77:** 887, 892
Welfare program, **1975:** 648 [6]
New York Society of Security Analysts, **1975:** 90
Newark, N.J., **1975:** 612; **1976–77:** 561
Newman, Edwin, **1976–77:** 803
Newport, R.I., **1975:** 511, 512
News conferences
1974
August 28, **1974:** 39
September 16, **1974:** 80
October 9, **1974:** 127
October 21, **1974:** 179
October 29, **1974:** 195

News conferences—*continued*
1974—*continued*
November 14, **1974:** 236
December 2, **1974:** 271
1975
January 21, **1975:** 36
February 4, **1975:** 72
February 11, **1975:** 85
February 26, **1975:** 109
March 6, **1975:** 125
March 17, **1975:** 138
April 3, **1975:** 166
May 6, **1975:** 243
May 30, **1975:** 290
June 9, **1975:** 316
June 25, **1975:** 354
July 12, **1975:** 396
September 16, **1975:** 565
October 9, **1975:** 620
October 10, **1975:** 622
November 3, **1975:** 657
November 14, **1975:** 678
November 26, **1975:** 695
December 20, **1975:** 739
1976
February 8, **1976–77:** 67
February 13, **1976–77:** 86
February 17, **1976–77:** 107
March 13, **1976–77:** 212
April 2, **1976–77:** 282
April 10, **1976–77:** 325
April 29, **1976–77:** 387
May 3, **1976–77:** 418
May 26, **1976–77:** 535 [1]
July 9, **1976–77:** 657
July 19, **1976–77:** 674
September 8, **1976–77:** 763
September 30, **1976–77:** 831
October 14, **1976–77:** 898
October 20, **1976–77:** 925
News media
Anderson Independent and Anderson Daily Mail building dedication, **1974:** 171
Black Press Week, message, **1975:** 130
Briefings and informal exchanges
Air Force One, exchange, **1975:** 717
Bonn, West Germany, exchange, **1975:** 440
California visit, remarks on return, **1975:** 583
Charleston, W.Va., exchange, **1975:** 669
Crime message, briefing, **1975:** 340
Dallas, Tex., exchange, **1975:** 558
Economic programs, briefing, **1975:** 54
Egyptian-Israeli troop disengagement agreement, exchange, **1975:** 517
Federal budget, briefing, **1975:** 62
Federal tax and spending reductions, briefing, **1975:** 626
Kansas City, Mo., exchange, **1975:** 555
News media—*continued*
Briefings—*continued*
Milwaukee, Wis., exchange, **1975:** 503
Northeastern State Governors meeting, exchange, **1975:** 42
Oil price decontrol, compromise with Congress, remarks, **1975:** 402, 429
Portland, Oreg., exchange, **1975:** 528
St. Louis, Mo., exchange, **1975:** 551
Salzburg, Austria, exchange, **1975:** 299
Warwick, R.I., exchange, **1975:** 510
Westover Air Force Base, Mass., exchange, **1975:** 662
Classified documents, publication, **1975:** 341
Coverage of the President, **1975:** 616 [10], 739 [11], 750 [12]
Equal time provision, **1975:** 615 [11]; **1976–77:** 964
Interviews and question-and-answer sessions
Air Force One, **1975:** 460
American Society of Newspaper Editors, **1975:** 189
CBS News, **1975:** 204
European journalists, **1975:** 276
Jacksonville, Fla., **1975:** 655
Knoxville, Tenn., **1975:** 615
Los Angeles, Calif., **1975:** 573, 648
"Meet the Press", **1975:** 666
Milwaukee, Wis., **1975:** 501
National Press Club, **1975:** 645
NBC News, **1975:** 45
Newport, R.I., **1975:** 511
Omaha, Nebr., **1975:** 600
Oval Office, **1975:** 750
Peterborough, N.H., **1975:** 548
Public Broadcasting Service, **1975:** 479
St. Louis, Mo., **1975:** 552
San Francisco, Calif., **1975:** 582
Japan Press Club, **1974:** 246
Judicial restraint of, **1976–77:** 523 [2]
National Association of Broadcasters, **1975:** 171
National Newspaper Association's Government Affairs Conference, **1975:** 135
National Newspaper Publishers Association, **1975:** 43
Presidential campaign coverage, **1976–77:** 763 [8], 964
President's relations, **1974:** 171, 236 [19], Appendix D
Radio and Television Directors' Association, **1974:** 76
Radio-Television News Directors Association, **1975:** 46
Sigma Delta Chi, Society of Professional Journalists, **1974:** 236
Washington Press Club, **1974:** 84
White House Correspondents Association, **1975:** 237

News media—*continued*
White House News Photographers Association, **1975:** 190
See also News conferences.
Newspaper Carrier Day, National, **1976–77:** 878
Newspaper Week, National, **1976–77:** 879
Newsweek magazine, interview, **1974:** Appendix D
Nicaragua, Ambassador to U.S., **1976–77:** 682
Nicholas Copernicus Medical Academy, Pediatric Institute, **1975:** 452
Niles, Mich., **1976–77:** 485
Nimitz, Adm. Chester W., **1975:** 236
Nimitz, U.S.S., **1975:** 236
Nixon, Pat, **1976–77:** 657 [18]
Nixon, Richard M., **1974:** 1, 3, 39 [1, 5, 24], 60, 61, 80 [1, 2, 13], 112, 127 [10, 15], 155, 195 [19], 212, 236 [13], 271 [7], 313, Appendix D; **1975:** 85 [14], 125 [7, 9], 189 [6], 204 [2], 396 [5], 479 [5], 573 [11], 582 [6], 615 [14], 622 [10], 666 [20]; **1976–77:** 63, 67 [11, 17], 86 [16], 107 [3, 15], 116, 138 [3], 185 [4], 192 [6], 209 [13], 210 [10], 325 [21], 387 [29], 657 [19], 674 [22], 763 [22], 803, 972
"No growth" policy, **1976–77:** 383
Nobel Prizes, **1976–77:** 933
Nogales, Mexico, **1974:** 177
Norfolk, Va., **1975:** 236; **1976–77:** 595
Norris, Lt. Thomas R., **1976–77:** 176
North Atlantic Treaty Organization
Administration policy, **1975:** 276 [4], 289, 650
Balance of payments, **1974:** 20, 242; **1975:** 101, 281
Campaign debate remarks, **1976–77:** 854
Communist membership, **1976–77:** 116, 318, 402 [1]
Council meeting, **1975:** 179, 186, 289, 290 [1, 4]
Cyprus dispute, **1974:** 145, 151, 195 [21]; **1975:** 718; **1976–77:** 283
Department of Defense Medal for Distinguished Public Service, **1976–77:** 267
French participation, **1974:** 302
Germany, Federal Republic of, Chancellor Helmut Schmidt, joint statement, **1974:** 284
Greek participation, **1975:** 290 [7]
Israeli participation, **1975:** 125 [10]
Italian participation, **1974:** 105
Middle East influence, **1975:** 276 [7]
Portuguese participation, **1974:** 168; **1975:** 276 [4], 354 [10]
Secretary General Joseph M. A. H. Luns, **1975:** 287, 290 [1]
Spanish participation, **1975:** 276 [4], 289, 290 [6]
Supreme Allied Commander, Europe
Gen. Alexander M. Haig, Jr., nomination, **1974:** 80 [12]
Gen. Andrew J. Goodpaster, retirement, **1974:** 312

NATO—*continued*
Turkey, suspension of U.S. military aid, effect, **1974:** 135, 145, 156, 195 [21]
Turkish participation, **1975:** 387
U.S. Permanent Representative to NATO Council, **1976–77:** 297
U.S. troop reductions, **1975:** 186, 276 [2], 387, 442
U.S.-Turkey defense cooperation agreement, **1976–77:** 598
North Carolina
Governor, **1976–77:** 212 [2], 369
Handicapped American of the Year, **1976–77:** 369
New River bill, **1976–77:** 771
President's visits, **1974:** 69–71, 174; **1975:** 271, 676, 677; **1976–77:** 213–214, 233–240, 949
Wilderness areas, **1974:** 277
North Carolina Central University, **1975:** 676
North Pacific fur seals, **1976–77:** 677
North Vietnam, **1976–77:** 354 [7]
Northbrook, Ill., **1976–77:** 969
Northeast Coalition, **1976–77:** 763 [13]
Northeast Republican Conference, **1976–77:** 62
Northern Mariana Islands, **1975:** 344, 368; **1976–77:** 255, 256
Northern Texas Panhandle Lion's Club, **1976–77:** 332
Northwest Atlantic Fisheries, International Commission for the, **1975:** 584
Northwest Compact, **1975:** 529
Norway
Bicentennial gift to U.S., **1976–77:** 636
Prime Minister Trygve Bratteli, **1975:** 290n.
Notre Dame University, **1975:** 137, 138
Nouira, Hedi, **1975:** 233
NRC.
See Nuclear Regulatory Commission.
NSC.
See National Security Council.
Nuclear energy
Enriched uranium production, **1975:** 357, 358, 359, 600 [9]
Exports, **1975:** 241, 276 [6]
Federal agency reorganization, **1974:** 138, 195 [1]
Legislation, **1974:** 141, 240; **1976–77:** 685
Messages to Congress, **1976–77:** 140, 1045
News conference remarks, **1976–77:** 67 [2, 6]
Non-proliferation, **1976–77:** 362 [2], 514, 569, 967, 985
Policy statement, **1976–77:** 980, 987
Powerplants, **1974:** 121, 141, 240; **1975:** 28, 60, 108, 488 [6], 582 [4], 600 [9], 615 [2], 741, 742; **1976–77:** 116, 118, 215 [2]
Reactors, negotiations with Egypt, **1975:** 655 [1]
Remarks at University of New Hampshire, **1976–77:** 68 [4]
Safeguards, **1975:** 241, 362, 520, 528 [4]; **1976–77:** 964

Nuclear energy—*continued*
Underground nuclear explosions, treaty with the Soviet Union, **1976–77:** 580, 700
U.S.-United Kingdom agreement, **1974:** 10
World proliferation, **1975:** 276 [6]
Nuclear Fuel Assurance Act of 1975, **1975:** 359
Nuclear Regulatory Commission
Activation, statement announcing, **1975:** 29
Chairman, **1974:** 195 [1]; **1976–77:** 315
Establishment, **1974:** 138
Functions, **1975:** 64; **1976–77:** 987
Regulatory agencies, meeting, **1975:** 392
Nuclear weapons, **1975:** 290 [3], 354 [2, 9], 450, 475
Nunn, Lee, **1975:** 620 [6]
Nurses, training programs, **1975:** 3, 436; **1976–77:** 385 [3]
Nursing Home Week, National, **1976–77:** 474
Nursing homes, **1975:** 424

Oath of Office, remarks following ceremony, **1974:** 1
Obenshain, Richard D., **1974:** 79, 88
O'Brien, Repr. George M., **1974:** 191
Occupational Safety and Health Act of 1970, **1975:** 65, 363
Occupational Safety and Health Administration, **1976–77:** 65, 181, 284 [9]
Ocean Ridge, Fla., **1976–77:** 154
Oceanic and Atmospheric Administration, National, **1976–77:** 824
Oceans
Federal program, **1976–77:** 1081
Intergovernmental Maritime Consultative Organization, **1974:** 157; **1975:** 391
Law of the Sea Conference, **1975:** 511 [8]; **1976–77:** 67 [4], 337
Resources, research and development, **1975:** 527 [14]
200-mile coastal fishing limit, **1975:** 527 [5]
Whale conservation, **1975:** 30; **1976–77:** 910
OECD.
See Organization for Economic Cooperation and Development.
Office.
See also other part of title.
Office of Economic Opportunity, **1975:** 12
Office of Economic Policy, **1974:** 39 [21]
Office of Education, **1974:** 93
Office of Minority Business Enterprise, **1974:** 291
Office of Science and Technology, **1975:** 315
Office of the Special Representative for Trade Negotiations, **1975:** 158, 311
Office of Watergate Special Prosecution Force, **1974:** 39 [6, 15], 80 [2, 11], 155, 195 [19], 313
Offutt Air Force Base, Nebr., **1975:** 599
Ogilvie, Donald G., **1976–77:** 23 (p. 59)
Ohio
Cuyahoga Valley National Recreation Area, **1974:** 324
Fort Hayes Career Center, **1976–77:** 1006
General revenue sharing, **1976–77:** 57
President's visits, **1974:** 42, 184; **1975:** 373–375; **1976–77:** 534, 566–581, 981–984, 1004–1006
Remarks at State Capitol, **1976–77:** 534, 1005
Ohio Farm Bureau Federation, **1976–77:** 217
Ohio Governor's Conference on Aging, **1976–77:** 533
Ohio River Basin Commission, **1975:** 425; **1976–77:** 594
Ohio State University, **1974:** 42
Oil
Alaska pipeline, **1975:** 703, 704
Allocations, **1975:** 26, 32, 45 [1], 109 [8]
Arab embargo, **1976–77:** 627 [28], 925 [9]
Campaign debate remarks, **1976–77:** 803
Concord, N.H., budget briefing, **1976–77:** 64
Decontrol, **1975:** 28, 54, 64, 85 [19], 225, 283, 396 [3], 402, 418, 420, 429, 460 [5], 484, 488 [1], 510, 511 [1], 528, 537, 538, 542, 548, 551, 562, 582 [9], 594, 602 [1], 678 [14], 741, 742; **1976–77:** 189 [11], 284 [3]
Deepwater ports, **1974:** 72, 240; **1975:** 8
Depletion allowances, **1974:** 127 [12], 240
Divestiture of companies, **1976–77:** 378 [6]
Domestic production, **1974:** 233; **1976–77:** 138 [9], 389, 401 [1]
Energy message, **1976–77:** 1045
Exchange for food exports, **1974:** 236 [8]; **1975:** 548, 552 [8], 582 [8], 616 [5], 620 [7], 622 [12, 14], 636
Florida budget briefing, **1976–77:** 89
Foreign supplies, **1976–77:** 385 [5]
Import fees, **1975:** 26, 28, 36 [17], 41, 54, 64, 70, 99, 108, 115, 120, 121, 225, 276 [5], 283, 485, 488 [1], 538, 741, 742
Imports, **1974:** 121, 195 [15], 274; **1975:** 8, 26, 28, 32, 36 [1, 17], 41, 42, 45 [1], 54, 60, 64, 90 [1], 108, 120, 121, 225, 270, 276 [5], 283, 418, 420, 485, 488 [1], 498, 537, 542, 562, 594, 636, 648 [3]
Industry
Illegal campaign contributions, **1976–77:** 159
Nationalization, **1975:** 109 [6]
Public trust, **1975:** 396 [15]
Israel, U.S. supplies, **1975:** 565 [4]
Mexican exports, **1974:** 179 [2, 6]
Monopolies, **1976–77:** 116
Naval petroleum reserves, **1974:** 72, 121, 240; **1975:** 28, 64, 189 [11], 742
Naval Petroleum Reserves Production Act of 1976, **1976–77:** 298, 299

Oil—*continued*
News conference remarks, **1976–77:** 86 [6], 325 [10], 387 [14]
Offshore resources, **1974:** 233, 262; **1975:** 64, 189 [11], 511 [10]
Organization of Petroleum Exporting Countries, **1975:** 45 [1], 90 [6], 91, 125 [13], 179, 276 [5], 354 [8, 14], 460 [17], 511 [5], 552 [8], 580, 592
Petroleum products, **1976–77:** 635
Pollution, legislation, **1975:** 388; **1976–77:** 685
Prices, **1974:** 39 [14], 121; **1975:** 28, 36 [25], 42, 54, 109 [7, 14], 121, 125 [13], 225, 276 [5], 312, 354 [8, 14], 396 [3], 418, 420, 460 [5], 484, 488 [1], 511 [1, 5], 537, 538, 542, 551, 562, 592, 602 [1], 678 [14]; **1976–77:** 541, 657 [6]
Research, **1974:** 138
Spill off Massachusetts coast, **1976–77:** 1036
Storage system, **1975:** 741, 742
Taxation, **1975:** 26, 60, 64, 70, 488 [7]
Transport on U.S. vessels, **1974:** 240, 327
Windfall profits tax, **1974:** 72, 240
O'Keefe, Georgia, **1976–77:** 1052
Oklahoma, President's visit, **1974:** 182, 183; **1975:** 571, 572; **1976–77:** 866
Oklahoma City, Okla., **1974:** 182, 183; **1975:** 571, 572
Oklahoma State Fair, **1975:** 571
Old North Bridge, Concord, Mass., **1975:** 198
Old North Church, Boston, Mass., **1975:** 197
Older Americans Act, **1976–77:** 70
Older Americans Amendments of 1975, **1975:** 698
Older Americans Month, **1976–77:** 300
Older persons
Administration on Aging, **1976–77:** 248
Federal activities, report transmittals, **1975:** 280, 424
Federal assistance, **1975:** 109 [12], 698; **1976–77:** 39, 69, 70, 92, 992
Food stamp program, **1975:** 36 [22], 634
Foster Grandparent program, **1975:** 550; **1976–77:** 318
Mandatory retirement, **1976–77:** 398 [3]
Message to Congress, **1976–77:** 708
News conference remarks, **1976–77:** 86 [3]
Older Americans Month, **1976–77:** 300
President's assessment, **1976–77:** 117
Radio address, **1976–77:** 971
Texas Nursing Home Association, **1976–77:** 388
Olson, Dr. Frank, **1976–77:** 883
Olson, John, **1974:** 152
Olympic Sports, President's Commission on, **1975:** 338
Olympic Winter Games Authorization Act, **1976–77:** 829
Olympics
International Olympic Committee, **1976–77:** 657 [9], 902
Olympics—*continued*
Summer games, **1976–77:** 674 [29]
United States Olympic Team, **1976–77:** 658, 659, 716
Winter games, 1980, **1976–77:** 438, 685
Omaha, Nebr., **1975:** 600, 602; **1976–77:** 439–443
OMB.
See Management and Budget, Office of.
O'Neill, Eugene, **1976–77:** 917
O'Neill, Paul H., **1976–77:** 23 (p. 66), 64
OPEC.
See Organization of Petroleum Exporting Countries.
Operation Sail, **1976–77:** 647
Opium, control, **1975:** 720
Opportunities Industrialization Centers of America, **1975:** 71
Oral Surgeons, American Society of, **1975:** 617
Oregon
Agricultural organizations, **1976–77:** 509
Flood control project, **1974:** 307
President's visits, **1974:** 214–17; **1975:** 528–30; **1976–77:** 501–09, 962–65
Republican Party-President Ford Committee reception, Portland, **1976–77:** 504
Warner Pacific College, **1976–77:** 506
Wilderness areas, **1974:** 276, 277
World Affairs Council, **1976–77:** 505
Oregon Museum of Science and Industry, **1974:** 216
Organization.
See also other part of title.
Organization of African Unity, **1975:** 739 [9], 750 [6]
Organization of American States, **1974:** 39 [23], 179 [5]; **1975:** 251
Organization for Economic Cooperation and Development, **1974:** 284
Organization for Economic Cooperation and Development Financial Support Fund, **1975:** 312
Organization of Petroleum Exporting Countries, **1975:** 45 [1], 90 [6], 91, 125 [13], 179, 276 [5], 354 [8, 14], 460 [17], 511 [5], 552 [8], 580, 592; **1976–77:** 89, 1031, 1045
Orlando, Fla., **1976–77:** 86, 87
Ortoli, François-Xavier, **1975:** 290n.
O'Scanlain, Diarmuid, **1974:** 215
OSHA.
See Occupational Safety and Health Administration.
Oswald, Lee Harvey, **1975:** 558
Ottoman, Mr. and Mrs. James R., **1975:** 409
Outer Continental Shelf, oil and gas development, **1974:** 233, 262; **1975:** 28, 64, 189 [11]; **1976–77:** 690, 691
Overland Park, Kans., **1975:** 556
Owens, Jesse, **1976–77:** 716

Pacific Doctrine, **1975:** 716
Pacific Northwest River Basins Commission, **1975:** 425; **1976–77:** 594
Packard, David, **1975:** 657 [12]
Packers and Stockyards Act of 1921, amendments, **1976–77:** 774, 775
Packwood, Sen. Bob, **1974:** 215
Page, Ray H. (Harry), **1974:** 191
Page, Ariz., **1974:** 202
Pahlavi, Shah Mohammad Reza, **1975:** 258, 261, 263, 276 [5]
Pakistan
  Joint statement, **1975:** 78
  Prime Minister Zulfikar Ali Bhutto, **1975:** 74, 78
Palestine Liberation Organization, **1974:** 195 [8], 236 [20], 271 [3, 12], Appendix D; **1975:** 204 [7], 695 [23]
Palmer, Arnold, **1975:** 734
Panama Canal
  Administration policy, **1976–77:** 356 [3], 362 [1], 376, 385 [6], 398 [10], 392 [4], 406, 415 [1], 416, 505
  Campaign debate remarks, **1976–77:** 854
  Negotiations, **1975:** 589, 615 [9]; **1976–77:** 185 [11], 231 [9], 354 [9], 378 [1]
  News conference remarks, **1976–77:** 212 [14], 282 [4], 325 [2], 387 [9, 31], 418 [8]
  Organization of American States, remarks to General Assembly, **1975:** 251
  Treaty, **1976–77:** 89
  U.S. control, termination, **1976–77:** 372
Paperwork, Commission on Federal, **1974:** 323
Paperwork reduction, **1975:** 220, 335, 500, 595, 602 [2], 631; **1976–77:** 181, 687, 862
Papua New Guinea, Generalized System of Preferences, **1975:** 668
Paramus, N.J., **1976–77:** 893
Pardons.
  See Executive clemency.
Park Chung Hee, **1974:** 252, 254, 255; **1976–77:** 854
Parker, Daniel, **1974:** 14; **1975:** 163; **1976–77:** 104, 493, 545, 1037
Parker, Marshall, **1974:** 170, 171, 173
Parks system, national, **1974:** 185; **1976–77:** 743, 745, 746
Parris, Repr. Stanford E., **1974:** 88
Pasadena, Calif., **1976–77:** 952, 953
Pascagoula, Miss., **1976–77:** 816
Paterson, N.J., **1976–77:** 562, 563
Patman, Repr. Wright, **1974:** 29
Patterson, Bradley H., Jr., **1976–77:** 741
Patterson, Tammy, **1975:** 734
Paul VI, Pope, **1975:** 304n.
Pauling, Linus Carl, **1975:** 568
Paulucci, Jeno, **1976–77:** 787
Payroll Savings Committee, U.S. Industrial, **1975:** 33
Peace, radio address, **1976–77:** 985
Pearl Harbor, Hawaii, **1975:** 715
Peck, Ralph Brazelton, **1975:** 568
Pekin, Ill., **1975:** 495
Peking, People's Republic of China, **1975:** 706, 708
Pendleton, Oreg., **1976–77:** 507–509
Pennsylvania
  President's visits, **1974:** 58, 65, 131; **1975:** 264, 265; **1976–77:** 643–646, 720, 803–806, 967, 975–978, 996
  Valley Forge State Park, **1975:** 380
Pennsylvania, University of, **1975:** 264
Pension Benefit Guaranty Corporation, **1974:** 46
Pension plans, **1974:** 45, 46, 72, 140, 262
Pension Reform Act of 1974, **1975:** 80
Peoria, Ill., **1975:** 496; **1976–77:** 184–187
Pepper, Repr. Claude, **1976–77:** 98
Pepper, Mildred, **1976–77:** 98
Pepperdine University, **1975:** 574
Percy, Sen. Charles H., **1974:** 191; **1976–77:** 209 [8]
Pereira, Aristides, **1975:** 404
Perk, Ralph, **1974:** 184
Permian Basin Petroleum Museum, **1975:** 562
Perry, Lowell W., **1975:** 282
Pershing missiles, **1975:** 565 [2, 11], 573 [4], 578 [5], 582 [3], 600 [17]
Peterborough, N.H., **1975:** 548
Petersen, Henry E., **1974:** 224
Peterson, Elly, **1976–77:** 722
Peterson, John C., **1974:** 220
Peterson, Russell W., **1974:** 233; **1976–77:** 143
Petroleum.
  See Energy; Gas; Oil.
Petroleum Reserves Production Act, Naval, **1976–77:** 789
Pettis, Repr. Jerry L., **1975:** 94
Philadelphia, Pa., **1974:** 58, 131; **1975:** 264, 265; **1976–77:** 576, 645, 646, 720, 803–806, 976, 977
Philippines
  Administration policy, **1975:** 716
  Joint communique, **1975:** 713
  President Ferdinand E. Marcos, **1975:** 711, 712, 713, 714
  President's visit, **1975:** 711–714
  Security assistance programs, **1975:** 649
Philippines, Convention on Income Taxation, United States-, **1976–77:** 1080
Phillips, Len, **1974:** 170, 172
Phnom Penh, Cambodia, **1975:** 182
Phoenix, Ariz., **1974:** 236
Phosphate interests, **1974:** 111
Physical Fitness and Sports, Council on, **1976–77:** 818
Piacentini, John, **1974:** 215
Pickering, William H., **1976–77:** 557, 914
Pike, Repr. Otis G., **1975:** 551
Pinehurst, N.C., **1974:** 70, 71
Pineland Hospital and Training Center, **1975:** 508

Pirrie, Jack A., **1976–77:** 663
Pittsburgh, Pa., **1974:** 65; **1976–77:** 967
Pitzer, Kenneth Sanborn, **1975:** 568
Plattsburgh, N.Y., **1976–77:** 658, 659
PLO.
  See Palestine Liberation Organization.
Plutonium, **1976–77:** 987
Point Reyes National Seashore, Calif., **1976–77:** 916
Poland
  Agricultural trade with U.S., **1975:** 602 [1, 5, 13]
  Chairman of the Council of Ministers Piotr Jaroszewicz, **1975:** 453n.
  First Secretary Edward Gierek, **1974:** 119, 123, 128, 129, 130, 143; **1975:** 448, 449, 450, 451, 454
  Fishery agreement with U.S., **1976–77:** 785
  Grain agreement with U.S., **1976–77:** 8
  Joint statements, **1974:** 128, 129, 130, 143; **1975:** 450, 454
  Joint U.S.-Polish Trade Commission, **1974:** 129, 130, 143; **1975:** 450
  President's visit, **1975:** 448–453
  Taxation convention with United States, **1975:** 40
  U.S. grain sales, **1975:** 600 [1], 622 [1]
Polar Bears, Agreement on the Conservation of, **1975:** 699
Police, International Association of Chiefs of, **1974:** 96; **1976–77:** 818
Polish-Americans, **1976–77:** 805
Political campaigns, **1976–77:** 212 [3, 18], 898 [1]
Political Rights of Women, Convention on the, **1976–77:** 241
Political system
  Citizen participation, **1974:** 184, 187, 195 [3], 209, 215, 219
  President's assessment, **1975:** 187, 666 [8], 750 [20, 25]; **1976–77:** 19
  President's philosophy, **1974:** 39 [2], 80 [17], 236 [22]; **1976–77:** 119, 387 [7]
  Public confidence, **1975:** 501 [4], 527 [7], 552 [4], 666 [10, 21]
Polls, public opinion, **1975:** 354 [4], 750 [3]
Pollution.
  See under Environment.
Pontiac, Ill., **1976–77:** 907
Pope, Eileen Wallace Kennedy, **1974:** 203
Pope Air Force Base, N.C., **1974:** 69
Population, United Nations Conference on World, **1974:** 86
Porter, Sylvia, **1974:** 109, 121, 150
Portland, Maine, **1975:** 509
Portland, Oreg., **1974:** 214, 215, 216, 217; **1975:** 528, 529, 530; **1976–77:** 503–506, 962–965
Ports, deepwater, **1974:** 72, 240
Portsmouth, N.H., **1975:** 549; **1976–77:** 121
Portsmouth, Ohio, **1976–77:** 854, 980, 981, 987
Portsmouth Navy Yard, **1976–77:** 118
Portugal
  Administration policy, **1975:** 166 [15], 492
  Guinea-Bissau, independence, **1974:** 4
  Joint communique, **1974:** 168
  NATO relationship, **1975:** 276 [4], 354 [10]
  Political situation, **1975:** 276 [2], 290 [5]; **1976–77:** 854
  President Francisco da Costa Gomes, **1974:** 168
  Prime Minister Vasco Gonçalves, **1975:** 289n., 290 [5]
  Security assistance programs, **1975:** 649
Postal Reorganization Act Amendments, **1976–77:** 810
Postal Service, United States, **1975:** 134, 496 [4]; **1976–77:** 185 [13], 288
Poston, Ersa, **1976–77:** 634
Powell, John H., Jr., **1975:** 141
Power Commission, Federal, **1974:** 243
Power of Years, The, presentation of book to President, **1976–77:** 24
Powerplants, **1974:** 121, 141, 240; **1975:** 28, 60, 108, 326, 488 [6], 582 [4], 600 [9], 615 [2], 741, 742
POW's.
  See Prisoners of war.
Prayer Breakfast, National, **1975:** 56; **1976–77:** 37
Prayer proclamations, Day-of-, **1975:** 416
Prayer in public schools, **1976–77:** 67 [8], 947
Presidency, President's views on, **1975:** 36 [28], 45 [7], 204 [4], 276 [9], 396 [6], 479 [1, 3], 615 [15], 620 [12], 666 [3, 4, 9], 750 [1, 4]; **1976–77:** 138 [7], 192 [9], 207 [9], 209 [7], 240 [8], 778
President, Executive Office of the, **1975:** 160
President Ford Committee
  Campaign advertisements, **1976–77:** 561, 566
  Establishment, letter authorizing, **1975:** 343
  Ethnic Affairs committee, **1976–77:** 846
  Federal Election Campaign Act Amendments of 1974, **1976–77:** 46
  News conference remarks, **1975:** 620 [6], 657 [12], 678 [1], 739 [6], 750 [13]; **1976–77:** 212 [1], 418 [10], 763 [21]
  President's assessment, **1976–77:** 657 [24]
  President's remarks to Kansas City staff, **1976–77:** 728
  Reorganization, **1976–77:** 740
  Visit to Washington, D.C., headquarters, **1976–77:** 10, 722
Presidential Clemency Board, **1974:** 77, 78, 266, 329; **1975:** 113, 243 [5], 566, 573 [12]
Presidential Initiatives Management program, **1976–77:** 1019
Presidential Medal of Freedom, **1976–77:** 76, 281, 716, 900, 1052, 1061
Presidential pardons.
  See Executive clemency.

Presidential Recordings and Materials Preservation Act, **1974:** 313
Presidential Scholars program, **1975:** 371
Presidential succession, 25th amendment to the Constitution, **1974:** 195 [12], 236 [2]
"Presidentials" youth group, **1976–77:** 727
President's Advisory Committee on Refugees, **1975:** 267, 415
President's Commission on Olympic Sports, **1975:** 338
President's Commission on White House Fellowships, **1975:** 269
President's Committee on Mental Retardation, **1974:** 136
President's Committee on Urban Development and Neighborhood Revitalization, **1976–77:** 625, 626, 787, 805, 846, 925 [14], 930, 931
President's domestic priorities, **1976–77:** 461, 523 [7]
President's Economic Policy Board
  Establishment, **1974:** 109
  Executive Director, **1975:** 92
  Food Committee, **1975:** 539
  Grain exports, monitoring, **1974:** 121
  Task Force on International Air Transportation Policy, **1976–77:** 765
President's financial records, **1976–77:** 107 [8], 898 [4, 21]
President's Foreign Intelligence Advisory Board, **1976–77:** 279
President's goals for America, **1976–77:** 210 [11], 240 [2], 1003
President's image, **1976–77:** 352 [9]
President's Labor-Management Committee, **1974:** 109; **1975:** 326, 600 [2]
President's Panel on Federal Compensation, **1975:** 328, 729
President's papers, donation to Government, **1976–77:** 1028
President's past campaign finances, **1976–77:** 831
President's views on the Presidency, **1976–77:** 333 [11], 406
President's views on religion, **1976–77:** 215 [3], 378 [11]
President's visits to other countries.
  See Travel, President's.
Press.
  See News media.
Press Club, National, **1975:** 645
Pressler, Repr. Larry, **1974:** 152
Prevailing Rate Advisory Committee, Federal, **1976–77:** 751
Price Stability, Council on Wage and, **1974:** 6, 19, 32, 33, 41, 72, 109, 121, 152, 241
Prices.
  See Wages and prices.
Primaries.
  See Elections, 1976; *specific States.*
Principe, **1975:** 668
Prisoners of war, **1974:** 83; **1975:** 411
Prisons, Federal Bureau of, **1975:** 341
Privacy
  Administration policy, **1974:** 6
  Legislation, **1974:** 31, 125
  Student records, **1974:** 25
Privacy, Domestic Council Committee on the Right of, **1974:** 39 [11], 125
Privacy Act of 1974, **1974:** 125; **1975:** 1, 577, 595
Privacy Protection Study Commission, **1975:** 1
Private enterprise, **1976–77:** 23 (p. 60)
Private organizations, **1976–77:** 107 [18]
Private property rights, **1976–77:** 89
Proclamations
  Bicentennial Independence Day, **1976–77:** 628
  Bicentennial Year, **1975:** 752
  Drug Abuse Prevention Week, signing ceremony, **1974:** 167
  Granting pardon to Richard Nixon, **1974:** 60, 61
  Japanese-American internment during World War II, **1976–77:** 111
  National Hispanic Heritage Week, 1974, **1974:** 48, 49
  National Saint Elizabeth Seton Day, **1975:** 546
  Oil import fees, **1975:** 41, 120
  Older Americans Month, **1976–77:** 300
  Vietnam era draft evaders and military deserters, clemency program, **1974:** 77, 78
  Vietnam era veterans benefits, termination of eligibility period, **1975:** 246, 247
  See also Appendix B, 1974, 1975, 1976–1977.
Productivity and Work Quality, National Commission on, **1974:** 121
Professional athletes prayer brunch, **1976–77:** 100
Professional Responsibility, Office of, proposed, **1976–77:** 675
Project Independence, **1974:** 6, 39 [14], 42, 94, 127 [6]; **1975:** 488 [13]
Psychotropic Substances, Convention on, **1975:** 748
Public broadcasting, **1976–77:** 354 [4]
Public Broadcasting, Corporation for, **1975:** 88
Public Broadcasting Financing Act of 1975, **1976–77:** 2
Public Broadcasting Service, **1975:** 276, 479
Public Documents Commission, **1974:** 313
Public Health Service Act, **1975:** 436
Public opinion, effect on decisions, **1976–77:** 240 [9], 674 [38]
Public opinion polls, **1975:** 354 [4], 750 [3]
Public Safety Officers' Benefits Act, **1976–77:** 818, 827, 828
Public service employment, **1974:** 39 [3], 121; **1975:** 479 [2], 602 [15], 616 [6, 12], 622 [21], 662, 666 [13], 678 [8]; **1976–77:** 311, 313, 356 [4]

Public Works and Economic Development Act of 1965, **1974:** 108
Public Works Employment Act, **1976–77:** 652, 653, 683, 686
Public Works Employment Appropriations Act, **1976–77:** 845
Public works employment bill, veto, **1976–77:** 83, 86 [9], 113
Public Works for Water and Power Development and Atomic Energy Commission Appropriation Act, 1975, **1974:** 40
Puerto Rico
  Cuban role in independence movement, **1975:** 739 [9]
  President's visit, **1976–77:** 618–621
  Statehood proposal, **1976–77:** 1041, 1042, 1065
  Summit conference, **1976–77:** 550, 580, 618–621
  U.S. policy, **1976–77:** 702
Pulliam, Eugene C., **1975:** 349
Purrington, J. Ward, **1974:** 174

Rabbit meat, mandatory inspection, **1976–77:** 911
Rabin, Yitzhak, **1974:** 66, 75; **1975:** 204 [7], 243 [2], 316 [9], 322, 516, 522; **1976–77:** 32, 34, 41, 560 [8], 648, 766, 854
Radiation Control for Health and Safety Act of 1968, **1975:** 362; **1976–77:** 584
Radio Free Europe, **1975:** 460 [14]
Radio interviews.
  See under News media.
Radio Regulations (Geneva, 1959), **1975:** 408
Radio and television, public broadcasting, **1976–77:** 354 [4]
Radio and Television Directors' Association, **1974:** 76
Radio-Television News Directors Association, **1975:** 46; **1976–77:** 48
Railroad Retirement Board, **1976–77:** 536
Railroad Retirement System, **1974:** 72, 140, 262
Railroad Retirement Trust Fund, **1974:** 140
Railroad Revitalization and Regulatory Reform Act of 1976, **1976–77:** 58, 59
Railroads
  Amtrak, **1975:** 279; **1976–77:** 95
  Concord, N.H., budget briefing, **1976–77:** 64
  ConRail, **1976–77:** 59
  Financial assistance, **1975:** 268, 279; **1976–77:** 38
  On-board customs procedures, **1975:** 279
  Regulatory reform, **1974:** 240; **1975:** 196, 268
  Retirement benefits, **1975:** 143
  Safety, **1975:** 9; **1976–77:** 209 [4]
  State programs, **1976–77:** 217
Railsback, Repr. Tom, **1974:** 191
Railway Association, United States, **1976–77:** 1046
Raleigh, N.C., **1975:** 677; **1976–77:** 949
Ramadan, **1974:** 159; **1975:** 605; **1976–77:** 821
Rambouillet, France, **1975:** 680
Rangeland Renewable Planning Act of 1974, Forest and, **1974:** 13
Rantoul, Ill., **1976–77:** 190
Ray, Dixy Lee, **1974:** 195 [1]
Ray, Gov. Robert D., **1974:** 187, 188, 210; **1976–77:** 551, 552
Razak, Tun Abdul, **1976–77:** 18
REA.
  See Rural Electrification Administration.
Reagan, Ronald, **1975:** 19, 396 [19], 501 [16], 530, 551, 552 [2, 3], 573 [1, 3], 582 [5], 622 [20], 648 [5], 657 [16], 666 [14, 16], 678 [20], 695 [7, 13], 739 [5], 750 [2, 14, 22]; **1976–77:** 67 [12–14, 16], 86 [10, 11], 107 [5, 16], 138 [11], 150, 159, 192 [4], 212 [3, 15, 18, 19], 287 [9], 354 [6], 385 [6], 387 [1, 5, 8, 15, 19], 400, 418 [13, 14], 535 [4], 552, 560 [1], 560 [4, 5], 566, 576, 581, 585, 657 [17], 657 [24], 674 [8], 674 [13], 694, 730, 733, 740, 742, 778, 1025
Real Property Acquisition Policies Act of 1970, Uniform Relocation Assistance and, **1975:** 49
Realtors, National Association of, **1974:** 234
Recession, **1974:** 127 [2], 195 [13], 236 [3]; **1975:** 36 [12, 27], 62, 64, 70, 72 [8], 85 [4], 147, 166 [8], 167, 189 [10], 204 [8], 410
Reclamation Authorization Act of 1975, **1976–77:** 201
Reclamation Development Act of 1974, **1974:** 202
Recombinant DNA experiments, **1976–77:** 801
Recordings and Materials Preservation Act, Presidential, **1974:** 313
Records, Keith, **1974:** 219
Recreation
  Cuyahoga Valley National Recreation Area in Ohio, **1974:** 324
  Wilderness areas, **1974:** 277
Red Cross, American National, **1974:** 11
Red Cross, International, **1974:** 83
Red Cross Month, **1975:** 104; **1976–77:** 134
Red River navigation project, **1976–77:** 373 [3]
Rees, Albert E., **1974:** 109
Refugee program, Indochina, **1975:** 267, 347, 415, 746; **1976–77:** 247
Regional Action Planning Commissions, **1974:** 108
Registration of Objects Launched Into Outer Space, Convention on, **1976–77:** 228
Regula, Repr. Ralph S., **1974:** 184
Regulations, Federal, Congressional review, **1975:** 279
Regulatory agencies, securities, **1974:** 199
Regulatory reform, **1974:** 121, 146, 150, 189, 240; **1975:** 9, 70, 144, 192, 196, 220, 268, 308, 335, 341, 374, 375, 392, 395, 396 [17], 496 [8], 500, 502 [2, 12], 527 [12, 13], 531, 585, 602 [2], 618, 675, 678 [6, 9], 723, 724; **1976–77:** 308, 315, 388, 468, 610, 685, 836, 1062, 1070

Regulatory Reform, National Commission on, **1974:** 121, 240
Regulatory Review Commission, **1975:** 192
Rehabilitation Act of 1973, **1975:** 156
Rehabilitation Loan Fund, **1976–77:** 9
Reifenberg, Jan, **1975:** 276
Religion
Christmas, **1974:** 304, 306; **1975:** 728, 736, 747; **1976–77:** 1030
Day-of-prayer proclamations, **1975:** 416
Jewish High Holy Days, **1974:** 55, 80; **1975:** 521; **1976–77:** 809
National Baptist Convention, **1975:** 553
National Prayer Breakfast, **1975:** 56; **1976–77:** 37
National Religious Broadcasters, **1975:** 50; **1976–77:** 125
National Saint Elizabeth Seton Day proclamation, **1975:** 546
President's views on, **1976–77:** 215 [3], 378 [11]
Ramadan, **1974:** 159; **1975:** 605; **1976–77:** 821
Renegotiation Board, Chairman, **1974:** 267
Reorganization Plan authority, **1974:** 72
Reports to Congress.
See Congress, communications to; Appendix C, **1974.**
Republican Congressional staff, **1974:** 98
Republican Leadership Conference, National Teenage, **1976–77:** 603
Republican National Committee
Chairman, **1976–77:** 657 [20]
Dinner, **1976–77:** 887
Executive Committee, reception, **1976–77:** 617
Federal Election Campaign Act Amendments of 1974, reaction of the committee, **1974:** 149
Kansas City, Mo., breakfast, **1976–77:** 734
Luncheon, **1974:** 79
Reception, **1976–77:** 142
Republican National Finance Committee, **1974:** 79
Republican National Hispanic Assembly, **1976–77:** 702
Republican Party
Administration's accomplishments, **1976–77:** 96
Campaign trips of administration officials, **1976–77:** 212 [7]
Dinners, rallies, etc.
See specific city or State.
Election results, **1974:** 195 [9], 236 [6]
Jarman, Repr. John, change in party affiliation, **1975:** 44
Leaders, question-and-answer session, **1976–77:** 1025
Michigan State Convention, **1974:** 35
National Federation of Republican Women, **1975:** 559
National Republican Club of Capitol Hill, **1975:** 213, 543
National Republican Heritage Groups Council, **1975:** 262
Republican Party—*continued*
National Teenage Republican Leadership Conference, **1975:** 339
News conference remarks, **1976–77:** 212 [7], 282 [13], 418, 674 [8, 23]
Northeast Republican Conference, **1976–77:** 62
Northwest Compact, **1975:** 529
Post-election philosophy, **1974:** 236 [16, 22]
President Ford Committee, chairman, **1976–77:** 273
President's assessment, **1975:** 125 [5], 352, 479 [3], 491, 493, 494, 509, 525, 529, 536, 572, 598, 612, 623, 647, 652, 664, 665, 677, 679, 695 [13], 750 [13]; **1976–77:** 253, 352 [8]
President's travel, **1975:** 396 [8], 552 [2, 4], 565 [13], 620 [6], 657 [17]
Republican National Associates, **1975:** 352
Republican National Committee, **1975:** 536
Republican National Leadership Conference, **1975:** 129
Southern State chairmen, meeting with the President, **1976–77:** 786
State party organizations
Illinois, **1975:** 138 [7], 396 [2]
Kansas, **1975:** 85 [13]
United Republican Fund of Illinois, **1974:** 191
Young Republican Conference, **1976–77:** 39
Young Republican Leadership Conference, **1975:** 116
See also Elections, 1976.
Republican Women, National Federation of, **1976–77:** 791
Republican Women's Task Force, **1976–77:** 264
Rescissions, budget.
See under Budget, Federal.
Research and development
Defense, **1976–77:** 736
Energy, **1976–77:** 68 [5], 71, 189 [6], 195, 417, 461, 1045
Space program, **1976–77:** 622
Reserve, La., **1976–77:** 812
Reserve Officers Association of the United States, **1975:** 103
Resignations and retirements
Agriculture Department, Secretary, **1976–77:** 849
Commerce Department, Secretary, **1975:** 657 [1]
Council on International Economic Policy, Executive Director, **1974:** 321
Defense Department, Secretary of the Army, **1975:** 376
Domestic Council, Executive Director, **1974:** 294
Equal Employment Opportunity Commission
Chairman, **1975:** 141
General Counsel, **1975:** 142
Export-Import Bank of the United States, President and Chairman, **1975:** 569
Federal Energy Administration, Administrator, **1974:** 196

Resignations and retirements—*continued*
Federal Power Commission, Commissioner, **1975:** 127
General Services Administrator, **1975:** 458
Health, Education, and Welfare Department, Secretary, **1975:** 360
Housing and Urban Development Department, Assistant Secretary for Housing Management, **1976–77:** 35
Interior Department, Secretary, **1975:** 431
Justice Department
Assistant Attorney General, Criminal Division, **1974:** 224
Attorney General, **1974:** 295
Deputy Attorney General, **1975:** 132
Labor Department, Secretary, **1975:** 80; **1976–77:** 15
North Atlantic Treaty Organization, Supreme Allied Commander, Europe, **1974:** 312
Office of Management and Budget, Director, **1974:** 303
President Ford Committee, chairman, **1976–77:** 273
Renegotiation Board, Chairman, **1974:** 267
Securities and Exchange Commission, Chairman, **1975:** 570
Special Representative for Trade Negotiations, **1974:** 321
Supreme Court of the United States, Associate Justice, **1975:** 673
Transportation Department, Secretary, **1974:** 308
United Nations, U.S. Representative, **1976–77:** 54
White House Staff
Assistant to the President, **1974:** 273, 283, 303
Assistant to the President for Domestic Affairs, **1974:** 294
Counsel to the President, **1975:** 93, 481
Counsellor to the President, **1974:** 265, 269
Deputy Assistant to the President, **1974:** 309
Press Secretary to the President, **1974:** 64
Special Assistant to the President, **1974:** 310; **1975:** 604
Resource Conservation and Recovery Act, **1976–77:** 938
Reston, James B., **1975:** 666
Retail Federation, American, **1976–77:** 469
Retired persons, **1976–77:** 24
Retirement Income Security Act of 1974, Employee, **1974:** 45, 46
Revenue Adjustment Act of 1975, **1975:** 735n.
Revenue sharing.
See General revenue sharing.
Reynolds, Frank, **1976–77:** 803
Rhoads, James B., **1976–77:** 1028
Rhoads, Jonathan E., **1974:** 169
Rhode Island
Bicentennial song, **1975:** 591
President's visit, **1975:** 510, 511, 512
Rhodes, James A., **1974:** 184; **1976–77:** 575
Rhodes, Repr. John J., **1974:** 236 [5]; **1976–77:** 617
Rhodesia
Campaign debate remarks, **1976–77:** 854
Chrome imports, **1976–77:** 420 [5]
Cuban involvement, **1976–77:** 207 [7], 415 [2]
Interview remarks, **1976–77:** 778
Soviet involvement, **1976–77:** 207 [7]
University of Michigan, remarks, **1976–77:** 784
U.S. assistance, **1976–77:** 159
U.S. policy, **1976–77:** 415 [2], 807
Ribicoff, Sen. Abraham A., **1975:** 192
Richardson, Bill, **1974:** 211
Richardson, Elliot L., **1975:** 23, 109 [17], 657 [1], 663, 678 [18]; **1976–77:** 53, 67 [18], 116, 277, 580 [3], 592, 626, 691, 709, 829, 859, 958, 1034
Richey, Charles R., **1974:** 195 [19]
Richmond, Va., **1976–77:** 948
Rikard, Ralph M., **1976–77:** 454
Riley, Tom, **1974:** 188
Ringsak, Elton W., Sr., **1975:** 229
Rio Treaty, **1975:** 700
Ritchie, Richard Steven, **1974:** 174
River Basins Commissions, report transmittals, **1975:** 425; **1976–77:** 594
Rizzo, Frank L., **1976–77:** 646
Robert H. Goddard Memorial Trophy, **1975:** 180
Roberts, William, **1974:** 2
Robinson, Charles W., **1975:** 552 [8]
Robinson, Repr. J. Kenneth, **1974:** 88
Robson, John E., **1975:** 203; **1976–77:** 315
Rocco, WO Louis R., **1974:** 293
Rochester, N.Y., **1976–77:** 999
Rock Hill, S.C., **1974:** 172
Rockefeller, Nelson A., **1974:** 17, 18, 39 [4, 11], 72, 79, 127 [16], 155, 195 [4, 11, 16], 236 [2, 4, 21, 24], 240, 288, 314, Appendix D; **1975:** 19, 91, 92, 125 [6], 138 [11], 204 [11], 396 [9, 19], 479 [11], 501 [15], 511 [11], 543, 552 [5], 565 [12, 14], 648 [1], 655 [4], 657 [2, 5, 10, 22, 27], 666 [1, 2], 684n., 729; **1976–77:** 23 (p. 55, 56), 24, 57, 62, 387 [25], 545, 551, 674 [15], 726, 732, 740, 742, 887, 1025, 1035, 1052
Rockefeller Public Service Awards, **1974:** 275
Rockford, Ill., **1976–77:** 202–206
Rockford Tool, Die and Machining Association, **1976–77:** 204
Rockwell, Norman, **1976–77:** 1052
Rockwell International Corporation, **1976–77:** 858
Rodenticide Act, Federal Insecticide, Fungicide, and, **1976–77:** 725
Rodino, Repr. Peter W., Jr., **1976–77:** 611, 797, 836
Rogers, Repr. Paul G., **1976–77:** 688

Rogers Memorial Hospital, **1976–77:** 697
Romania
  Fishery agreement with United States, **1976–77:** 1048
  Generalized System of Preferences, beneficiary, **1975:** 668
  Joint communique, **1975:** 465
  President Nicolae Ceausescu, **1975:** 460 [14], 461, 462, 463, 464, 465
  President's visit, **1975:** 461–465
  Romanian-American Joint Economic Commission, **1975:** 465
  Romanian-U.S. Economic Council, **1975:** 465
  U.S. trade relations, **1975:** 210, 211, 463, 464, 465, 668
  Waiver authority extension, **1976–77:** 548
Rome, Italy, **1975:** 301, 302, 304
Ronan, William J., **1974:** 127 [16]
Rose, Gregory, **1975:** 356
Rosenbaum, Richard, **1976–77:** 729
Roseville, Mich., **1976–77:** 463
Rossmoor Golden Rain Foundation, **1976–77:** 529
Rossmoor President Ford Committee, **1976–77:** 530
Roudebush, Richard L., **1974:** 16, 139, 192; **1976–77:** 449, 590, 832
Rowan, Roy, **1975:** 426 ftn.
Rubber workers strike, **1976–77:** 461
Rubinstein, Arthur, **1976–77:** 281
Ruckelshaus, William D., **1976–77:** 740
Rudman, Warren, **1976–77:** 118
Ruff, Charles F. C., **1976–77:** 831
Rumsfeld, Donald H., **1975:** 138 [7], 657 [1, 5, 6, 9, 11, 19], 663, 666 [5], 678 [18], 688
Runaway fathers, **1976–77:** 116
Rundlett Junior High School, **1976–77:** 66
Rural areas
  Development legislation, **1976–77:** 301
  Employment, **1975:** 32
  Energy development, **1975:** 488 [10]
  Environmental programs, **1975:** 15
  Health and education programs, availability, **1975:** 616 [9]
  Transportation, **1975:** 383
Rural Electric Cooperative Association, National, **1975:** 321
Rural Electrification Administration, **1974:** 318; **1975:** 321
Rural Electrification Administration Technical Amendments Act, **1976–77:** 928
Rural electrification and telephone program, budget rescission, **1974:** 89
Rural Environmental Assistance program, **1974:** 318; **1975:** 15
Rural Environmental Conservation program, **1975:** 15
Rush, Kenneth, **1974:** 41
Russell, Kans., **1976–77:** 735
Ruth, Repr. Earl B., **1974:** 174
Ruth, Henry S., Jr., **1974:** 155

Sacramento, Calif., **1975:** 531, 532, 533
Sadat, Anwar el-, **1975:** 243 [2], 297, 298, 299, 300, 316 [9, 11], 516, 522, 565 [11], 642, 643, 644, 654, 657 [25]; **1976–77:** 766
Safe Drinking Water Act, **1974:** 305
Safety
  Airlines, **1975:** 725
  Airport and airway, **1975:** 136
  Consumer products, **1975:** 392
  Fire prevention and control, **1974:** 197
  Highway, **1974:** 50, 194; **1975:** 613; **1976–77:** 616, 753
  Nuclear materials, **1975:** 241, 362, 520, 582 [4]
  Occupational safety programs, **1975:** 65, 363
  Railroads, **1975:** 9
  Schoolbus, **1974:** 194
Safety Administration, National Highway Traffic, **1974:** 50
Safety Officers' Benefits Act, Public, **1976–77:** 818, 827, 828
Saginaw, Mich., **1976–77:** 487
Saigon, Republic of Vietnam, **1975:** 168
St. Christopher-Nevis-Anguilla, Generalized system of Preferences, **1975:** 668
St. Clair, James D., **1974:** 155
St. Edward Mercy Medical Center, **1975:** 483
Saint Elizabeth Seton Day, National, **1975:** 546
Saint Lawrence Seaway Development Corporation, annual report, transmittal, **1975:** 535
St. Louis, Mo., **1975:** 551, 552, 553, 554; **1976–77:** 7, 8, 909, 991, 993
St. Petersburg, Fla., **1976–77:** 92, 93
Salem, Dr. Khalil, **1974:** 14
SALT.
  See Strategic arms limitation talks.
Salt Lake City, Utah, **1974:** 218
Salzburg, Austria, **1975:** 296, 297, 298, 299, 300
Sampson, Arthur F., **1974:** 195 [19], 313; **1975:** 458
San Antonio, Tex., **1976–77:** 316–319
San Diego, Calif., **1975:** 167; **1976–77:** 518–521, 958, 965
San Diego Chamber of Commerce, **1976–77:** 51
San Diego Council of the Navy League, **1976–77:** 519
San Fernando Valley Business and Professional Association, **1976–77:** 862
San Francisco, Calif., **1975:** 169, 580, 581, 582, 650; **1976–77:** 259–261, 852, 854–857
San Francisco Bay Area Council, **1975:** 169
San Jose, Calif., **1976–77:** 524–526, 532
San Jose Foreign Trade Zone, **1976–77:** 527
Sanchez, Phillip V., **1976–77:** 702
São Tomé and Principe, Generalized System of Preferences, **1975:** 668

Sarasota, Fla., **1976–77:** 163, 164
Sarett, Lewis H., **1976–77:** 557, 914
Sato, Eisaku, **1975:** 303
Saudi Arabia, King Faisal Ibn Abdul Aziz, **1975:** 155
Savings bonds, **1975:** 33, 159, 228, 627; **1976–77:** 13
Savings and Loan Insurance Corporation, Federal, **1974:** 200
Savings and loans associations, **1975:** 144
Sawhill, John C., **1974:** 195 [10, 20], 196
Saxbe, William B., **1974:** 80 [2 ftn.], 155, 295
SBA.
See Small Business Administration.
Schaufele, William E., Jr., **1976–77:** 763 [1]
Schaumberg, Ill., **1976–77:** 970
Scheel, Walter, **1975:** 330, 331, 334, 443
Scherle, Repr. William J., **1974:** 188
Schieffer, Bob, **1975:** 204; **1976–77:** 560
Schlesinger, James R., **1975:** 276 [5], 600 [17], 657 [1, 4, 14, 15, 29], 666 [1, 7, 11]; **1976–77:** 23 (p. 59), 854
Schmidt, Helmut, **1974:** 279, 282, 284; **1975:** 54, 289n., 440, 441, 444, 457n., 680n.; **1976–77:** 621, 668, 669, 671
Schmults, Edward C., **1976–77:** 315
School Lunch Act and Child Nutrition Act of 1966 Amendments of 1975, National, **1975:** 609, 615 [8], 616 [15], 620 [11]
School Lunch program, National, **1974:** 210
Schoolbus Safety Amendments of 1974, Motor Vehicle and, **1974:** 194
Schools
Busing, **1975:** 496 [6], 511 [6], 552 [10], 554 [3], 565 [7, 8], 573 [10], 578 [9], 620 [5], 622 [17], 648 [2]; **1976–77:** 118, 209 [9], 210 [13], 240 [10], 282 [1]
Coed athletic programs, **1976–77:** 356 [8]
Desegregation, **1974:** 24, 25, 127 [20], 142; **1976–77:** 118
Federal loans, **1975:** 554 [4]
Impact aid program, **1976–77:** 373 [10]
Lunch programs, **1974:** 210; **1975:** 609, 615 [8], 616 [15], 620 [11]
Medical, **1976–77:** 288
Prayers in public schools, **1976–77:** 118
Private, assistance, **1974:** 127 [13]; **1975:** 496 [7], 502 [11], 560, 574
See also Education.
Schweiker, Sen. Richard S., **1974:** 131
Science, National Medal of, **1975:** 345, 568; **1976–77:** 557, 914
Science Board, National, **1975:** 150; **1976–77:** 130, 839
Science Foundation, National, **1975:** 114, 568
Science and Technology, Office of, **1975:** 315
Science and Technology Exposition, Bicentennial, **1976–77:** 591
Science and Technology Policy, Office of, **1976–77:** 244, 724
Science and Technology Policy, Organization, and Priorities Act of 1976, National, **1976–77:** 451, 452
Scott, Sen. Hugh, **1974:** 131; **1975:** 265, 657 [21]; **1976–77:** 617, 836
Scott, Stanley S., **1975:** 604
Scowcroft, Brent, **1975:** 657 [1, 19]
Scranton, William W., **1974:** 131; **1976–77:** 133, 138 [5], 218
Sea, Conference on the Law of the, **1975:** 450, 511 [8], 527 [5]
Sea, 1960, International Convention for the Safety of Life at, amendments, **1974:** 157
Sea, 1974, International Convention for the Safety of Life at, **1976–77:** 748
Sea, United Nations Conference on the Law of the, **1974:** 86
Sea Grant Program Improvement Act of 1976, **1976–77:** 874
Seabrook, N.H., **1976–77:** 67 [2, 6], 68 [4]
Seals, Convention for the Conservation of Antarctic, **1975:** 730
Seals, North Pacific fur, **1976–77:** 677
Seamans, Robert C., Jr., **1974:** 195 [1]; **1976–77:** 23 (p. 75), 86 [2], 980
Seatbelt interlock systems, **1974:** 194
Seaton, Elizabeth Bayley, **1974:** 296
Seattle, Wash., **1975:** 524, 525, 526, 527; **1976–77:** 959–961
Sebelius, Repr. Keith G., **1974:** 220
SEC.
See Securities and Exchange Commission.
Second Supplemental Appropriations Act, **1976–77:** 545
Second United Nations Development Decade, **1974:** 86
Secret Service, temporary protection for certain Government officials, **1976–77:** 1064
Securities Acts Amendments of 1975, **1975:** 308
Securities and Exchange Commission
Chairman, **1975:** 570; **1976–77:** 315, 709
Regulatory agencies, meeting, **1975:** 392
Securities Acts Amendments of 1975, **1975:** 308
Security, national.
See Defense and national security.
Security, President's, **1975:** 551, 552, 555, 565 [10], 582 [2], 615 [6], 620 [5], 655 [7]; **1976–77:** 215 [13]
Security and Cooperation in Europe, Conference on, **1976–77:** 283
Seidman, L. William, **1974:** 109
Selective Service
Director, **1974:** 77, 78
Draft evaders, clemency, **1974:** 16, 77, 78, 80 [10], 236 [13], 266, 329; **1975:** 36 [14], 58, 113, 243 [5], 566, 573 [12]
Selective Service Act, Military, **1975:** 58
Senate.
See under Congress.

Senate Subcommittee on Internal Security, **1976–77:** 352 [10]
Seoul, Korea, **1974:** 252, 254
SER-Jobs for Progress, **1975:** 410
Serafini, Marcello, **1976–77:** 545
Seton Day, National Saint Elizabeth, **1975:** 546
Sevareid, Eric, **1975:** 204
Sevilla-Sacasa, Guillermo, **1976–77:** 682
Sewage treatment facilities, **1974:** 262
Shafer Commission, **1975:** 565 [19]
Shaker, Maj. Gen. Zaid bin, **1974:** 14
Shanghai communique, **1975:** 706, 716
Shannon, Edgar F., **1975:** 19
Shannon, James Augustine, **1975:** 568
Sharp, Nolan, **1974:** 204
Shiing-Shen Chern, **1976–77:** 557
Ships and Shipping
  Cargo preference, **1975:** 527 [8]
  Defense appropriations, **1976–77:** 667
  Deepwater ports, **1974:** 72, 240; **1975:** 8
  Grain exports, **1975:** 497 [4], 539, 571, 602 [5]
  Great Lakes, military cargo, **1975:** 502 [20]
  Longshoremen's strike, **1975:** 497 [1, 3], 539
  Merchant marine, **1975:** 207
  Oil pollution control, legislation, **1975:** 388
  Petroleum imports, **1974:** 240, 327
  U.S. flag fishing vessel, **1975:** 18
Shoe industry, import effects, **1976–77:** 284 [1]
Shopping Centers, International Council of, **1976–77:** 516
Shouse, Catherine Filene, **1976–77:** 559, 1052
Shreveport, La., **1976–77:** 375
Shrimp, agreement with Brazil, **1975:** 320
Shriver, Repr. Garner E., **1974:** 220
Shultz, George P., **1975:** 240
Sickle cell anemia, **1975:** 77, 530; **1976–77:** 425
Sihanouk, Norodom, **1975:** 189 [2]
Sijan, Capt. Lance P., **1976–77:** 176
Silberman, Lawrence H., **1975:** 132; **1976–77:** 26
Silbert, Earl J., **1975:** 460 [7]
Silcio, Benedict, **1975:** 582 ftn.
Silver, stockpile disposal, **1974:** 240
Simon, William E., **1974:** 41, 195 [10], 214, Appendix D; **1975:** 189 [9], 228, 626; **1976–77:** 1, 86 [7], 562, 626
Simpson, Richard O., **1976–77:** 315
Sinai agreement.
  See under Middle East.
Sinaia, Romania, **1975:** 464
Singapore, Prime Minister Lee Kuan Yew, **1975:** 249
Sioux City, Iowa, **1974:** 210
Sioux Falls, S. Dak., **1974:** 152
Sioux Indians, **1974:** 198
Sisco, Joseph J., **1976–77:** 23 (p. 54)
Sixth Circuit Judicial Conference, **1975:** 400
Skinner, Jonty, **1976–77:** 420 [10]
Skubitz, Repr. Joe, **1974:** 220
Skylab, **1974:** 223; **1975:** 180, 313
Skylar, David, **1976–77:** 984
Slayton, Donald K., **1975:** 412, 428, 482
Small business, **1976–77:** 333 [9], 398 [2], 470, 685, 862
Small Business Administration
  Administrator, **1976–77:** 81, 626, 805
  Legislation, **1974:** 34
  Loan programs, **1976–77:** 685
  Minority businesses, **1974:** 291
  Programs, bill signing statement, **1976–77:** 558
  Rescissions and deferrals, **1976–77:** 1069
  Small Business Awards, ceremony, **1975:** 272
Small Business Amendments of 1974, 1974: 34
Small Business Awards, **1975:** 272
Smith, Alfred E., Memorial Dinner, **1976–77:** 935
Smith, Repr. Henry P., III, **1974:** 155
Smith, Ian, **1976–77:** 807, 854
Smith, Jack, **1975:** 691
Smith, Margaret Chase, **1976–77:** 116
Smith, Mary Louise, **1974:** 79; **1976–77:** 264, 657 [20]
Smith, Mrs. Merrill, **1975:** 238
Smith, Virginia, **1974:** 153
Smithsonian Institution, **1975:** 576
Snyder, Repr. Gene, **1974:** 175
Social Security Administration, **1974:** 140; **1976–77:** 779
Social security benefit indexing act, proposed, **1976–77:** 601, 602
Social security system
  Benefit structure, **1975:** 126; **1976–77:** 321 [9]
  Benefits increase, **1975:** 26, 28, 32, 36 [22], 46, 64, 143; **1976–77:** 24, 533
  Child support, **1975:** 487
  Deficits, **1976–77:** 362 [3], 533, 580 [5], 1044
  Federal budget, impact at local level, **1976–77:** 89
  Funding, **1975:** 554 [15]
  Improvement amendments, **1976–77:** 685
  Older Americans, special message to the Congress, **1976–77:** 70
  St. Petersburg, Fla., remarks to senior citizens, **1976–77:** 92
  Social Security Trust Fund, **1976–77:** 207 [2], 210 [8], 266 [9], 287 [5], 362 [3], 385, 432, 433
  State of the Union Address, **1976–77:** 19
  Tax decrease, **1976–77:** 415
  Tax increase, **1976–77:** 23 (p. 64), 24, 95, 433, 1044
  Title, **1976–77:** 20, 64
  Voluntary program, possibility, **1976–77:** 209
Social Services Amendments of 1974, **1975:** 14
Solar energy, **1974:** 138; **1975:** 108, 488 [9]; **1976–77:** 86 [2], 118, 356 [9]
Solzhenitsyn, Aleksandr, **1975:** 666 [19]
Somalia, Generalized System of Preferences, **1975:** 154, 668

Sonnenfeldt, Helmut, **1976–77:** 805
South Africa, Republic of, **1976–77:** 68 [10], 207 [7], 763 [1], 807, 854
South Bend, Ind., **1975:** 137, 138
South Carolina
  President's visits, **1974:** 170–173; **1976–77:** 950, 951
  Wilderness area, **1974:** 277
South Dakota
  Black Hills, Sioux Indian claim, **1974:** 198
  President's visit, **1974:** 152
Southeast Asia
  Administration policy, **1975:** 125 [4], 138 [2], 179, 716
  Domino theory, **1975:** 166 [2], 750 [23]
  Postwar reconstruction funding, **1975:** 161
  Refugee resettlement program, **1975:** 267, 347, 415, 746
  U.S. missing in action, **1975:** 411, 552 [9], 600 [13], 716; **1976–77:** 546
Southeast Asia, National League of American Prisoners and Missing in, **1976–77:** 689
Southern Baptist Convention, **1976–77:** 595
Southern Methodist University, **1975:** 560; **1976–77:** 321
Southwest Border Economic Development Region, **1976–77:** 958
Southworth, Frank, **1974:** 219
Soviet Union.
  See Union of Soviet Socialist Republics.
Space Museum, National Air and, **1976–77:** 631
Space program
  Apollo-Soyuz Test Project, **1974:** 59; **1975:** 405, 406, 412, 428, 482, 624
  Bicentennial Science and Technology Exposition, **1976–77:** 71, 591
  Communications satellites, **1975:** 313
  Convention on Registration of Objects Launched Into Outer Space, **1976–77:** 228
  Funding, **1976–77:** 215 [7]
  NASA Distinguished Service Medal, award ceremony, **1975:** 482
  National Space Club, **1975:** 180
  Observation satellites, **1975:** 313, 317
  Planetary exploration, **1975:** 313
  Report to Congress, **1976–77:** 622
  Skylab, **1974:** 223; **1975:** 180, 313
  Space shuttle, **1976–77:** 356 [9]
  Viking I, **1976–77:** 679
Spain
  Generalissimo Francisco Franco, **1975:** 291, 292n., 294, 684
  Juan Carlos
    As King, **1976–77:** 547, 549, 553
    As Prince, **1975:** 293n., 684n.
  NATO relationship, **1975:** 276 [4], 289, 290 [6]
  President of Government Carlos Arias Navarro, **1975:** 292n., 293, 459n.
Spain—*continued*
  President's visit, **1975:** 291–295
  United States-Spain Extradition Treaty, **1976–77:** 56
  United States-Spain Friendship and Cooperation Treaty, **1976–77:** 108
  U.S. Ambassador, **1975:** 684n.
Spanish-speaking Americans
  Economic and social statistics, publication legislation, **1976–77:** 596, 597
  Employment, **1975:** 410
  National Hispanic Heritage Week, **1974:** 48, 49; **1976–77:** 768, 788
  Republican National Hispanic Assembly, First annual banquet, **1976–77:** 702
  Voting rights, **1975:** 410, 422, 477
Sparkman, Sen. John J., **1974:** 29, 315; **1975:** 347; **1976–77:** 611, 797
Spartanburg, S.C., **1974:** 170
Special Coordinator for Disaster Relief, **1975:** 163
Special Prosecutor, Office of, proposed, **1976–77:** 675
Special Prosecutor Force, Office of Watergate, **1976–77:** 831
Special Representative for Trade Negotiations, **1974:** 121, 321; **1975:** 158, 311; **1976–77:** 346, 409, 410
Speedy Trial Act of 1974, **1975:** 7
Spence, Repr. Floyd, **1974:** 170, 173
Spencer, Stuart K., **1975:** 620 [6]; **1976–77:** 657 [24], 740
Spivak, Lawrence E., **1975:** 666
Sports
  American Football Coaches Association, **1975:** 25
  China, People's Republic of, national women's basketball team, **1975:** 696
  Elder, Lee, reception, **1974:** 268
  International Star Class Yacht Racing Association dinner, **1975:** 499
  Jackie Gleason Inverrary Classic, **1975:** 110
  Little League World Series, **1974:** 36
  National Collegiate Athletic Association, **1975:** 22
  National Football Foundation and Hall of Fame, **1974:** 289
  President's Commission on Olympic Sports, **1975:** 338
  Walter Hagen Invitational Golf Tournament, **1975:** 398
  Wimbledon tennis champions, **1975:** 417
  World Golf Hall of Fame, **1974:** 70, 71
Springfield, Ill., **1976–77:** 180–183, 907
Springfield, Mo., **1976–77:** 588, 589
Springfield, Ohio, **1976–77:** 576, 577
Spruce Pine, N.C., **1976–77:** 239
Stabler, Wells, **1975:** 684n.
Staebler, Neil, **1975:** 184

Stafford, George M., **1976–77:** 315
Stafford, Brig. Gen. Thomas P., **1975:** 412, 428, 482, 624
Staggers, Repr. Harley O., **1975:** 192
Stainless steel flatware industry, **1976–77:** 410, 412
Stames, Nick F., **1976–77:** 664
Stamm, Gilbert G., **1976–77:** 583
Stanford, Calif., **1975:** 577, 578
Stanford University School of Law, **1975:** 577, 578
Stanley, David M., **1974:** 188, 210
Stanton, Frank, **1974:** 11
Stanton, Repr. J. William, **1974:** 184
State, Department of
  Appropriations, **1974:** 72; **1975:** 681
  Assistant Secretary, **1974:** 195 [1]
  Budget deferrals, **1975:** 681
  Chief of Protocol, **1976–77:** 680
  Consular Agent, **1975:** 117, 118
  Counselor, **1976–77:** 805
  Foreign boycott practices, investigation, **1975:** 690
  Indochina refugees, **1975:** 347, 415
  Nuclear policy functions, **1976–77:** 987
  Rescissions and deferrals, **1976–77:** 1069
  Secretary, **1974:** 22, 81, 109, 124, 127 [7, 18], 132, 195 [14], 226, 236 [10], 259, 271 [1], 291; **1975:** 20, 85 [1], 153, 204 [5], 311, 324, 479 [9], 489, 516, 523, 600 [17], 657 [1, 3, 15, 19], 662, 666 [7], 678 [2], 685, 695 [5, 18], 718; **1976–77:** 16, 60, 133, 159, 207 [1], 209 [14], 212 [16, 17], 215 [1], 287 [9], 293 [2], 308, 325 [20], 339 [3], 352 [2], 362 [8], 396, 406, 418 [15], 523 [3], 560 [12], 599, 709, 763 [1], 770, 778, 784, 850, 854, 856, 959, 1061
  Under Secretary, **1975:** 311, 552 [8]
  Under Secretary for Political Affairs, **1976–77:** 23
  U.S. Ambassadors, **1974:** 16, 22, 237, 295; **1975:** 32, 239, 303, 657 [12], 684n.; **1976–77:** 16
  U.S. Representative to the United Nations, **1975:** 365
  See also specific constituent agencies.
State and Local Fiscal Assistance Amendments of 1976, **1976–77:** 890
State and local government
  Airport and airway development, **1975:** 136
  Antitrust legislation, **1976–77:** 417
  Budget news briefing, **1976–77:** 23 (p. 54–56, 60, 62)
  Budgets, spending levels, **1975:** 195
  Child day care, legislation, **1976–77:** 305, 760
  Child support programs, **1976–77:** 116
  Community development program, **1976–77:** 138 [11]
  Community services, **1975:** 502 [18]; **1976–77:** 127
  Concord, N.H., budget briefing, **1976–77:** 64
State and local government—*continued*
  Courts, Federal assistance, **1975:** 400
  Criminal justice programs, **1974:** 62, 96, 181
  Education, Federal aid, **1976–77:** 105, 168, 169, 185 [14], 189 [13], 192 [2], 284 [2], 352 [12], 402 [3]
  Emergency medical services, **1976–77:** 420 [2]
  Employment programs, Federal assistance, **1974:** 72, 108, 121, 328; **1975:** 616 [4], 678 [8]
  Energy, **1974:** 176, 201; **1975:** 32, 42, 85 [11, 17]
  Fair trade laws, **1975:** 192, 196, 220, 723, 724
  Federal assistance, **1975:** 102, 214, 215, 750 [19]; **1976–77:** 39, 185 [3], 398 [6]
  Federal Executive Boards, **1975:** 151
  Federal policies
    Economy, **1975:** 32
    Energy, **1975:** 32
  Federal role, **1975:** 554 [14]
  Federal-State relationship, **1976–77:** 131
  Fire prevention and control programs, **1974:** 197
  Fiscal policy, **1975:** 72 [18]
  Florida budget briefing, **1976–77:** 89
  Food and nutrition programs, Federal assistance, **1975:** 609, 615 [8], 616 [15], 620 [11]
  Gasoline taxes, State revenue, **1975:** 678 [16]
  General revenue sharing, **1974:** 271 [18]; **1975:** 28, 32, 64, 69, 70, 90 [1], 102, 138 [16], 169, 214, 215, 216, 393, 554 [14], 678 [8]; **1976–77:** 38, 49, 57, 65, 95, 209 [1], 210 [1], 215 [4], 216, 231 [1], 284 [5], 321, 352 [11], 354 [2], 372, 551, 552, 782, 947
  Governors, meetings, **1975:** 42, 102
  Grant programs, **1976–77:** 116
  Health programs, **1975:** 363, 436; **1976–77:** 38, 135, 136, 209 [10]
  Highway construction, **1975:** 72 [9], 84, 85 [3], 108, 309, 367, 382, 383, 393, 622 [21]
  Housing programs, Federal assistance, **1975:** 350, 351, 372, 496 [3], 622 [11]
  Impact aid, **1976–77:** 118, 373 [10]
  Inflation, telegram to officials, **1974:** 146, 151
  Labor-management relations, **1976–77:** 293 [3]
  Law enforcement and crime, **1975:** 341, 532, 554 [5, 10], 590; **1976–77:** 97, 818
  Legislation, **1976–77:** 685
  Loans, usury law exemptions, **1974:** 199
  Mass transportation, **1974:** 261
  Mayors, U.S. Conference of, **1976–77:** 38
  National Conference on State Legislatures, **1975:** 216
  News conference remarks, **1976–77:** 898 [8]
  Occupational safety and health programs, **1975:** 363
  Offshore oil and gas development, **1974:** 233, 262
  Offshore oil rights, **1975:** 511 [10]
  Oil pollution control, legislation, **1975:** 388
  Older persons, programs, **1975:** 424; **1976–77:** 92
  Public employees strikes, **1975:** 502 [10], 554 [11], 582 [1]

State and local government—*continued*
Public works projects, **1974:** 108; **1975:** 616 [6]
Regional cooperation, **1975:** 616 [19]
Remarks at National Governors' Conference, **1976–77:** 126
State legislatures
Awards, **1975:** 34
President's addresses, **1975:** 84, 195, 532
State of the Union Address, **1976–77:** 19
States' rights, **1976–77:** 356 [1]
Unemployment benefits, **1975:** 508
Virginia General Assembly, **1976–77:** 51
WIN consumer pledges, **1974:** 232
State of the Union Address, **1975:** 28; **1976–77:** 19, 1057
Statements by the President
Abrams, Gen. Creighton W., Jr., death, **1974:** 51
Advisory Council on Social Security, report, **1975:** 126
American prisoner, release from Laos, **1974:** 83
Anthony, Susan B., birthday, **1976–77:** 85
Automobile emission standards deadline, extension, **1975:** 364
Aviation, international, **1976–77:** 765
Bell, Jack, death, **1975:** 563
Biological and chemical weapons, ratification of treaties, **1975:** 38
Calder, Alexander, death, **1976–77:** 1018
California cannery strike settlement, **1976–77:** 695
Cambodia
Evacuation of U.S. Mission in Phnom Penh, **1975:** 182
Fall of government, **1975:** 191
Chiang Kai-shek, death, **1975:** 170
Child day care, legislation, **1976–77:** 424, 430
Chou En-lai, death, **1976–77:** 12
Clemency and pardons, **1974:** 68, 329; **1975:** 58, 113, 566
Commission on CIA Activities Within the United States, establishment, **1975:** 19
Commission on Revision of the Federal Court Appellate System, report submittal, **1975:** 342
Common situs picketing bill, veto, **1975:** 743
Considine, Bob, death, **1975:** 588
Consumer representation in Federal departments and agencies, **1975:** 658
Corporation for Public Broadcasting, support for Federal funding, **1975:** 88
Council on Wage and Price Stability
Appointment of Chairman and members, **1974:** 41
Congressional action establishing, **1974:** 19
Cultural Challenge Grant Program, **1976–77:** 899
Daley, Richard J., death, **1976–77:** 1035
de Valera, Eamon, death, **1975:** 507
District of Columbia, Fiscal Year 76 budget, amendment transmittal, **1976–77:** 345

Statements by the President—*continued*
District of Columbia city council, decisions concerning two bills, **1976–77:** 147
Domestic Council Drug Abuse Task Force report, **1975:** 628
Domestic Council Review Group on Regulatory Reform, report, **1976–77:** 1062
Drug abuse
Law enforcement, **1976–77:** 128
Programs, **1975:** 748
Economic data, **1976–77:** 921
Economic Impact Statements program, **1976–77:** 1043
Egan, John Patrick, death, **1975:** 117
Egyptian-Israeli troop disengagement agreement, **1975:** 515
Election results for 1974, **1974:** 225
Electric utilities construction, President's Labor-Management Committee recommendations, **1975:** 326
Emergency agricultural bill, House action sustaining veto, **1975:** 252
Emergency livestock feed assistance, **1976–77:** 1029
Energy conservation, **1974:** 166; **1975:** 149
Energy Research and Development Administration, activation, **1975:** 29
"Expo 81," recognition as a world's fair, **1976–77:** 1034
Faisal Ibn Abdul Aziz, death, **1975:** 155
Federal Election Commission
Reconstitution by Congress, **1976–77:** 370
Statement on proposed legislation, **1976–77:** 123
Federal Energy Office, establishment, **1976–77:** 705
Federal labor-management relations in the Federal service, **1975:** 76
Federal pay increase, **1974:** 82, 87, 115
Federal spending ceiling, congressional adoption, **1975:** 223; **1976–77:** 472
Foreign boycott practices, **1975:** 689
Foreign Intelligence Advisory Board, announcement of expansion, **1976–77:** 199
Forest and Rangeland Renewable Resources Planning Act of 1974, statement of policy, **1976–77:** 171
Franco, Francisco, death, **1975:** 684
General Motors, prices, **1974:** 5, 23
General revenue sharing, **1976–77:** 586, 835
Grain sales agreement with the Soviet Union, **1975:** 539, 636
Guinea-Bissau, Portuguese recognition of independence, **1974:** 4
Haile Selassie, death, **1975:** 505
Hart, Sen. Philip A., death, **1976–77:** 1038
Hastie, William H., death, **1976–77:** 344
Hearing-impaired, visual television aids, **1976–77:** 929

Statements by the President—*continued*
Highway safety over Labor Day weekend, **1976–77:** 753
Hoffman, Paul G., death, **1974:** 122
Income tax
Exemption proposal, **1976–77:** 719
Reduction extension, **1976–77:** 747
Withholding rate extensions, **1976–77:** 756
Independence Day, **1975:** 377
Indochina refugee resettlement program, **1975:** 415, 746
Inter-American Convention on the Granting of Political Rights to Women and Convention on the Political Rights of Women, statement on signing, **1976–77:** 241
International Fund for Agricultural Development, **1976–77:** 1037
Japanese Diet's approval of non-proliferation of nuclear weapons, **1976–77:** 514
Jarman, Repr. John, change in party affiliation, **1975:** 44
Jewish High Holy Days, **1976–77:** 809
Job Corps, 10th anniversary, **1975:** 52
Keating, Kenneth B., death, **1975:** 239
King, Martin Luther, Jr., anniversary of birth, **1976–77:** 17
Kissinger, Secretary of State Henry A., trip to Middle East, **1975:** 489
Kluczynski, Repr. John C., death, **1975:** 51
La Guardia Airport, bombing incident, **1975:** 749
Labor Day, **1974:** 44
Lebanon, evacuation of American citizens, **1976–77:** 604, 607
Legislative priorities, **1976–77:** 674 [1], 684
Lincoln, George A., death, **1975:** 284
Lindbergh, Charles A., death, **1974:** 37
Lippmann, Walter, death, **1974:** 298
Lisagor, Peter, death, **1976–77:** 1027
Little, Franklin Rockefeller, death, **1975:** 205
Litton, Repr. Jerry, death, **1976–77:** 713
Mao Tse-tung, death, **1976–77:** 767
Mindszenty, József Cardinal, death, **1975:** 242
Mississippi River, Locks and Dam 26, replacement, **1976–77:** 738
Moley, Raymond, death, **1975:** 98
National Endowment for the Humanities, **1976–77:** 1079
National Epilepsy Month, **1975:** 638
National Labor Relations Act, 40th anniversary, **1975:** 378
National Medal of Science, awards, **1975:** 345; **1976–77:** 557
New York City's financial situation, **1975:** 683
93rd Congress, **1974:** 316
94th Congress, **1976–77:** 851
Nobel Prizes, **1976–77:** 933
Northern Mariana Islands, Commonwealth status, **1975:** 344

Statements by the President—*continued*
Nuclear policy, **1976–77:** 987
Nuclear Regulatory Commission, activation, **1975:** 29
Oil
Import fee-setting authority, **1975:** 99
OPEC price decision, **1975:** 592; **1976–77:** 1031
Price decontrol, **1975:** 420, 542
Prices, international, **1976–77:** 541
Spill off Massachusetts coast, **1976–77:** 1036
Older Americans programs, **1976–77:** 992
Paperwork reduction, **1976–77:** 687
Pardon of Richard Nixon, **1974:** 155
Petroleum products, termination of price controls, **1976–77:** 635
Pettis, Repr. Jerry L., death, **1975:** 94
Presidential Clemency Board, termination, **1975:** 566
Presidential Management Initiatives program, **1976–77:** 1019
President's Commission on Olympic Sports, establishment, **1975:** 338
President's Committee on Mental Retardation meeting, **1974:** 136
President's Committee on Urban Development and Neighborhood Revitalization, **1976–77:** 625, 930
Privacy Act of 1974, **1974:** 125; **1975:** 595
Public Works Employment Act, congressional override of veto, **1976–77:** 683, 686
Public works employment bill, Senate action sustaining veto, **1976–77:** 113
Puerto Rico, proposed statehood, **1976–77:** 1041
Pulliam, Eugene C., death, **1975:** 349
Razak, Tun Abdul, death, **1976–77:** 18
Report of the Select Committee on Intelligence, House of Representatives vote on the release of, **1976–77:** 40
Richardson, Elliot L., nomination to be U.S. Ambassador to the United Kingdom, **1975:** 23
Rockefeller, Nelson A., confirmation to be Vice President of the United States, **1974:** 288, 314
Sato, Eisaku, death, **1975:** 303
School busing, **1976–77:** 543
Seaton, Elizabeth Bayley, canonization, **1974:** 296
Skylab crystal presentation, **1974:** 223
Small business, **1976–77:** 81
Social Security Trust Fund, proposed payroll tax increase, **1976–77:** 433
Southern Africa, **1976–77:** 763 [1]
Soviet Mission to United Nations, gunfiring incident, **1976–77:** 286
Spain, President's departure, **1975:** 295
Sugar imports, **1974:** 241; **1976–77:** 795

Statements by the President—*continued*
Supreme Court decision concerning Federal Election Campaign Act amendments of 1974, **1976–77:** 46
Task Force on Questionable Corporate Payments Abroad, **1976–77:** 276, 593
Tax reduction extension bill, House action sustaining veto, **1975:** 735
Tel Aviv, Israel, terrorist attack, **1975:** 123
terHorst, J.F., resignation as Press Secretary, **1974:** 64
Trade reform legislation, Senate action, **1974:** 299
Trucking industry contract negotiations, **1976–77:** 294
Turkey, U.S. military assistance, **1975:** 73, 608
Suspension, **1974:** 113, 120, 147; **1975:** 427, 434
U Thant, death, **1974:** 260
United Kingdom, economic situation, **1976–77:** 986
Veterans Administration hospitals, **1976–77:** 456
Vietnam, Republic of
Refugees assistance, **1975:** 163, 231
U.S. humanitarian assistance, **1975:** 161 [1], 231
U.S. mercy flight crash near Saigon, **1975:** 168
U.S. personnel, evacuation, **1975:** 221
Vietnam era veterans benefits, termination of eligibility period, **1975:** 246
Welch, Richard, death, **1975:** 745
White House Conference on Handicapped Individuals, **1976–77:** 242
White House Conference on Library and Information Services, **1976–77:** 678
Williams, Repr. Lawrence G., death, **1975:** 407
World Environment Day, **1975:** 310; **1976–77:** 556
Zionism, United Nations resolution, **1975:** 640
See also Legislation, remarks and statements on approval.
Stein, Herbert, **1974:** 38, 39 [12]
Stevens, Bill, **1974:** 174
Stevens, John Paul, **1975:** 697, 750 [1]; **1976–77:** 947
Stevens, Roger L., **1976–77:** 623
Stevens, Sen. Ted, **1975:** 704
Stever, H. Guyford, **1975:** 568; **1976–77:** 724
Stinson, George, **1976–77:** 28
Stock market, **1976–77:** 48 [17]
Stock ownership, **1976–77:** 685
Stockdale, Rear Adm. James P., **1976–77:** 176
Stockpiles disposal, **1974:** 240; **1976–77:** 685
Stockyards Act of 1921, Packers and, amendments, **1976–77:** 774, 775
Stone, Clement, **1974:** 155
Stone, Mr. and Mrs. Don J., **1975:** 272
Strategic arms limitation
Joint statements
France, **1974:** 302
Germany, Federal Republic of, **1974:** 284
Japan, **1974:** 249
Union of Soviet Socialist Republics, **1974:** 257, 258
News conference responses, **1974:** 39 [27], 127 [8], 195 [14], 236 [21], 271 [1, 2, 4, 5, 6, 7, 9, 10]
Newsweek magazine interview, **1974:** Appendix D
Union of Soviet Socialist Republics, remarks following visit, **1974:** 259
Strategic arms limitation talks, **1975:** 64, 96, 119, 179, 186, 243 [7], 276 [3], 290 [8], 316 [5], 354 [10], 456, 459, 460 [1, 4], 479 [7], 492, 501 [8, 9], 502 [5], 512, 526, 581 [8], 600 [10], 650, 657 [13], 666 [25], 695 [5, 16], 717, 750 [5]; **1976–77:** 23 (p. 72), 48 [1], 569, 657 [22, 23], 701, 763 [6], 854, 967
Strausz-Hupé, Robert, **1976–77:** 297
Streeter, Sgt. John V., **1974:** 59
Strip mining.
See Surface mining.
Student Loan Marketing Association, **1975:** 55
Study of Afro-American Life and History, Association for the, **1976–77:** 74
Stump, Harvey, Jr., **1975:** 272
Submarines, **1974:** 271 [16]
Sugar imports, **1974:** 241; **1976–77:** 795, 796
Sugar Policy, Task Force on, **1976–77:** 795
Suharto, **1975:** 381, 709, 710
Sullivan, Repr. Leonor K., **1974:** 99
Summer youth program, **1976–77:** 23 (p. 74)
Summit conference in Puerto Rico, **1976–77:** 550, 580 618–621
Sun Newspaper Good Neighbor Awards, **1976–77:** 984
Supersonic transport, **1976–77:** 933
Supplemental Security Income Amendments, Food Stamp and, **1976–77:** 708, 721, 943
Supplemental Security Income program, **1975:** 64, 143
Supplies and Shortages, National Commission on, **1974:** 114
Supreme Court of the United States
Abortion decision, **1976–77:** 189 [15], 287 [2], 674 [34]
Antitrust appeals, **1974:** 317
Associate Justice, **1975:** 673, 697, 750 [1]
Brown v. Board of Education of Topeka, Kansas, **1975:** 565 [8]
Chief Justice, **1974:** 1; **1975:** 692
Criteria for nominee selection, **1975:** 578 [1], 678 [4, 7, 18]
Death penalty decision, **1976–77:** 657 [25]

Supreme Court—*continued*
Federal Election Campaign Act amendments of 1974, **1976–77:** 46, 48 [2]
Federal Election Commission, **1976–77:** 103
Philosophy, **1975:** 678 [7]
Selection process for Justices, **1976–77:** 185 [6], 947
Vacancy, **1975:** 695 [9, 14, 17]
Surface mining, **1974:** 72, 121, 131, 240, 326; **1975:** 28, 64, 75, 152, 270, 488 [9], 615 [10], 616 [16]; **1976–77:** 209 [12], 947
Surinam
Generalized System of Preferences beneficiary, **1975:** 668
President Johan Henri Eliza Ferrier, **1975:** 693
Swank, C. William, **1976–77:** 217
Swearing-in ceremonies
Attorney General of the United States, **1975:** 79
Civil Aeronautics Board, Chairman, **1975:** 203
Commerce Department, Secretary, **1975:** 227
Consumer Advisory Council, membership, **1975:** 230
Council of Economic Advisers, Chairman, **1974:** 52
Defense Department, Secretary, **1975:** 688
Equal Employment Opportunity Commission, Chairman, **1975:** 282
Federal Election Commission, membership, **1975:** 184
Federal Reserve System, Board of Governors, member, **1975:** 403
Health, Education, and Welfare Department
Assistant Secretary of Health, **1975:** 370
Secretary, **1975:** 480
Housing and Urban Development Department, Secretary, **1975:** 131
Interior Department, Secretary, **1975:** 327, 633
Labor Department, Secretary, **1975:** 140
Librarian of Congress, **1975:** 672
National Institutes of Health, Director, **1975:** 370
National Labor Relations Board, Chairman, **1975:** 97
Office of Management and Budget, Director, **1975:** 81
President of the United States, **1974:** 1
Special Representative for Trade Negotiations, **1975:** 158
Transportation Department, Secretary, **1975:** 128
U.S. Representative to the United Nations, **1975:** 365
Veterans Administration, Administrator, **1974:** 139
Swine flu immunization program, **1976–77:** 257, 258, 280, 341, 342, 685, 688, 715, 718, 723
Switzerland Treaty on Mutual Assistance in Criminal Matters, United States, **1976–77:** 109
Synthetic fuels, **1976–77:** 685
Syracuse, N.Y., **1976–77:** 997
Syria
Disengagement of forces with Israel, **1975:** 648 [7]
Lebanon, involvement in, **1976–77:** 282 [5], 505, 560 [8]
Security assistance programs, **1975:** 649

Taft, Julia, **1975:** 415
Taft, Sen. Robert, Jr., **1974:** 184; **1976–77:** 578, 983
Taft-Hartley Act, **1976–77:** 287 [3], 293 [3]
Taiwan.
See China, Republic of.
Tampa, Fla., **1976–77:** 165–167
Tanaka, Kakuei, **1974:** 244, 249
Tape recordings.
See Documents and recordings, Presidential.
Tariffs and Trade, General Agreement on, **1974:** 130, 274
Task Force on Questionable Corporate Payments Abroad, **1976–77:** 275–77, 592, 593, 709
Task Force on Sugar Policy, **1976–77:** 795
Tax Reduction Act of 1975, **1975:** 164
Tax Reform Act, **1976–77:** 847, 848
Taxation
Bilateral conventions
Iceland, **1975:** 385
Poland, **1975:** 40
Business taxes
Exempt securities, **1976–77:** 558
Investment tax credit, **1974:** 121, 240; **1975:** 69, 70, 71, 84, 602 [8], 614, 616 [1], 623
Reduction, **1975:** 26, 28, 32, 64, 90 [3, 4], 614, 616 [1], 623, 629, 630, 631; **1976–77:** 406 [3], 416, 967, 1044
Reform, **1975:** 616 [14]
Windfall profits, **1974:** 240; **1975:** 32, 60, 64, 70, 85 [6], 109 [7], 283, 488 [7], 538
Campaign debate remarks, **1976–77:** 803, 947
Capital gains, **1974:** 121
Casualty losses, **1974:** 264
Church properties, **1976–77:** 846
Concord, N.H., budget briefing, **1976–77:** 64
Congressional action, **1975:** 109 [5, 20], 135, 138 [10], 164
Congressional Members, exemption from local income taxes, veto of bill, **1976–77:** 710
Conventions on taxation
Korea, Republic of, **1976–77:** 754
United Kingdom, **1976–77:** 613, 799
Domestic International Sales Corporation, **1975:** 554 [7]
Economic Report of the President, **1976–77:** 1070
Education, private assistance, **1975:** 496 [7]

Taxation—*continued*
Elderly persons, **1975:** 424
Energy conservation, **1975:** 26
Energy tax rebate, **1975:** 121, 582 [9]
Estate tax, **1976–77:** 181, 189 [7], 203, 287 [14], 333 [3], 389, 512, 610
Fuel, **1974:** 121, 127 [5], 135, 152, 153, 154, 210, 236 [9], 271 [17], Appendix D; **1975:** 60, 64, 70, 138 [17], 383, 393, 678 [16]
Income taxes
Exemption proposal, **1976–77:** 719, 735
Rebates, **1975:** 26, 28, 32, 36 [2, 29], 39, 46, 54, 70, 71, 72 [14], 90 [3]
Reduction, **1975:** 26, 28, 32, 36 [12], 54, 62, 64, 69, 85 [17], 90 [1, 3, 4], 121, 125 [8], 157, 164, 171, 354 [7, 17], 379 [1, 2, 10], 501 [1], 565 [6], 600 [2], 614, 615 [1], 616 [1], 617, 620 [3, 13], 622 [5, 16, 22], 623, 626, 629, 630, 631, 647, 650, 666 [15], 695 [20], 717, 731, 732, 735, 750 [10]; **1976–77:** 406 [3], 416, 610, 628, 747, 966, 1044
Return inspection, **1974:** 80 [7], 127 [14]
Legislation, **1976–77:** 685
Long-term investments, **1976–77:** 293 [9]
Mortgage interest tax credit, **1974:** 234; **1975:** 144
News conference remarks, **1976–77:** 67 [10], 86 [7], 387 [12], 898 [19]
Radio-Television News Directors Association, **1976–77:** 48 [14]
Reductions, **1976–77:** 185 [8], 327 [3], 339 [10], 406, 416, 610, 628, 747, 966, 967, 1044
See also specific areas of taxation.
Reform, **1974:** 72, 121, 271 [13]; **1975:** 157, 164, 169, 171, 616 [14]; **1976–77:** 287 [6], 362 [4], 383
State of the Union Address, **1976–77:** 19, 1057
Surcharge, **1974:** 121, 127 [3, 11], 131, 135, 154, 236 [12], 240, Appendix D
Windfall profits tax, **1974:** 72, 240; **1975:** 32, 60, 64, 70, 85 [6], 109 [7], 283, 488 [7], 538
Withholding rates extension, bill signing, **1976–77:** 756
Taylor, Repr. Gene, **1974:** 151
Teague, Repr. Olin E., **1975:** 112
Teamsters.
See Trucking industry.
Teeter, Robert, **1976–77:** 740
Tel Aviv, Israel, **1974:** 39 [22]; **1975:** 123, 125 [10]
Telecommunication Convention, International, **1974:** 158
Telecommunications Policy, Office of, **1976–77:** 964
Television
Cable, **1976–77:** 964
Hearing-impaired, visual aids, **1976–77:** 928
Industry, self-regulation, **1976–77:** 964
Television Directors' Association, Radio and, **1974:** 76
Television interviews.
See under News media.
Television News Directors Association, Radio-, **1975:** 46
Teller, Edward, **1976–77:** 199
Teng Hsiao-ping, **1975:** 706, 708
Tennessee
Commerce Square Fountain, Memphis, dedication ceremonies, **1976–77:** 478
President Ford Committee, **1976–77:** 479
Presidential primary, **1976–77:** 523
President's visits, **1975:** 615, 616; **1976–77:** 475–480
Republican Party reception, **1976–77:** 480
Wilderness area, **1974:** 277
Tennessee-Tombigbee Waterway, **1975:** 616 [12]; **1976–77:** 817
Tennessee Valley Authority, **1974:** 320; **1975:** 615 [4], 616 [13], 678 [17]
terHorst, J. F., **1974:** 2, 64
Terman, Frederick E., **1976–77:** 557, 914
Terrorism, international prevention, **1976–77:** 876
Teton Dam, Idaho, **1976–77:** 583, 587, 758, 783
Texas
Abilene Jaycees, **1976–77:** 406, 408
Baylor University, **1976–77:** 392
Bicentennial commemoration ceremony, El Paso, **1976–77:** 329
Fort Worth/Tarrant County Bar Association, **1976–77:** 380
Grain and Feed Association, Texas, **1976–77:** 327
Greater Houston Builders and Contractors Associations, **1976–77:** 383
Houston campaign rally, **1976–77:** 385
Houston Music Theatre, **1976–77:** 995
Irving Bar Association Law Day dinner, **1976–77:** 323
Northern Texas Panhandle Lion's Club dinner, **1976–77:** 332
President Ford Committee
Conroe, **1976–77:** 390
Dallas, **1976–77:** 324, 871
El Paso, **1976–77:** 328
Houston, **1976–77:** 384, 386
San Antonio, **1976–77:** 319
Tyler, **1976–77:** 377
Waco, **1976–77:** 394
West Texas, **1976–77:** 403
Presidential primary, **1976–77:** 325 [9, 22], 372, 378 [10], 382
President's visits, **1975:** 82, 558–562; **1976–77:** 316–324, 326–333, 376–386, 388–408, 868–872, 994, 995
Public forum, Dallas, **1976–77:** 398
Republican delegation, **1976–77:** 253
Republican Party functions, **1976–77:** 318, 397
Southern Methodist University, **1976–77:** 321

Texas—*continued*
Tyler Junior College, **1976–77:** 378
Waco Suspension Bridge, **1976–77:** 393
West Texas State University, public forum, **1976–77:** 333
Texas Nursing Home Association, **1976–77:** 388
Texas State Fair, **1976–77:** 869
Texas State Fair Board, **1976–77:** 870
Texas Technological University, **1976–77:** 401, 402
Textile Agreements, Committee for the Implementation of, **1975:** 311
Textile industry, **1974:** 173
Textile Trade Policy Group, **1975:** 311
Thailand, security assistance programs, **1975:** 649
Thanksgiving Day, **1975:** 694, 695 [24]
Theodore Roosevelt Award, **1975:** 22
Theresa Janene, **1976–77:** 523
Thieu, Nguyen Van, **1975:** 85 [12], 166 [2, 6], 189 [6], 204 [2]
Third century goals, **1976–77:** 356 [6]
Thomas, Helen, **1976–77:** 560
Thomas, Jerry, **1976–77:** 86 [11]
Thomas, Lowell, **1976–77:** 1052
Thomson, Gov. Meldrim, Jr., **1976–77:** 67 [2, 6]
Thomson, Vernon, **1975:** 184
Thone, Repr. Charles, **1974:** 153
Thorelli, Hans B., **1975:** 230
Thorn, Gaston, **1975:** 289n., 674
Thorsness, Leo, **1974:** 152
Thurmond, Sen. Strom, **1974:** 170, 172, 173; **1976–77:** 951
Tiernan, Robert, **1975:** 184
Timmons, William E., **1974:** 273
Tin, stockpile disposal, **1974:** 240
Tin Agreement, International, **1976–77:** 612
Tindemans, Leo, **1975:** 287n.
Tito, Josip Broz, **1975:** 466, 467, 468, 469, 471
Tobacco price support levels, **1975:** 601
"Today" program, interview, **1976–77:** 778
Tokyo, Japan, **1974:** 244, 245, 246, 247, 248, 250
Tolbert, William R., Jr., **1976–77:** 794, 798
Toledo, Ohio, **1976–77:** 581
Tomb of the Unknowns, **1974:** 192; **1975:** 278
Topeka, Kans., **1975:** 83, 84, 85
Torell, Bruce, **1975:** 272
Tourism programs, **1975:** 285, 389
Tower, Sen. John G., **1974:** 29; **1976–77:** 394
Toxic Substances Control Act, **1976–77:** 882
Trade.
See International Commerce.
Trade, General Agreement on Tariffs and, **1974:** 130, 274
Trade Commission, Joint Polish-American, **1974:** 129, 130
Trade Commission, United States International.
See United States International Trade Commission.
Trade Commission Act of 1974, Commodity Futures, **1974:** 189, 240
Trade Negotiations, Advisory Committee for, **1976–77:** 11
Trade Negotiations, Office of the Special Representative for, **1975:** 158, 311
Trade Negotiations, Special Representative for, **1974:** 121, 321
Trademark Registration Treaty, **1975:** 519
Traffic and Motor Vehicle Safety Act of 1966, National, **1974:** 194
Traffic safety, **1974:** 50, 194; **1975:** 613; **1976–77:** 616
Traffic Safety Administration, National Highway, **1974:** 50
Trans-Canada gas pipeline, **1976–77:** 657 [21]
Transportation
Customs procedures, **1975:** 279
Hazardous materials, regulation, **1975:** 9
International, customs inspection, **1974:** 201
Legislation, **1976–77:** 685
Mass transit, **1975:** 85 [3], 128, 393
Regulatory reform, **1975:** 70, 196, 220, 678 [6]
Legislation, **1974:** 72, 240; **1975:** 268
Safety programs, **1974:** 50, 197; **1975:** 9, 613, 725
Saint Lawrence Seaway Development Corporation report, **1975:** 535
Urban, **1974:** 65, 72, 127 [17], 240, 261
See also specific mode of transportation.
Transportation, Department of
Automotive transport research and development bill, veto, **1976–77:** 811
Budget deferrals and rescissions, **1975:** 11, 72 [9], 84, 367; **1976–77:** 802, 1069
Concorde, **1976–77:** 356 [10]
Deputy Secretary, **1976–77:** 657 [12]
La Guardia Airport, bombing incident, investigation, **1975:** 749
Military incentive awards program, **1975:** 139
Secretary, **1974:** 72, 109, 132, 291, 308; **1975:** 20, 92, 128, 268, 725, 749; **1976–77:** 38, 58, 661, 934, 941, 959, 972, 1073
War Risk Insurance Program, **1976–77:** 230
See also specific constituent agencies.
Transportation Assistance Act of 1974, National Mass, **1974:** 240, 261
Transportation Safety Act of 1974, **1975:** 9
Travel, President's
Domestic.
See specific State or city.
Foreign.
See specific country.
News conference responses, **1974:** 236 [15], 271 [1]
Newsweek magazine interview, **1974:** Appendix D
Travel Program for Foreign Diplomats, **1975:** 148
Travel Service, United States, **1975:** 285

Traverse City, Mich., **1975:** 398, 401n.
Treasury, Department of the
  Alexander Hamilton Award, **1975:** 240
  Budget rescissions and deferrals, **1975:** 541, 681; **1976–77:** 364, 739, 1017, 1022
  Foreign investment activity in the United States, study, **1974:** 193
  Secretary, **1974:** 41, 109, 132, 291; **1975:** 20, 92, 189 [9], 214, 228, 240, 311, 324, 626; **1976–77:** 1, 86 [7], 562, 626
  Under Secretary, **1975:** 311
  See also specific constituent agencies.
Treaties and other international agreements
  Antarctic Seals, Convention for the Conservation of, **1975:** 730
  Antiballistic missile systems limitation, protocol to treaty with Union of Soviet Socialist Republics, **1974:** 85
  Atomic energy, amendment to agreement with United Kingdom, **1974:** 10
  Biological weapons convention, **1975:** 37, 38
  Consular convention with Bulgaria, **1974:** 73
  Extradition treaties
    Australia, **1974:** 28
    Canada, **1974:** 74
  Geneva Protocol of 1925, **1975:** 37, 38
  Inter-American Treaty of Reciprocal Assistance (Rio Treaty), protocol, **1975:** 700
  Intergovernmental Maritime Consultative Organization convention, amendments, **1975:** 391
  International Coffee Agreement of 1968, protocol, **1975:** 188
  International Office of Epizootics, agreement creating, **1974:** 270
  International telecommunication convention, **1974:** 158
  International Wheat Agreement, 1971, protocols, **1975:** 319
  Internationally protected persons, convention on prevention and punishment of crimes against, **1974:** 86, 230
  Nuclear weapons, nonproliferation treaty, **1975:** 450
  Polar bears, agreement on the conservation of, **1975:** 699
  Psychotropic substances, convention, **1975:** 748
  Radio Regulations (Geneva, 1959), partial revision, **1975:** 408
  Safety of life at sea convention, amendments, **1974:** 157
  Shrimp agreement with Brazil, **1975:** 320
  Taxation conventions
    Iceland, **1975:** 385
    Poland, **1975:** 40
  Trade agreement with Romania, **1975:** 210, 211, 668
  Trademark Registration Treaty, **1975:** 519
Trewhitt, Henry L., **1976–77:** 854
Trident submarine, **1974:** 271 [16]
Trivette, Alpha, **1975:** 419
Trucking industry
  Compensatory legislation, **1974:** 240; **1975:** 11
  Contract negotiations, **1976–77:** 294
  Deregulation, **1975:** 502 [12]
  Freight rates, **1976–77:** 308
  Motor carrier reform legislation, **1975:** 675, 678 [6]
  News conference remarks, **1976–77:** 282 [3]
  Teamsters, Chauffeurs, Warehousemen and Helpers of America, International Brotherhood of, **1976–77:** 284 [4], 308
  Weight standards, **1976–77:** 210 [3]
Trudeau, Pierre Elliott, **1974:** 278; **1975:** 290n.; **1976–77:** 600, 621
Truman, Harry S., **1975:** 6, 85 [16], 479 [6], 582 [7]; **1976–77:** 447
Tubac, Ariz., **1974:** 178, 179
Tucson, Ariz., **1974:** 180
Tulane University, **1975:** 208
Tunisia, Prime Minister Hedi Nouira, **1975:** 233
Turkey
  Arms embargo, Congressional action, **1975:** 479 [10]
  Cyprus dispute, **1975:** 390, 718; **1976–77:** 60, 68 [9], 118, 283, 314, 582, 717, 1051
  Defense cooperation agreement with United States, **1976–77:** 598, 685, 1074
  Foreign Minister Caglayangil, **1976–77:** 60
  Generalized System of Preferences, beneficiary, **1975:** 668
  Illicit drug trafficking, **1975:** 748
  NATO involvement, **1975:** 387
  Opium poppies, control, **1975:** 720
  Prime Minister Süleyman Demirel, **1975:** 289n., 457, 720
  Security assistance programs, **1975:** 649
  U.S. military assistance, **1974:** 113, 120, 135, 144, 145, 147, 151, 156, 164, 195 [21], 236 [21], 325; **1975:** 73, 91, 179, 276, [2], 387, 390, 427, 440, 447, 479 [10], 492, 565 [18], 608
  U.S. military operations, suspension, **1975:** 434, 447, 457, 460 [2]
Tuss McLaughry Award, **1975:** 25
25th Amendment to the Constitution, **1974:** 195 [12], 236 [2]
Tyler, Tex., **1976–77:** 377
Tyler Junior College, **1976–77:** 378

U Thant, **1974:** 260
Ueki, Mitsunori, **1976–77:** 623
Uganda
  Generalized System of Preferences, **1975:** 154
  Rescue of Israeli hostages, **1976–77:** 648, 657 [4, 10]

Ullman, Repr. Al, **1976–77:** 23 (p. 70)
Unemployment.
See Employment and unemployment.
Unemployment Assistance Act, Emergency Jobs and, **1974:** 328; **1975:** 32, 64, 209
Unemployment Assistance Extension Act of 1975, Emergency Compensation and Special, **1975:** 366
Unemployment Compensation Act, Emergency, **1974:** 328; **1975:** 32, 64, 209
Uniform Code of Military Justice, **1974:** 16, 78; **1975:** 58
Uniform Relocation Assistance and Real Property Acquisition Policies Act of 1970, **1975:** 49
Uniformed Services University of Health Sciences, **1975:** 394
Union, N.J., **1976–77:** 894, 895
Union of Soviet Socialist Republics
Administration policy, **1974:** 6; **1975:** 179, 186
Angola, involvement, **1975:** 695 [22], 738, 739 [7, 8], 750 [5, 21]; **1976–77:** 138 [14]
Antiballistic missile systems, protocol to treaty with United States, **1974:** 85
Apollo-Soyuz Test Project, **1974:** 59; **1975:** 405, 406, 412, 428, 482, 624
Arms and weapons, **1976–77:** 405
Backfire bomber, **1975:** 666 [25]
Campaign debate remarks, **1976–77:** 854
Democratic Republic of Vietnam, aid, **1975:** 189 [5]
Détente with United States, **1975:** 36 [15], 276 [3], 289, 290 [2], 354 [10], 459, 492, 501 [8], 502 [5], 530, 581 [8], 657 [7], 663, 666 [19, 22], 695 [22], 739 [8], 750 [5]; **1976–77:** 6, 210 [5], 283, 362 [2], 392 [6]
Fishery agreement with United States, **1976–77:** 1050
Florida budget briefing, **1976–77:** 89
General Secretary L. I. Brezhnev, **1974:** 127 [7], 256, 257, 258, 259, 271 [1], Appendix D; **1975:** 36 [23], 72 [4], 316 [5], 456, 460 [1, 8, 13], 622 [4], 657 [14], 666 [25], 695 [16]
Grain
Agreement with U.S., **1976–77:** 8, 48 [13], 181, 192 [2], 288, 333 [17], 904
U.S. sales, **1974:** 210; **1975:** 396 [13], 460 [10], 490, 497 [1, 4], 511 [3, 12], 539, 548, 552 [8], 554 [2], 571, 581 [6], 582 [8], 598, 600 [1, 6], 602 [1, 5, 7, 13], 616 [5], 620 [7], 622 [1], 636, 750 [7]
Intelligence activities, **1975:** 354 [16]
Jewish emigration, **1976–77:** 766
Joint statements, **1974:** 257, 258
Middle East involvement, **1975:** 45 [2], 204 [7], 276 [7], 479 [8]; **1976–77:** 402 [2]
Military capabilities, **1976–77:** 327 [11]
Naval policy, **1975:** 207
News conference remarks, **1976–77:** 67 [20], 387 [4], 763 [23]
USSR—*continued*
Newsweek magazine interview, **1974:** Appendix D
Oil, exchange for U.S. grain, **1975:** 582 [8], 620 [7], 622 [12, 14], 636
President's intention to visit, **1974:** 195 [14]
President's visit, **1974:** 238, 256–59
Strategic arms limitation, **1974:** 39 [27], 127 [8], 195 [14], 257, 271 [1, 2, 5, 6, 7, 9, 10]; **1975:** 64, 96, 119, 179, 186, 243 [7], 276 [3], 290 [8], 316 [5], 354 [10], 456, 459, 460 [1, 4], 479 [7], 492, 501 [8, 9], 502 [5], 512, 526, 581 [8], 600 [10], 650, 657 [13], 666 [25], 695 [5, 16], 717, 750 [5]
Transpolar aviators, **1975:** 348
Underground nuclear explosions, treaties, **1976–77:** 580, 700
U.S. trade relations, **1974:** 72, 210, 274; **1975:** 36 [15], 91, 179, 226; **1976–77:** 185 [5]
Whaling operations, **1975:** 30
UNITA.
See Angola—Union for the Total Independence of Angola.
United Auto Workers, **1976–77:** 778, 947
United Fund, **1974:** 57
United Kingdom
Agreement with United States on atomic energy, **1974:** 10
Economic situation, **1976–77:** 986
European participation, **1975:** 276 [4]
Magna Carta delegation, **1976–77:** 554
Prime Minister Harold Wilson, **1975:** 54, 57, 61, 290n., 456n., 457n., 680n.
Prime Minister James Callaghan, **1976–77:** 807
Queen Elizabeth II, **1976–77:** 654, 656
Summit conference in Puerto Rico, **1976–77:** 621
Taxation and fiscal evasion convention, message to Senate, **1976–77:** 613, 799
United States-United Kingdom Extradition Treaty, **1976–77:** 55
U.S. Ambassador, **1975:** 23, 657 [12]; **1976–77:** 16, 112
United Mine Workers of America, **1975:** 47
United Nations
Charter on Economic Rights and Duties of States, **1975:** 578 [4]
Cyprus conflict, **1975:** 718; **1976–77:** 850
Fund for Drug Abuse Control, **1975:** 720
General Assembly, address, **1974:** 81
Israeli membership, **1975:** 552 [9], 581 [10]
Korea, Republic of, membership, **1975:** 552 [9]
Korean question, **1974:** 255
Middle East, involvement, **1975:** 276 [7], 517, 526, 648 [7], 655 [5]
NBC News interview, **1976–77:** 6
News conference remarks, **1976–77:** 86 [5]
President's assessment, **1975:** 650
Secretary General, **1975:** 718; **1976–77:** 60
Soviet Mission, gunfiring incident, **1976–77:** 286

United Nations—*continued*
U.S. Participation
Annual report, transmittals, **1974:** 86; **1975:** 656; **1976–77:** 842
Question-and-answer sessions, remarks, **1976–77:** 138 [5], 189 [8], 362 [14], 385 [7]
U.S. Representative, **1975:** 365; **1976–77:** 54, 89, 133, 218
Vietnamese membership, **1975:** 552 [9]
Zionism resolution, **1975:** 640, 655 [6], 669, 678 [12]
United Nations Conference on the Human Environment, **1975:** 310
United Nations Conference on the Law of the Sea, **1974:** 86
United Nations Conference on World Population, **1974:** 86
United Nations Development Decade, Second, **1974:** 86
United Nations Development Program, **1975:** 161
United Republican Fund of Illinois, **1974:** 191
United States Arms Control and Disarmament Agency, **1975:** 96, 119; **1976–77:** 701, 1085
United States-Bulgaria International Fishery Agreement, **1976–77:** 1067
United States-China International Fishery Agreement, **1976–77:** 1047
United States Civil Service Commission, **1975:** 111, 124, 328, 690
Chairman, **1974:** 91, 115, 117; **1976–77:** 808, 844
Citizenship requirements for employment, **1976–77:** 752
United States Court of Appeals for the District of Columbia Circuit, **1975:** 485
United States Court of Claims, **1974:** 203
United States District Court for the District of Columbia, Judge, **1974:** 195 [19]
United States district judges, Louisiana, **1976–77:** 373 [6]
United States-Egypt Convention on Income Tax, **1976–77:** 79
United States-German Democratic Republic International Fishery Agreement, **1976–77:** 1049
United States Grain Standards Act, **1976–77:** 939
United States Industrial Payroll Savings Committee, **1975:** 33; **1976–77:** 28
United States Information Agency, **1974:** 72; **1976–77:** 1046
United States International Trade Commission
Chairman, **1976–77:** 268, 780
Sugar imports, **1976–77:** 795, 796
United States-Israel Convention on Income Tax, **1976–77:** 78
United States-Japan Cooperative Medical Science Program, **1975:** 384
United States Jaycees, **1975:** 540; **1976–77:** 610, 790
United States Metric Board, **1975:** 744
United States Military Academy, **1975:** 306
United States-Philippines Convention on Income Taxation, **1976–77:** 1080
United States Postal Service, **1975:** 134, 496 [4]; **1976–77:** 231 [2], 293 [6], 308, 810
United States Railway Association, **1976–77:** 1046
United States-Romania International Fishery Agreement, **1976–77:** 1048
United States Sinai Support Mission, **1976–77:** 411, 1056
United States-Soviet Treaty on Underground Nuclear Explosions for Peaceful Purposes, **1976–77:** 540
United States-Soviet Union International Fishery Agreement, **1976–77:** 1050
United States-Spain Extradition Treaty, **1976–77:** 56
United States-Spain Friendship and Cooperation Treaty, **1976–77:** 108
United States-Switzerland Treaty on Mutual Assistance in Criminal Matters, **1976–77:** 109
United States Travel Service, **1975:** 285
United States-Turkey Defense Cooperation Agreement, **1976–77:** 1074
United States-United Kingdom Extradition Treaty, **1976–77:** 55
United States world image, **1976–77:** 354 [8]
United Way campaign, **1974:** 57
University of Hawaii, **1975:** 716
University of Michigan, **1976–77:** 783, 784, 1028, 1033
University of Michigan Club, **1975:** 122
University of Nebraska, **1976–77:** 444
University of New Hampshire, **1976–77:** 68
University of Pennsylvania, **1975:** 264
University of Southern California, **1976–77:** 860
Upper Mississippi River Basin Commission, **1975:** 425; **1976–77:** 594
Uranium enrichment, **1975:** 357, 358, 359, 600 [9]; **1976–77:** 685, 854, 980, 987
Urban areas
Administration policy, **1975:** 396 [11], 397
Campaign debate remarks, **1976–77:** 947
Community development, **1974:** 29, 30, 39 [21], 72, 121; **1975:** 12, 167, 351
Federal assistance, **1975:** 254, 578 [8], 602 [17], 622 [3]; **1976–77:** 561
Fiscal problems, **1975:** 479 [3]
General revenue sharing, **1975:** 214
Health care programs, **1975:** 436
Housing, assistance programs, **1974:** 29, 30, 234; **1975:** 622 [11]
Model Cities program, **1974:** 29, 30, 39 [21]
Municipal bankruptcy legislation, **1975:** 646, 648 [1], 655 [8], 683, 695 [1]
Municipal bonds, **1975:** 648 [1], 655 [8]
Municipal workers, strikes, **1975:** 582 [1]

Urban areas—*continued*
News conference remarks, **1976–77:** 763 [13], 925 [14]
Polish-American Congress, remarks, **1976–77:** 805
Transportation, **1974:** 65, 127 [17], 240, 261; **1975:** 85 [3], 128, 383, 393
Urban Development and Neighborhood Revitalization, President's Committee on, **1976–77:** 625, 626, 787, 805, 846, 925 [14], 930, 931, 947
Urban League, **1974:** 217
Urban Mass Transportation Administration, **1974:** 65; **1976–77:** 64
U.S. merchant marine, **1974:** 327
Usery, W. J., Jr., **1976–77:** 25, 75
Utah
President's visit, **1974:** 218
Wilderness area, **1974:** 277
Utilities
Advertising, **1975:** 554 [13]
Conversion from oil to coal, **1975:** 616 [11]
Development, **1975:** 321, 326
Legislation, **1976–77:** 685
Rate increases, **1975:** 615 [2]

VA.
See Veterans Administration.
Vail, Colo., **1975:** 485, 488, 497; **1976–77:** 737, 740, 742, 1032, 1039, 1040, 1042
Vail Symposium, **1975:** 488
Valeriani, Richard, **1976–77:** 854
Valley Forge, Pa., **1976–77:** 643
Valley Forge State Park, **1975:** 380
Valley Forge National Historic Park, Pa., **1976–77:** 644
Van Camp, Brian R., **1974:** 211
Van Elslande, Renaat, **1975:** 287n.
Van Meter, Sharon, **1976–77:** 454
Van Nuys, Calif., **1976–77:** 522
Vandenberg, Sen. Arthur H., **1974:** 207, 209; **1975:** 91
Vanderhoof, John D., **1974:** 219
Vatican, Pope Paul VI, **1975:** 304n.
Vermont, President's visit, **1974:** 118
Veterans
Benefits, **1974:** 39 [18], 192
Disability compensation, **1975:** 478
Educational, **1974:** 16, 39 [18], 72, 195 [6]; **1975:** 246, 247
Medical, allied wartime veterans, **1976–77:** 897
Relief of Nolan Sharp, **1974:** 204
Concord, N.H., budget briefing, **1976–77:** 64
Disabled American Veterans National Service and Legislative Headquarters, **1976–77:** 174

Veterans—*continued*
Employment, **1974:** 192; **1975:** 156, 174, 502 [7]
GI bill, **1975:** 554 [4]
Handicapped, **1976–77:** 415 [6]
Hospitals, **1976–77:** 94, 95
Legislation, **1976–77:** 685, 832, 833
News conference remarks, **1976–77:** 387 [23, 24]
Remarks at University of New Hampshire, **1976–77:** 68 [22]
Survivor benefits, **1975:** 478
Travel expenses, **1975:** 21
Vietnam era, **1974:** 192, 240, 263
Veterans Administration
Administrator, **1974:** 16, 139, 192; **1975:** 92; **1976–77:** 832
Benefit reduction rates, **1976–77:** 708
Hospital construction, **1976–77:** 456
Veterans Administration Hospital, Seattle, Wash., remarks, **1976–77:** 961
Veterans Day, **1974:** 192; **1975:** 575, 641
Veterans Disability Compensation and Survivor Benefits Act of 1975, **1975:** 478
Veterans' Education and Employment Assistance Act, **1976–77:** 903
Veterans of Foreign Wars, **1974:** 16; **1976–77:** 197
Veterans Omnibus Health Care Act, **1976–77:** 940
Veterans Readjustment Assistance Act of 1974, Vietnam Era, **1975:** 156
Veto messages and memorandums of disapproval
Agricultural resources conservation act, memorandum, **1976–77:** 922
Animal health research, message, **1974:** 9
Atomic Energy Act amendments, message, **1974:** 141
Automotive transport research and development bill, message to House of Representatives, **1976–77:** 811
Child day care bill, message, **1976–77:** 305
Common situs picketing bill, message, **1976–77:** 4
Congressional Members, exemption from local income taxes, message to Senate, **1976–77:** 710
Continuing appropriations resolution, messages, **1974:** 144, 145, 156
Departments of Labor and Health, Education, and Welfare Appropriation Act, 1976, **1975:** 737
Departments of Labor and Health, Education, and Welfare Appropriation Act, 1977, message to House of Representatives, **1976–77:** 830
Education Division and Related Agencies Appropriation Act, 1976, **1975:** 433
Electric and hybrid vehicle research, development, and demonstration bill, message to House of Representatives, **1976–77:** 777
Emergency agricultural bill, message, **1975:** 232

Veto messages—*continued*
Emergency employment appropriations bill, message, **1975:** 288
Emergency housing bill, message, **1975:** 351
Farm Labor Contractor Registration Act amendments, message, **1974:** 205
Federal coal leasing amendments bill, message to the Senate, **1976–77:** 640
Federal fire prevention and control act, message to House of Representatives, **1976–77:** 655
Federal grant and cooperative agreement act, memorandum of disapproval, **1976–77:** 944
Federal Insecticide, Fungicide, and Rodenticide Act, extension, message to House of Representatives, **1976–77:** 725
Filberts, import bill, memorandum, **1975:** 16
Foreign diplomatic missions, protection, message, **1975:** 701
Foreign sovereign immunities bill, memorandum of disapproval, **1976–77:** 936
Freedom of Information Act amendments, message, **1974:** 160
Grand Rapids, Mich., naming of Federal building for the President, memorandum, **1975:** 17
Hatch Act amendments, message to House of Representatives, **1976–77:** 335
Health revenue sharing and health services legislation, memorandum, **1974:** 319
Hester, Camilla A., relief disapproval, memorandum, **1976–77:** 884
Indian employees, retirement benefits, message to House of Representatives, **1976–77:** 808
International Navigational Rules Act of 1976, memorandum of disapproval, **1976–77:** 877
Maritime Administration appropriations, memorandum, **1975:** 18
Marshals, Deputy U.S., wage increase, message, **1974:** 7
Military construction bill, message to House of Representatives, **1976–77:** 638
Milk price support bill, memorandum, **1975:** 4; **1976–77:** 47
National School Lunch Act and Child Nutrition Act of 1966 Amendments of 1975, message, **1975:** 609
National Security Act of 1947, amendment, message, **1976–77:** 1
National Wildlife Refuge System Administration Act amendment, message, **1974:** 185
Nurses, training appropriations, memorandum, **1975:** 3
Oil import fees bill, message, **1975:** 121
Oil price control extension, message, **1975:** 538

Veto messages—*continued*
Petroleum price review bill, message, **1975:** 418
Phosphate interests in Florida, sale, message, **1974:** 111
Public health services bill, **1975:** 436
Public Works Employment Act, message to Senate, **1976–77:** 653
Public works employment bill, message, **1976–77:** 83
Rabbit meat, mandatory inspection, memorandum, **1976–77:** 911
Railroad retirement benefits legislation, message, **1974:** 140
Relief for private citizens, messages, **1974:** 203, 204
Rural environmental programs, funding, memorandum, **1975:** 15
Surface mining control and reclamation legislation, messages, **1974:** 326; **1975:** 270
Tax reduction extension bill, message, **1975:** 732
Tennessee Valley Authority legislation, memorandum, **1974:** 320
Tobacco price support levels bill, message, **1975:** 601
Tourism programs appropriations, message, **1975:** 285
Travel expense allowances for Federal civilians, memorandum, **1975:** 21
Turkey, U.S. military assistance, messages, **1974:** 144, 145, 156
U.S. oil tankers preference legislation, memorandum, **1974:** 327
Vietnam era veterans' education and training benefits legislation, message, **1974:** 263
Vocational rehabilitation amendments, message, **1974:** 206
Willow Creek, Oreg., flood control legislation, message, **1974:** 307
Zinc tariff legislation, message, **1974:** 264
See also Addresses and remarks; Statements by the President.
Veto power, President's views, **1975:** 356, 374, 375, 423, 512, 557, 598, 630; **1976–77:** 189 [9]
Vetoes, President's record, **1976–77:** 406
VFW.
See Veterans of Foreign Wars.
Vice President of the United States
Duties, **1974:** 39 [11]
Rockefeller, Nelson A., **1974:** 17, 18, 39 [11], 72, 127 [16], 195 [4, 11, 16], 236 [2, 4, 24], 240, 288, 314, Appendix D; **1975:** 19, 91, 92, 316 [8], 328 [9], 479 [11], 501 [15], 511 [11], 552 [5], 665 [4], 657 [2, 5, 10, 22], 666 [1, 2], 684n., 729; **1976–77:** 23 (p. 55, 56), 24, 57, 62, 387 [25], 493, 1016
Running mate, **1975:** 479 [11], 501 [15], 511 [11], 552 [5], 602 [6], 665 [4], 657 [2, 5, 10, 22], 666 [1, 2]; **1976–77:** 210 [7], 240 [1], 282

Vice President—*continued*
Running mate—*continued*
[12], 318, 321 [4], 325 [15], 327 [6], 338 [18], 339 [4, 7], 354 [6], 387 [25], 392 [3], 406, 461, 535 [8]
Vice Presidential staff, Presidential transition, memorandum, **1974:** 3
Vientiane Accords, **1974:** 83
Vietnam, Democratic Republic of
Administration policy, **1975:** 479 [8]
Campaign in South Vietnam, **1975:** 204 [2]
Soviet Union, assistance, **1975:** 189 [5]
Vietnam, Republic of
Administration policy, **1975:** 479 [8]
Executions, **1975:** 243 [12]
Orphans, evacuation, **1975:** 166 [1, 4], 168, 169
President Nguyen Van Thieu, **1975:** 85 [12], 166 [2, 6], 189 [6], 204 [2]
Refugees, **1975:** 163, 166 [1, 7], 167, 169, 179, 181, 189 [12], 204 [2], 224, 231, 243 [3, 10], 260, 262, 267, 347, 415, 484, 530, 746
United Nations membership, **1975:** 552 [9]
U.S. Ambassador, **1975:** 243 [10]
U.S. assistance, **1974:** 126, 325; **1975:** 36 [6, 13, 18], 45 [3], 53, 72 [1], 85 [15], 109 [3], 125 [1], 161 [1], 166 [2, 11, 14], 167, 179, 181, 189 [6, 13], 204 [2], 224, 231, 347
U.S. personnel, evacuation, **1975:** 179, 189 [12], 204 [2], 221, 243 [10]
Vietnam conflict
Cease-fire efforts, **1975:** 189 [2]
Communist actions, **1975:** 166 [2], 179
Congressional inquiry, **1975:** 243 [1]
Draft evaders and military deserters, clemency, **1974:** 16, 77, 80 [10], 236 [13], 266, 329; **1975:** 36 [14], 58, 113, 243 [5], 566, 573 [12]; **1976–77:** 585
Missing in action, **1974:** 192; **1975:** 411, 552 [9], 600 [13], 716; **1976–77:** 762
1976 election campaign issue, **1975:** 204 [2]; **1976–77:** 854
Paris accords, U.S. support, **1975:** 166 [2], 179, 189 [5]
Peace agreement, **1974:** 83
President's assessment, **1975:** 36 [18, 21], 316 [3]
Refugees, **1975:** 163, 166 [1, 7], 167, 169, 179, 181, 189 [12], 204 [2], 224, 231, 243 [3, 10], 260, 262, 267, 347, 415, 484, 530, 746; **1976–77:** 611
Selective service discharges, **1976–77:** 1076
South Vietnamese efforts, **1975:** 166 [2], 204 [2]
U.S. involvement, **1975:** 36 [21], 109 [3], 166 [2, 11, 14], 179, 189 [13], 204 [2], 243 [1, 6]
Veterans, **1974:** 192, 263
Vietnam Era Veterans Readjustment Assistance Act of 1974, **1975:** 156
Vietnam Humanitarian Assistance and Evacuation Act of 1975, **1975:** 224
Viking I, **1976–77:** 679
Villa Maria Nursing and Retirement Center, **1976–77:** 819
Villanova University, **1976–77:** 975
Violators Unit, Major, **1974:** 96
Virginia
General Assembly, joint session, Williamsburg, **1976–77:** 51
Governor, **1976–77:** 52
President's visits, **1974:** 59, 88, 311; **1975:** 95, 218, 219, 236, 410, 411, 667; **1976–77:** 50, 595, 649, 947, 948
Wilderness areas, **1974:** 277
Viscardi, Dr. Henry, Jr., **1975:** 691
Vladivostok, Union of Soviet Socialist Republics, **1974:** 256
Vocational rehabilitation, **1974:** 206, 240
Vogel, Orville Alvin, **1976–77:** 557, 914
Voice of America, **1975:** 460 [14]
Volpe, John A., **1976–77:** 545, 787
Von Stackelberg, Hans, **1976–77:** 671
Vorster, B. J., **1976–77:** 763 [1], 807, 854
Voting Rights Act of 1965, **1975:** 27, 43, 48, 410, 422, 477

Waco, Tex., **1976–77:** 391–395
Waco Suspension Bridge, **1976–77:** 393
Wage and Price Stability, Council on, **1974:** 41, 109, 121, 152, 241; **1976–77:** 220, 466, 764, 1054
Wage and Price Stability Act, Council on, **1974:** 19, 32, 33, 72
Wages and Prices
Agricultural commodities, **1975:** 232, 501 [13], 602 [16], 616 [17], 636
Airline rates, **1975:** 618
Congressional pay increase, **1974:** 195 [17]; **1975:** 620 [10]
Controls, **1974:** 39 [10, 12], 67, 116, 236 [3, 11], Appendix D; **1975:** 36 [26], 64, 72 [17], 402, 429, 565 [17]; **1976–77:** 207 [2], 967
Dairy products, **1974:** 152, 153
Economic Report of the President, **1976–77:** 31
Fair trade laws, **1975:** 196
Federal employees, **1974:** 39 [26], 43, 72, 82, 87, 115, 117, 262; **1975:** 26, 28, 32, 46, 64, 143, 328, 506, 554 [15], 729; **1976–77:** 401 [5]
Food, **1974:** 121, 150
Gasoline, **1974:** 271 [15]; **1975:** 26, 45 [1], 396 [4], 582 [9]
General Motors, prices, **1974:** 5, 23
Grain, **1975:** 396 [13], 497 [2, 3]
Housing, **1975:** 243 [15]
Increase rate, **1975:** 64, 68
Livestock prices, farmers' protest, **1974:** 152, 153
Marshals, Deputy U.S., **1974:** 7

Wages and Prices—*continued*
Milk price support bill, **1975:** 4
Minimum wage, **1976–77:** 231 [5]
Monitoring agency, **1974:** 6, 19, 32, 33, 41, 72, 109, 121, 152, 241; **1975:** 31, 176, 328, 438, 486, 687
Motor carrier rates, **1975:** 675
Natural gas, **1975:** 28, 64, 82, 84, 85 [19], 220, 374, 375, 496 [1], 502 [17], 527 [16], 562, 612, 663, 742
Oil, **1974:** 39 [14], 121; **1975:** 28, 36 [25], 42, 54, 109 [7, 14], 121, 225, 276 [5], 312, 354 [8, 14], 396 [3], 418, 420, 460 [5], 484, 488 [1], 511 [1, 5], 537, 538, 542, 551, 562, 592, 602 [1], 678 [14]
Price-fixing legislation, **1974:** 218
Rate-setting, **1976–77:** 383
Regulatory reform, **1974:** 121, 128 [9]; **1975:** 220
Securities transactions, **1975:** 308
Tobacco, **1975:** 601
Wagonseller, James M., **1975:** 421
Waldheim, Kurt, **1975:** 718; **1976–77:** 60, 850
Wallace, Gov. George C., **1975:** 678 [15, 19]; **1976–77:** 48 [10], 159, 817
Walnut Creek, Calif., **1976–77:** 528, 531
Walter Hagen Invitational Golf Tournament, **1975:** 398
Walters, Barbara, **1976–77:** 947
Walters, John, **1976–77:** 372
War Powers Act, **1975:** 166 [3, 11], 183
War Powers Resolution, **1975:** 257, 276 [2]
War Risk Insurance Program, **1976–77:** 230
Waring, Robert O., **1976–77:** 599, 604, 606
Warner, Rawleigh, Jr., **1974:** 109
Warner Pacific College, **1976–77:** 506
Warren Commission, **1975:** 166 [13], 243 [8], 558, 695 [19]; **1976–77:** 560 [11]
Warsaw, Poland, **1975:** 448, 449
Warwick, R.I., **1975:** 510
Washington
President's visits, **1975:** 524–527; **1976–77:** 959–961
Wilderness area, **1974:** 277
Washington, D.C.
See District of Columbia.
Washington Energy Conference, **1974:** 94
Washington Press Club, **1974:** 84
Waste treatment, **1974:** 89; **1976–77:** 923
Water Act, Safe Drinking, **1974:** 305
Water Conservation Fund bill, Land and, **1976–77:** 825, 826
Water and waterways
Dams, Federal projects, **1976–77:** 201
Locks and Dam, **1976–77:** 26, 181
Lubbock, Tex., **1976–77:** 402 [5]
Pollution, **1976–77:** 240 [4], 373 [9]
Red River navigation project, **1976–77:** 373 [3]
Waste treatment plants, **1976–77:** 923
Watergate
Effect on 1976 Presidential elections, **1976–77:** 185 [9], 207 [1], 396
Investigations, **1976–77:** 925 [15], 947, 972
News conference remarks, **1975:** 479 [5]; **1976–77:** 212 [5], 325 [3], 387 [17], 898 [2, 6], 925 [1, 2]
Pardons, **1975:** 109 [13]
Watergate Special Prosecution Force, Office of, **1974:** 39 [6, 15], 80 [2, 11], 155, 195 [19], 313; **1976–77:** 831
Watkins, Bob, **1974:** 170, 173
Watson, James D., **1976–77:** 1052
Weapons.
See Arms and weapons; Missiles; Strategic arms limitation.
Weather Program, World, **1975:** 317; **1976–77:** 824
Weinberger, Caspar W., **1974:** 109, 206; **1975:** 360
Weitz, Capt. Paul J., **1975:** 235
Welch, Richard, **1975:** 745
Welfare
Administration policy, **1976–77:** 402 [6]
Budget news briefing, **1976–77:** 23 (p. 54, 58)
Federal programs, **1976–77:** 284 [6]
Food stamp program, **1976–77:** 321 [2], 327 [9], 420 [9]
Minimum wage, **1976–77:** 287 [15]
News conference remarks, **1976–77:** 535 [16]
President's assessment, **1976–77:** 207 [3]
Reform, **1975:** 479 [4], 600 [12], 626, 648 [6]; **1976–77:** 68 [16]
State of the Union Address, **1976–77:** 19
West Bend, Wis., **1976–77:** 287
West Berlin, **1974:** 285
West Germany.
See Germany, Federal Republic of.
West Orange, N.J., **1976–77:** 564, 565
West Palm Beach, Fla., **1976–77:** 150, 151
West Point, N.Y., **1975:** 306
West Texas State University, **1976–77:** 333
West Virginia, President's visits, **1975:** 611, 669–671
West Wilkes High School, Wilkesboro, N.C., **1976–77:** 215
Westover Air Force Base, Mass., **1975:** 662
Wetlands Loan Extension Act of 1976, **1976–77:** 106
Whale Conservation and Protection Study Act, **1976–77:** 910
Whalen, Repr. Charles W., Jr., **1974:** 184
Whaling Commission, International, **1975:** 30; **1976–77:** 910
Wheat.
See Grain.
Wheat Agreement, 1971, International, **1975:** 319; **1976–77:** 605
Wheat Council, International, **1976–77:** 769
Wheat Trade Convention, **1975:** 319

Wheatgrowers organizations, **1975:** 497
Wheaton, Ill., **1976–77:** 207
White, Robert M., **1974:** 275
White House Conference on Handicapped Individuals, **1975:** 691; **1976–77:** 242
White House Conference on Library and Information Services, **1976–77:** 266 [6], 678
White House Conference on Domestic and Economic Affairs
Atlanta, Ga., **1975:** 69
Cincinnati, Ohio, **1975:** 374
Concord, N.H., **1975:** 196
Hollywood, Fla., **1975:** 108
Knoxville, Tenn., **1975:** 616
Milwaukee, Wis., **1975:** 502
Omaha, Nebr., **1975:** 602
Peoria, Ill., **1975:** 496
Portland, Ore., **1974:** 214
St. Louis, Mo., **1975:** 554
San Diego, Calif., **1975:** 167
Seattle, Wash., **1975:** 527
White House Correspondents Association, **1975:** 237
White House Fellows, **1976–77:** 471
White House Fellowships, President's Commission on, **1975:** 269
White House News Photographers Association, **1975:** 190
White House Staff
Assistants to the President, **1974:** 273, 283, 303; **1975:** 657 [1]; **1976–77:** 626
Assistant to te President for Domestic Affairs, **1974:** 294; **1975:** 91, 92
Assistant to the President for Economic Affairs, **1974:** 109; **1975:** 328
Assistant to the President for National Security Affairs, **1975:** 311, 657 [1]
Assistant to the President for Public Liaison, **1975:** 20
Christmas party, remarks, **1975:** 728
Counsel to the President, **1974:** 155; **1975:** 93, 481
Counsellors to the President, **1974:** 41, 155, 265, 269
Deputy Assistant to the President, **1974:** 309
Deputy Counsel to the President, **1976–77:** 315
Physician to the President, **1974:** 154
Presidential transition, memorandum, **1974:** 3
President's assessment, **1976–77:** 392 [9]
Press Secretary to the President, **1974:** 2, 64, 92; **1976–77:** 566
Special Assistant to the President for Consumer Affairs, **1974:** 41; **1975:** 230
Special Assistant to the President for Ethnic Affairs, **1976–77:** 283
Special Assistant to the President for Women, **1976–77:** 193
White House Staff—*continued*
Special Assistants to the President, **1974:** 310; **1975:** 604; **1976–77:** 670, 702, 741
Special Coordinator for Disaster Relief, **1975:** 163
White Plains, N.Y., **1976–77:** 891
Whitehead, William S., **1974:** 267
Wholesale Price Index, **1976–77:** 86 [9], 89, 107 [19], 118, 555, 657 [16]
Whyte, William G., **1976–77:** 831
Wichita, Kans., **1974:** 220
Widnall, Repr. William B., **1974:** 29
Wilderness areas, **1974:** 276, 277
Wilderness Preservation System, National, **1974:** 276, 277; **1975:** 726
Wildlife
Antarctic seals, **1975:** 730
Polar bears, **1975:** 699
Preservation, **1975:** 488 [12]
Whales, **1975:** 30
Wildlife Refuge System, National, **1976–77:** 746
Wildlife Refuge System Administration Act of 1966, National, **1974:** 185
Wiley, Richard E., **1976–77:** 315
Wilkesboro, N.C., **1976–77:** 215
Will, George F., **1975:** 666
Willett, Edward R., **1975:** 230
Williams, Edward Bennett, **1976–77:** 199
Williams, Repr. Lawrence G., **1975:** 407
Williams, Maurice J., **1974:** 275
Williamsburg, Va., **1976–77:** 51, 52, 947
Willow Creek, Oreg., **1974:** 307
Wilson, E. Bright, Jr., **1976–77:** 557, 914
Wilson, Harold, **1975:** 54, 57, 61, 290n., 456n., 457n., 680n.
Wimbledon tennis champions, **1975:** 417
WIN (Whip Inflation Now) program, **1974:** 121, 127 [1, 4], 131, 135, 150, 170, 171, 172, 175, 195 [2], 214, 232, 290; **1975:** 54
Windfall profits tax, **1974:** 72, 240; **1975:** 32, 60, 64, 70, 85 [6], 109 [7], 283, 488 [7], 538
Winn, Repr. Larry, Jr., **1974:** 220
Winston, Nat T., Jr., **1976–77:** 932
Winston-Salem, N.C., **1976–77:** 214
Wisconsin
Association of Manufacturers and Commerce, economic forum, **1976–77:** 284
Farm forum, **1976–77:** 288
Ford-Dole Committee, **1976–77:** 990
Green Bay Packers Hall of Fame, **1976–77:** 291
Livestock farmers' protest, **1974:** 152, 153
Presidential primary, **1976–77:** 282 [2], 307
President's visits, **1975:** 501–503, 651, 652; **1976–77:** 265, 266, 283–285, 287–293, 989, 990
Public forums, **1976–77:** 287, 293
Wilderness area, **1974:** 276, 277
Wisconsin Education Association, **1976–77:** 989

Wolf Trap Farm Park, Va., **1976–77:** 559
Wolman, Abel, **1975:** 568
Women
  Citizen's Advisory Council on the Status of Women, **1976–77:** 363
  Educational programs, **1976–77:** 402 [8]
  Employment, **1975:** 124, 185, 209
  Equal rights amendment, **1975:** 24, 185, 307, 396 [14], 578 [2], 616 [21]; **1976–77:** 406
  Federal affirmative action programs, **1975:** 616 [8]
  Inter-American Convention on the Granting of Political Rights to Women and Convention on the Political Rights of Women, **1976–77:** 241
  National Federation of Business and Professional Women's Clubs, **1976–77:** 179
  Roles in administration, **1976–77:** 308, 321 [10], 366
  Special Assistant to the President for Women, **1976–77:** 193
  Supreme Court nomination, consideration, **1975:** 695 [14]
  Vice-Presidential running mate, consideration, **1975:** 602 [6], 662; **1976–77:** 189 [3], 376
Women Voters, League of, **1976–77:** 750
Women's Equality Day, 1975, **1975:** 504
Women's Forum on National Security, **1975:** 106
Women's Year, 1975, National Commission on the Observance of International, **1975:** 24, 185; **1976–77:** 634
Women's Year, World Conference of the International, **1976–77:** 842
Wood, Arthur M., **1974:** 109
Woodcock, Leonard, **1974:** 109; **1976–77:** 947
Woodruff, Douglas O., **1976–77:** 24
Woodson, Carter G., **1976–77:** 74
Work incentive program, **1976–77:** 685
Work Quality, National Commission on Productivity and, **1974:** 121
World affairs, U.S. role, **1976–77:** 356 [11], 405
World Affairs Council, **1975:** 581
World Affairs Council of Oregon, **1976–77:** 505
World Bank.
  See International Bank for Reconstruction and Development.
World Conference of the International Women's Year, **1976–77:** 842
World Conference on Law, **1975:** 632
World Energy Conference, **1974:** 94
World Environment Day, **1975:** 310; **1976–77:** 556
World Food Conference, **1974:** 80 [15], 81, 86; **1975:** 64, 137, 147, 179
World Food Program, **1974:** 102; **1976–77:** 36
World Golf Hall of Fame, **1974:** 70, 71
World Weather Program, **1975:** 317; **1976–77:** 824
Wright-Patterson Air Force Base, **1976–77:** 575
Wriston, Walter B., **1974:** 109
Wu, Chien-Shiung, **1976–77:** 914
Wylie, Repr. Chalmers P., **1974:** 184
Wyman, Louis, **1975:** 511 [9], 547, 548, 549, 573 [2]
Wyoming
  President's visit, **1976–77:** 743
  Wilderness areas, **1974:** 277

Yacht Racing Association, International Star Class, **1975:** 499
Yale University Law School, **1975:** 217
Yellowstone National Park, Wyo., **1976–77:** 743
Yemen, People's Republic of, Generalized System of Preferences, **1975:** 154
Yeshiva High School, New York City, **1976–77:** 885
YMCA Youth Governors Conference, National, **1975:** 356
Young, Repr. Edward, **1974:** 170, 173
Young, Repr. Samuel H., **1974:** 191
Young Republican Conference, **1976–77:** 39
Young Republican Leadership Conference, **1975:** 116
Younger, Evelle J., **1974:** 211
Youth
  Alcohol and drug abuse, **1974:** 93
  Budget news briefing, **1976–77:** 23 (p. 54, 60, 67)
  Crime, **1975:** 341, 532
  Employment, **1974:** 47; **1975:** 172, 174, 178, 243 [11], 333, 511 [7], 554 [8], 616 [7]; **1976–77:** 138 [9], 266 [18], 293 [4], 310–313
  Florida budget briefing, **1976–77:** 89
  Foster Grandparent program, **1975:** 550
  Groups
    Boys Nation, **1975:** 421
    Boys/Girls Nation, **1976–77:** 714
    Capitol Page School class, **1975:** 314
    CLOSE-UP, **1975:** 172
    Cub Scouts, induction ceremonies, **1975:** 671
    Future Farmers of America, **1975:** 419
    Girls Nation, **1975:** 414
    Holton-Arms School, **1975:** 307
    Loy Norris High School students, **1975:** 337
    National Explorer Presidents' Congress, **1975:** 177
    National Teenage Republican Leadership Conference, **1975:** 339
    Presidential Scholars, **1975:** 371
    Youth Bicentennial rally, **1975:** 530
    See also specific organizations.
  Handicapped, education, **1975:** 707
  Juvenile delinquency, **1974:** 62, 181; **1976–77:** 685
  Minority unemployment, **1975:** 602 [9]
  Nonvoting role in elections, **1976–77:** 266 [16]
  Presidential Scholars Program, **1975:** 371
  President's advice, **1975:** 582 [11]

Youth—*continued*
School lunch and child nutrition programs, **1975:** 143, 609, 615 [8], 616 [15], 620 [11]
Summer employment
Appropriation bill, **1975:** 333
Federal program, **1976–77:** 310–313
Youth Conservation Corps, **1974:** 47
Yugoslavia
Belgrade City Assembly, **1975:** 470
Joint statements, **1975:** 146, 471
President Josip Broz Tito, **1975:** 466, 467, 468, 469, 471
President's visit, **1975:** 466–471
Prime Minister Dzemal Bijedic, **1975:** 145, 146, 468n.

Zablocki, Repr. Clement J., **1975:** 387
Zaire, security assistance programs, **1975:** 649
Zambia, President Kenneth D. Kaunda, **1975:** 200
Zapanta, Albert C., **1976–77:** 702
Zarb, Frank G., **1974:** Appendix D; **1975:** 564, 593, 661; **1976–77:** 23 (p. 52), 177, 789
Zinc, tariff legislation, **1974:** 264
Zion, Repr. Roger H., **1974:** 154
Zionism, **1975:** 640, 655 [6], 669, 678 [12]

DATE DUE